Political Animal

Political Animal
I'd Rather Have a
Better Country

Brian Wendell Morton

Apprentice House
Baltimore, Maryland

Library of Congress Cataloging-in-Publication Data

Morton, Brian Wendell, 1961-
Political animal : I'd rather have a better country / Brian Wendell Morton.
p. cm.
Collected columns, first published in Baltimore's City paper.
ISBN 978-1-934074-35-0
I. Title.

PN4874.M5874A25 2008
808.8'0358--dc22
2008027235

Printed in the United States of America
First Edition

Jacket art: Todd Shearer
Jacket design: Andrew Zaleski

Published by Apprentice House
The Future of Publishing...Today!

Apprentice House
Communication Department
Loyola College in Maryland
4501 N. Charles Street
Baltimore, MD 21210
410.617.5265 • 410.617.5040 (fax)
www.ApprenticeHouse.com

For my parents, Herwald and Christine Morton, and my brother, Keith Morton, for being there, putting up with me, encouraging me, tolerating me, and loving me across two hemispheres, five continents, and forty-six years.

Table of Contents

Foreword

Once upon a time—back when Gerald Ford was president—there was a famous "mentalist" known as the Amazing Kreskin. He had his own syndicated TV show and was familiar to millions of Americans as a regular guest on the late-night talkers. Kreskin, a fabulous self-promoter, was one of the biggest names in entertainment in the 1970s. He was no magician; he didn't do card tricks. His shtick was drawn from the realm of the psychic. If Johnny Carson hid a $20 bill under a newspaper in the bottom of a bird cage, Kreskin could find it. I mean, the guy was awesome.

Push up the clock to the late 1990s. I hosted a live, two-hour Sunday-morning show in Baltimore on WMAR-TV, the ABC affiliate here. Kreskin, in the has-been stage of life but still doing hundreds of shows a year, had arrived in Maryland to perform at a suburban high school. The producers of *Rodricks For Breakfast* lined him up as a guest. Thinking in segues, they thought it would be a good idea to book Brian Morton, Baltimore political columnist and magician, on the same show.

Brian appeared on the show first and he was wonderful. He cleverly mixed politics with sleight of hand, and he pretty much dazzled everyone in the studio that day. His magic was original, sharp, and witty—and so was his commentary. The audience and crew applauded him enthusiastically.

Watching from the wings was the Amazing Kreskin. He was not so impressed. In fact, he was pissed.

Kreskin had no intention of performing on my program; he was there to do a brief interview and plug his high school show, and he hated an upstart showing him up. Breaking out in a rash of offended ego, he copped an attitude about our having booked Brian just before his appearance on *RFB*, and he got in Brian's face during a commercial break. It was all very weird and awkward and, in the moment of a live TV show, upsetting.

But, soon as the insulted Kreskin finished his interview segment and left the building, we all had a pretty good laugh.

It seems to me that Brian Morton did that day what he has always done as the Political Animal columnist for the *City Paper* in Baltimore: Perform well and piss somebody off.

He's one of the most talented and intelligent people I've ever encountered—quick with an astute observation or witty comment, a provocative and amusing conversationalist blessed with a broadcast-quality voice, a gifted writer, a font of information about politics and popular culture, and a devoted student of the magical arts. I have known him as a radio journalist, talk-show host, clever magician, congressional press spokesman and handgun-control advocate, and for the last several years as a consistently strong, smart, and liberal voice in the *CP*.

Those of us who have worked for many years for *The Baltimore Sun*, and who remain proud of that paper and prideful in our work, give props—at least in private—to our brother and sister journalists at the city's alternative weekly. Baltimore is better for *CP*'s existence over the last 30 years, and it continues to produce fine and important work. One of management's best decisions was giving Brian Morton his column in 1994, and it was to our benefit that Brian settled down to write it.

He found his voice with Political Animal. These columns are worth another read.

It is clear that Brian takes time to read and think about current events and political trends and to distill his thoughts into one well-crafted column per week. This is his gift—the ability to take a large view, see the field clearly, extract what he finds important, and write an effective essay. Over the years, from the Clinton era into Bush—and, in Maryland, from the time of Parris Glendening to Bob Ehrlich and now Martin O'Malley—he has offered many trenchant comments about the political scene nationally and in the state, and he has developed a style that artfully balances a liberal's tendency toward idealism with the journalist's cynical view of the world. His prose runs from street to elegant, from quick jab to long flourish. He uses information to build arguments; he's sarcastic and angry when he needs to be, reflective and reminding when required, and always provocative. Brian does his job. He performs well and pisses somebody off.

Dan Rodricks
Columnist, *The Sun*
Host, WYPR's "Midday"

Introduction

While the Political Animal column was born in 1994, the political-animal writing it hatched sometime around 1984. I wrote a weekly column for the University of Maryland daily student newspaper, the *Diamondback*. It dabbled in social issues, primarily from a humorous perspective (my first column was centered around a pun based on the *vas deferens*, which is why you won't be reading it or anything else I wrote in college in this book), and I had no particular axe to grind.

And then Ronald Reagan ran for re-election.

While the state of Maryland now is what the national media calls a "blue" state (let us all thank the television networks for further dividing the nation by color), in 1984 "The Gipper" was king, and the quiet, apathetic campus at UM became a raging hotbed of nascent conservatism. And like my father in 1972—the only man wearing a McGovern button in a sea of Nixonites—I took up the cause of "the liberals."

Reagan talked about "welfare queens" and "quotas." He argued against sanctions on the racist apartheid regime of South

Africa and claimed Nelson Mandela was a communist. He fought against a national holiday for Martin Luther King, Jr. In my eyes, whatever Reagan was for, it wasn't hard for me to be against—he seemed to be the worst thing, politically, that could happen to America.

Hoo boy, was I wrong, and not for the first time.

The title of this book stems from a comment I made to a reader at a speaking engagement (you'll have to read it yourself—it's in the chapter titled "Outrages," listed as "A Different Kind Of Year") when someone asked if I was happy for all the material the Bush administration had been giving me.

Unlike some columnists, such as Maureen Dowd of *The New York Times* or Richard Cohen of *The Washington Post*, I don't spend a lot of time trying to figure out ways to yell, "A pox on both your houses!" in between catty theatre-criticism of national politics typed out on my Blackberry, while tossing off catty bon mots en route to the next party on Foxhall Road in Georgetown. I care about this stuff.

Peggy Noonan of *The Wall Street Journal* jabbers on about her Irish working-class roots, as does Bill O'Reilly. Dowd talks about her dad being a D.C. cop, but she hasn't had to scrape for a paycheck in a long, long time. I wish I had the same luxury, and I'm sure more of my extended family feels the same way than hers does.

I *do* wish we had a better country—and the fact that we don't provides me with a limitless well of outrage, no matter how much that makes me (gasp!) one of those "angry black men" that the mainstream media does so much to marginalize. But many clichés are born in fact, and this is one of them.

I have no illusions what you're holding here in your hand: It's a collection of my previously written crap, weekly recorded moments of the country's political pulse. But it's also a time capsule of sorts—it's a picture of Baltimore and Maryland and the nation taken in two separate eras, separated almost by a generation. One part exists in the 1990s before the nation was ripped into two primary colors, and the other is life after politics became a constantly-warring clash of armed camps, each side warily circling the other, jockeying for advantage.

You'll note that while I try not to primarily be a typical "black columnist," there still exists a thread that runs through much of the writing. This is, amazingly enough, due to the fact that I am a black columnist. "The problem of the color line" runs thick through the politics of the twenty-first century, and it seems that today's media spends as much time trying to ignore it as they do trying to deny it.

When I first went to Joe Stearne (the former editorial page editor of the Baltimore *Sun*) back in 1994 and proposed the idea of this column, he told me that if it were up to him, the paper would have fewer columnists, not more. When the paper folded the *Evening Sun* into the morning paper and laid off their African-American columnist, they hired another one—a somewhat reactionary black conservative that had to speak to a city that was more than 60 percent black with a ratio of 9 Democrats for every Republican.

I used to challenge politically astute and well-read friends to name five nationally syndicated black columnists (go ahead, try it yourself), a test almost no one passed. Yet, if you're a regular reader of op-ed pages, a list of their counterparts—George Will, William Safire, Jack Germond (both now retired), David Broder, Richard Cohen, Robert Novak, David Brooks, Cal Thomas—just trips off the tongue.

So I decided that I'd write about anything and everything that had a political angle to it, be it entertainment, sports, religion, movies, music, foreign affairs, or, well—politics. "Man is by nature a political animal," Aristotle said, and just about everything we do can in some way be affected by the political world.

The contents of this book comprise the columns I wrote for the Baltimore *City Paper* from the years 1994 to 1996, when Bill Clinton was president (and right when Newt Gingrich and his "Republican Revolution" took both houses of Congress), and then later, from September 2002 until this time went to press at the start of 2008. Scattered throughout the book are some unpublished columns that I attempted to get placed in *The Washington Post* "Outlook" section or the op-ed pages of the Baltimore Sun. The earliest of the unpublished ones, "The Glitch In The Machine," dates to the end of 1993, when Bill Clinton was being savaged for his gentle early foreign policy, which wasn't much different from the policy he inherited from George H. W. Bush with the exception of the rash that was the Somalia invasion which Bush Sr. bequeathed to him.

Writing from Baltimore has its advantages in that it's far enough away—35 miles—to not be affected by that peculiar airless attitude that afflicts one living in the center of the universe. When I moved here in 1990 after years of sucking in the heady, "this is where it all happens" smell of people running the country, I realized that Baltimore is more like America in many ways than D.C. will ever be. *The New York Times* writer Hedrick Smith wrote that Washington is "the ultimate company town," a city unique in that its output requires no smokestacks. And Baltimore exists just outside the edges of D.C.'s "ten square miles surrounded by reality," as Eric Engberg of CBS put it.

When I worked in the Clinton White House on the drug issue, the chief of staff (a former high-level State Department official) wandered into my office and asked me, "So when are you moving back to D.C.?"

I told her, "When I can invite two of my friends out to a neighborhood bar, order a round of beers, pay with a five-dollar bill, and get change back."

I'm still here.

Outrages

There's a spot on the banks of the Patapsco River flowing out of Baltimore where you can stand and look up at I-95, one of the busiest highways in America, right as it leads into the Fort McHenry tunnel. Stand there and look up as trucks and cars surge by, on their way to Philadelphia, New York, and Boston.

It is no greater an engineering miracle than any other section of highway, but look at it as a microcosm of a whole. Try and imagine the entire Eisenhower Interstate Highway System being built on the tax revenues of today. Today, we can barely maintain it—and it's an outrage.

Stand in the heart of the French Quarter, in downtown New Orleans, and look around you—you'll see partying tourists and convention-goers, same as ever. Now take a walk out northward, out Canal Street. Head northward and take a right when you get to North Broad, and note the difference as you walk along. You're witnessing the heart of the Ninth Ward, and the epicenter of the destruction of an American city. It's an outrage.

Take a trip into Washington, via Route 50—it's the one that

turns into New York Avenue, one of the city's main entry and exit routes. In 1989, you could drive all the way down New York Avenue, pass in front of the White House, and with only a slight turn, you would be on Pennsylvania Avenue, headed out toward Foggy Bottom and Georgetown. Almost twenty years later and you can't drive by "The People's House." You couldn't even see your president in a public place unless you were a signed and sworn supporter of his policies. In 2005, Alex Young, Leslie Weise, and Karen Bauer were ejected from a public forum in Denver featuring President Bush despite having done nothing to disrupt the event. In August of 2007, the federal government had to pay out $80,000 of your tax money to Jeff and Nicole Rank of Charleston, West Virginia because presidential advance staffers got the couple arrested for the crime of wearing anti-Bush t-shirts at a public event. Oh—and it was on the Fourth of July. Outrage.

For nearly every week of the last eight years, there is a story to tell guaranteed to raise your blood pressure a few points at the very least. This chapter will catalogue a few of them, and I'm sure they'll jog your memory of a few more. Torture, deceit, malfeasance, obfuscation—if there's any way possible the government of the United States could have been used as a partisan political tool, if you look hard enough, you could probably find it in the news stories of the last two terms.

*   *   *

The Party's Starting
October 11, 1995

Quick, while no one's looking, let's merge. All of us. Simultaneously. Remember back in the seventies when Steve Martin said "Let's get small?" Well, let's get big, real big, so big that no one can tell us what to do anymore, and if they don't like it, we'll blackmail them by taking our toys and going elsewhere.

This sounds like nonsense—a lot of what you read here does, doesn't it?—until you pick up the paper and think of all the mergers that you've read about within the last year or so.

Lockheed and Martin Marietta. Westinghouse and CBS. Disney and ABC. Ted Turner's TBS and Time-Warmer. PEPCO and BGE. What's going on here?

Remember the little Loyola Bank of Maryland? The bank that waved its small size and independence like a banner, with TV commercials that trumpeted how they remained the same while other banks around them were being eaten up by bigger banks? Remember them?

A bigger bank ate them.

The Bank of Baltimore, which years ago began as the Savings Bank of Baltimore, last year was taken over by First Fidelity, an out-of-state bank. Those of us who had accounts at the Bank of Baltimore were forced to buy new checks and accept banking plans less advantageous to us, the consumers who settled on the Bank of Baltimore in the first place. Then, barely after the ink is dry on the new checks, along comes First Union, which merges with First Fidelity to form the fourth largest bank in Maryland and the sixth largest in the country.

What does this mean, other than having to buy new checks again when the fully-merged bank changes its name to something ludicrous like Sigran or Sovnet or FirstBiz or something? For starters, usually layoffs.

Of course, a spokesman for First Fidelity, quoted in *The Sun*, says that though some consolidation is expected, reductions will be made through attrition and cuts will be minimal. "[We're] trying as hard as we can to minimize staff cuts," according to the spokesman.

Ask anyone from the old Maryland National Bank if that sounds familiar.

And the banks, which seem to be going through a merger frenzy normally only associated with rabbits, don't seem to be getting a clue either. They merge in order to "be more competitive," yet all the while either incurring debt in order to buy smaller banks or raising fees in order to placate shareholders.

And miffed consumers are starting to get the picture. The Associated Press reported that a poll commissioned by the American Bankers Association found that forty-nine percent of consumers believed that bank fees are inappropriate and most believe they already pay too much for services. Seventy percent of those polled said bankers don't care about the communities they serve.

Well, duh. It's kind of hard to localize sentiment for the community you serve when the community comprises the eastern half of the contiguous United States. Better charge them a fee to finance a poll to figure out why.

If you're already hot under the collar about that, just remember it'll cost you more for the heat as well. A week after Baltimore Gas and Electric announced an impending merger with the Potomac Electric Power Company, the Public Service Commission allows BGE to raise the cost of natural gas to consumers to the tune of $19.45 million a year.

Now, waitaminit. Wasn't the merger of the two supposed to bring about *lower* costs to the consumer? So what's the deal—they now get the money for the merger up front?

There really is no secret what's going on here. We're seeing the fruits of increased deregulation. What advocates of deregulation see as "increased competition" actually provides cover for those who steadily want to form monopolies. In the end, there'll be a handful of large corporations who have little interest in areas other than as markets for services that increase in cost out of proportion to their value.

Remember Standard Oil? The Rockefeller family held control of oil and gas, coal, the railroads and banking, and were able to control whole facets of society. Theodore Roosevelt campaigned against "malefactors of great wealth" and the newspapers owned by Rockefeller printed stories hinting that the president was insane.

Now Ted Turner has fallen in with Time Warner, one of the largest media conglomerates in history is being formed, with control over the last true commodity still manufactured in America: information. How is the deal being financed? Through banks, of course.

We don't like to sound like conspiracy theorists here—the world has quite enough in Oliver Stone and Zoh Hieronymus. But it doesn't take much effort to look back in a history book and see what happened at the end of the last great spree of mergers.

Turn out the lights at the BGE building. The party's just starting.

Another America
July 10, 1996

Even as we slide into the end of the summer and toward the presidential conventions, marking the start of the real political contest this fall, a disturbing trend continues to appear on the national socio-political radar screens. It encompasses race, taxes, guns and the law, and at its heart is the issue of who and what really constitutes America.

At the end of the smoldering ruins created by the riots of the late sixties, the Kerner Commission pointed out that we were moving toward two Americas, separate and unequal. We may not be there yet, so completely polarized that neither can see the views of the other, but we have clearly made it to the point where there are three—the two ends polarized against one another and the nether region in the middle, comprising the mainstream, the apathetic and the nihilist portions of the political spectrum.

We have had no less a personage than a Supreme Court justice, Antonin Scalia, recently state in a dissenting opinion that the court is reading a Constitution with which he is not familiar. Presidential candidate Pat Buchanan calls for a "culture war" and increasingly depicts America as a place where those whose value systems are out of line with his ride the line of being seditious.

Religion is used both as a litmus test and a wedge. Religious leaders make piousness a political standard to which candidates must make homage, and use their arbitrary checklists to define and separate those who are "right" from those who are "wrong." Children of all races are taught to stand and recite a pledge to the "Christian flag," thereby co-opting symbols and affirmations of ultra-patriotism that started years ago as a notice in a Baltimore newspaper. In the meantime, those who practice religions other than Christianity, or none at all, gather in the corners of the national debate, almost afraid to speak up lest they be branded as infidels and unworthy of citizenship. We decry fundamentalism in Eastern and Middle Eastern cultures, yet we seem ever more gradually to be heading toward it on our own.

And the hottest fires in the crucible are reserved for those who feel that the America of the Constitution as it had been read for the first two hundred years no longer seems to serve themselves and their interests. The flash point occurs when those individuals take matters into their own hands. We are seeing more and more of them every week, with names linked to places or sects—Ruby Ridge, Waco, the Freemen, the Viper Militia. Opposed to taxes, government, the United Nations, gun control, race-mixing, even some amorphous and undefined "New World Order," they are amassing weapons, gathering intelligence, and planning revolt. And they live among us.

A friend of this writer stated vehemently this past week that "there is no difference between Bob Dole and Bill Clinton." To much of the mainstream, and nearly all of the polarized ends, this is certainly true. The rest participate in politics as the major parties have defined them, or opt out altogether and accept the results with a resignation normally one associates with the fickleness of fate.

Minorities and ultra-liberals feel that the corporate power structure has pre-empted government as the true power in the country, having bought it wholesale through large campaign contributions and intensive lobbying campaigns and the inculcation of the ethic that big business keeps America afloat. The ever-growing so-called "fringe" of the right feels abandoned by a government that they see no longer addresses their needs while giving away "handouts" to the undeserving. Mainstream politicians, both on the left and the right accept money from tobacco and chemical interests and fritter away time pandering to the absolute center with promises of miniscule tax breaks and useless, meaningless or dangerous issues such as flag-burning, and victims-rights and balanced-budget amendments to the Constitution.

Bill Clinton veers to the right saying, "the era of big government is over." Bob Dole announces he will not veto the idea of accepting a pro-choice running mate. Neither's foreign policy initiatives differ greatly from the other—to do so would make the United States appear unstable and unpredictable in the eyes of our international allies.

Some time in the not-so-distant future, the center will not hold. The extremes, from Farrakhan to Falwell and from Earth First! to the Viper Militia and Operation Rescue will leave us all wondering from where the next act of political destruction will come. Our borders have ceased to be the interdiction point. The battleground is on our own territory, not from without. And the mainstream, from the very top levels to those who steer them and on down to those who pull the levers in every city and town in America are complicit in that they do not demand more attention be paid to what is really important.

But in the meantime, when mass media delivers entertainment as news or prattling talk labeled as unvarnished truth, we spend more and more of our time devoted to the lives of the rich and famous. And the fissure will quietly widen until there remains nothing left but two sides, with nothing left to say to one another and no option left save violence.

Dangerous Games
October 1, 2003

Some years ago, your humble Political Animal went to college with the son of the CIA station chief in the Philippines. At the time, this Animal's father worked in the U.S. embassy in Manila.

It seems that everyone knew the occupation of the other student's father—except the student himself (and his mother). A book came out later on the subject of the Philippines' "People Power Revolution," and the author wrote in one chapter that the student's father "was the CIA station chief in Manila, but nobody held it against him." The fact is, sometimes it becomes common knowledge who the American spook is in a given embassy, but it's still not meant for use as political currency, especially by one's own government.

This, however, has not been the case for the Bush administration, a group of arrogant hard-core politicos who think only of the goal, not who is crushed on the way toward it. Back in July, Joseph Wilson, a prominent diplomat and former ambassador to Gabon, wrote a piece for *The New York Times* op-ed page questioning the reliability of British claims that Iraq was seeking to buy yellowcake uranium from Africa for a nuclear weapons program. At the time, the Bush administration was first trying to buttress the president's State of the Union claim that Iraq had nuclear weapons, and then the flimsier argument that the nation was trying to build a nuclear weapons "program."

In order to retaliate against the Wilson article, the identity of Wilson's wife, Valerie Plame, was leaked to the conservative syndicated columnist Robert Novak, who then wrote that "two senior administration officials" told him Plame was an undercover CIA agent specializing in weapons of mass destruction.

In addition to ending Plame's career in intelligence, and quite possibly endangering the lives of anyone with whom she associated while overseas, this leak is a federal offense—but that shows you how far the people in this White House will go to make sure that their company line is toed.

On Sept. 28, *The Washington Post* published a piece quoting another senior administration official saying that Plame's identity had been shopped around to at least six Washington journalists. Following the story, CIA director George Tenet recommended that the Justice Department look into the leak—an amusing turn of events, as it was Tenet whom the White House tried to hang the blame on for the credulous "16 words" regarding yellowcake and the Iraqi nuclear program in the State of the Union.

The problem with this Keystone Kops scenario is that the Bush administration has already made sure that the henhouse is guarded by the most political fox in the administration, Attorney General John Ashcroft. After dragging the Clinton administration and the country through a partisan impeachment process centering on the flimsy issue of consensual behavior between two adults, Republicans wanted to make sure that the independent counsel mechanism could never be used with such broad and sweeping latitude against someone of their own party.

So where a special counsel used to be named by a panel of federal judges (albeit in the case of Bill Clinton, three partisan judges collaborated with Republican senators to name Kenneth Starr), now one would be appointed by Ashcroft and answer only to Ashcroft. And Ashcroft has always shown a spectacular ability to make sure his side's oxen are never the ones to get gored, so to speak.

Now trial balloons are being launched in which administration toadies, flunkies, and minions in the partisan press start trying to find an appropriate excuse for this leak/federal offense. National Review Online's Clifford May this week trotted out the argument that, gee, if everybody knew that Plame was a spook, it's not so bad, and why does it matter? In other words, just like saying that Bush's State of the Union allegation "was *only* 16 words," this little leak was no big deal, and by the way, since Joseph Wilson doesn't agree with Bush and because he's written for publications that don't agree with Bush, he's hopelessly partisan and therefore without credibility.

Is it any wonder that, despite Vice President Dick Cheney's constant dissembling and deception about Iraq's connection to Sept. 11 and international terrorism, support for the administration's handling of the Iraq venture is beginning to circle the drain?

It will be interesting to see how this plays out, as it is of dire importance to Karl Rove and the Bush re-election campaign that this dies out—a long drip-drip-drip of stories regarding someone in the White House committing a federal offense that comes closer to dealing with issues of national security than the stains on a blue Gap dress can't be useful. At the same time, anyone overseas who ever dealt with Valerie Plame should probably hope that, like the father of that unaware college student, nobody holds it against them.

Have a Banana
August 18, 2004

Grab your bags, make sure your passport is up to date, and take your shoes off, because we're about to head through the metal detectors and get on a plane for a coast-to-coast tour of the planet's newest banana republic. Like many banana republics, it's safe for tourism. (How else can you get money for the cronies of the Fearless Leader if you don't have tourists?) And as always, there's plenty to see and do.

In this banana republic, like most, the currency is at a good exchange rate, because the people in charge tend to have a lot of overseas investments that they want to get a good return on, so feel free to cash in some gold, and let's go.

Our first stop is in the warmer, southern climes of the nation, a neat little place called Rio Rancho in a charming parish called New Mexico. The Deputy Fearless Leader spoke here just a few short weeks ago, at the end of July, to 2,000 of his faithful followers. If you look on the ground, you can still see a few of the oaths they had to sign to pledge fealty to their leadership. A newspaper called *The Boston Globe* reported Aug. 9 that 72-year-old retiree John Wade, of that quaint little town Albuquerque, asked, "Whose vice president is he?" when presented with the form when he went to get tickets for the event. "I just wanted to hear what my vice president had to say, and they make me sign a loyalty oath."

Quite the amusing customs they have here. Step lively now, we're getting back on the plane.

This little country is famous for its farming and agrarian traditions, so we'll touch down in the middle of the country to see some of the peasants as they go about their chores. Maybe you can pick up some colorful trinkets during the stop.

Don't be surprised if you see some local dissent in our next stop, a sleepy hamlet called Dubuque—some of the folk here haven't been happy since the last coup. Why, a local veteran of the military, a 64-year-old guy named Nick Lucy, had a ticket to see Dear Leader speak in May, but the police were told to escort him out because he wasn't a registered member of the Party. Lucy said he'd seen every leader speak since the old premier, who just died back at the start of June, but they still wouldn't let him in.

Reminds you of 1970s Latin America, doesn't it?

Before we continue, the captain has asked us to listen to an announcement being piped in over the loudspeakers. It seems the presidential palace has issued a terrorism warning, and we must be on our guard. The announcement, coming from an unnamed palace official, says there is no new information causing them to issue the alert, but they are saying that there is a possibility that, right before the elections, there is a good chance of some sort of attack from the enemy.

"You will get intelligence which suggests they're targeting the election time frame," an unnamed palace official, as reported Aug. 13, told reporters of a little news sheet called *The Washington Post*. "In addition to that, you get other intelligence that suggests there is planning for an ongoing operation that may not specifically mention the election."

The same official said, "No question some of this information was accessed in 2004 and indications are more recently than January—spring." However, the palace official added, "I have seen no indication of an imminent operation."

Now that we've got that out of the way, we want to remind you not to let these periodic announcements ruin your vacation—so make sure you spend that money.

Our local "minders" have informed us that in order not to

run afoul of government information ministers we are obliged to announce that the newspapers in this country are not tools of the government in any way. Just to prove that this is the case, we will be handing out to all passengers copies of the apologies printed by two of the country's bigger and more popular papers, *The Washington Post* and *The New York Times*, where the editorial staff have recently acknowledged they gave more credence to the claims made by the Fearless Leader than they did the opposition. You'll note some of the scandal sheets are more humble than others: the *Times* printed its apology back in May, while the *Post* issued its just last week.

But that's enough of the local current events—won't you have a tale to tell your relatives when you get back home. But before you go, we have been given one last note to read to you, from the attorney general; something he said right after the last terrorist attack on the country. He said, "To those who scare peace-loving people with phantoms of lost liberty, my message is this: Your tactics only aid terrorists." So, with that, we hope you enjoyed your stay, and don't forget the duty-free shop in the airport. Gotta keep that economy humming!

An Allegory
March 9, 2005

"Good morning. I'd like you to look at the new insurance plan I have for you. Your old policy, while it's worked well enough for the past 70 years, just isn't right for you anymore."

"Wait—I'm perfectly happy with my old plan."

"Well, you know, it's in a crisis—it's going to fail on you in, oh, 30 years or so."

"They said that before, in the mid-1980s, and with a few

tweaks it was fixed. Why can't you do that this time?"

"That would cost money."

"But wouldn't your plan cost money?"

"Not really. There's just a few transitional things—we'll call them 'fees.' How's that?"

"Oh, really? And what are we talking about in the way of these 'transitional fees?'"

"Something on the order of maybe $750 billion over 10 years."

"Is that *all*? Just $750 *billion* over 10 years? And this is supposed to fix my current plan?"

"Wellll—no. But the new plan, my plan, will be better than your old plan."

"And how will this be better?"

"It will be *personal. Yours.*"

"So this private plan . . . "

"Uhhh—we don't use that word anymore. It's your *personal* plan, see?"

"Right. So this 'personal' plan of mine, it's not going to cost anything except for the $750 billion in 'transition financing'— how come the people who say my plan isn't in any danger are saying that your plan is going to cost $4.9 trillion?"

"What do they know? They haven't seen my plan yet."

"But wait—even your own No. 2 guy said not so long ago that your plan's costs would run into 'trillions of dollars.'"

"Did he say that? What a kidder he is."

"Now wait a second—just a second ago, you said my plan was in a crisis, and your plan for privatization wouldn't really fix that crisis."

"I never said that."

"Yes, you did, just a second ago."

"Nope. Never said it. Anyway, I told you—we don't use the terms 'privatization' or 'private accounts'—they're so . . . impersonal."

"But you were using them not long ago! And this business about a 'crisis' . . . "

"OK, it's not a crisis. It's a problem. A problem. A really big problem. Really, really big. It's a problem with a capital 'P.' Problem with a 'P' that rhymes with 'T' that stands for trouble. It's a troubling problem. Problematic trouble. Maybe not a crisis, but a serious problem."

"OK, I get it. So what's such a big deal about these 'personal' accounts?"

"It's your money—you should be able to do what you want with it."

"That's not what you said when I didn't want my money going to invade some country that didn't attack us for weapons that weren't there."

"Hey, buddy—for a second there, I thought you might have said something that shows you don't support our brave American troops…"

"And anyway, wasn't my current plan designed to help not just me, but also my grandparents and my grandchildren? My grandmother isn't going to be pleased if I pull my money out to stick it in your 'personal accounts' if it means she's going to end up eating Alpo in some piss-smelling rest home."

"That's nonsense. We'd never do that to your sweet old grandmother. Her benefits will be paid the same as they always were."

"I don't see how you can say that when your own guy said that your costs are going run trillions of dollars."

"And didn't I say that your grandkids will be taken care of?

See, this poll shows that your kids already think that your plan isn't going to be there for them when they get older."

"Lemme see that—*Hey*! You had the people running my current plan print out this brochure! That's not right!"

"What, are you going to tell them that what they know in their hearts is wrong?"

"Now wait just a minute: I read something a while back that said you've been saying my plan was going to fail back in 1988."

"I was right, wasn't I?"

"You were saying this in 1978."

"So my math was a little off."

"Your math was 'a little off'? Back in 2000, you were saying that we could afford a tax cut and never have to dip into my plan's surplus money. Your competitor said he wanted to put that surplus money into a 'lock box,' and you ridiculed him for it. Two years later, not only had you blown the entire surplus, but your company had to bum $159 billion more!"

"Well, Sept. 11 changed everything."

"It changed everything all right—you've since rung up two more tax cuts and two separate wars, and now you want me, my grandmother, and my grandkids to eat trillions of dollars in up-front costs for your supposedly spectacular plan? Lemme see this plan, then!"

"Well, it's not really on paper yet."

"What? You've lied about the existence of WMDs, your Medicare plan, your military record, and your drug use! What possible reason is there for us to trust you with our retirement money?"

"Now you've gone too far—why do you hate America?"

The Times, They Have a-Changed
April 20, 2005

Ten years ago this week, the world changed. Or so we thought.

One hundred sixty-eight people died when the Alfred P. Murrah Federal Building in Oklahoma City was brought down by people we initially thought were Middle Eastern terrorists in the first few panicky hours after the destruction. Ten years ago, in this column, I tore into a local radio shock jock who started up a drumbeat of anti-Middle Eastern rhetoric—the usual "nuke them until they glow" threats—until it became apparent that it wasn't Muslim fanatics, but our own homegrown nutjobs that did it. And up until 2001, it was the biggest example of terrorism on our native soil in history.

But back then we didn't drastically curtail civil rights. We didn't declare war on a scapegoat who had nothing to do with it. And we methodically and legally tracked down, prosecuted, and convicted the criminals who perpetrated the crime.

I note this in order to point out that I am not the same columnist that I was 10 years ago. I'm more shrill, more biting, and more impatient of the ridiculousness I see in public life than I was a decade ago. Back then I saw it as a game.

Nowadays, it's still a game. But the stakes are far higher, the scope is larger, and the terms are far uglier than they ever were, not that the loss of 168 lives is anything to sneeze at. But let's look at it in context:

In 10 years, a concerted effort has been made by a hard-right conservative minority to drive an elected president from office over a lie about a consensual sex act. A president was installed, via the Supreme Court, after a contested state election whose apparatus was run questionably at best by his brother.

The largest terrorist attack on U.S. soil occurred after a clear-cut warning was issued to the president, who remained on his vacation after receiving this warning. A president and his vice, who maintain ties to the energy industry, succeeded in hiding their policy apparatus from the public, while their main campaign contributors gamed the energy system in the largest Democratic state in the union, thereby causing the ejection of its governor and the election of a Republican actor to the job. The illegal shenanigans of that same energy company caused one of the largest public bankruptcies in U.S. history.

In five years, we went from a balanced budget with a surplus to a budget hole with deficits as far as experts can project, with not one, not two, not three, but four tax cuts (if the permanent repeal of the estate tax the House passed last week is fully enacted) for the wealthy since this president was elected. And he presently campaigns to destroy the safety net that is Social Security.

I'd love to laugh at politics like I did 10 years ago. I'd love to be able to say, "This is only a silly game—they're funny people doing stupid things, and in a few years it'll be a different set of clowns doing the same thing." Only I can't.

The same clowns have been running the show for the last five years, and many of them have been there for the last 10. With total control of the machinery, they have gradually given the lead to the most fundamentalist, most reactionary, and most intolerant of their kind, and we have seen more than 1,500 Americans die in an unnecessary war whose end can only be declared by the man who began it, because Congress has abdicated its constitutional role. We are nation-building in a land that has historically been resistant to the idea, and it's being run by a man who declared that he was against nation-building before he even became president.

Ten years ago, I would have loved to have kept laughing and pointing out how silly politics is. But I was woken up by 168 people dying in an Oklahoma office building. Now, we are at war abroad, the right-wing crazies are not only still among us but also running our government (ask Terri Schiavo's husband), and Americans working to scrape together a living have no idea what to make of their future.

Times have changed. Politics just isn't funny anymore.

No Government Required
September 7, 2005

Ronald Reagan used to joke about it. He'd say one of the biggest lies in the world is "I'm from the government and I'm here to help you." Americans for Tax Reform executive director Grover Norquist wants to shrink the federal government down to the size "where we can drown it in the bathtub." Government is the enemy.

A government that checks the meat that is sold so you don't end up with trichinosis or *E. coli*, apparently it can't help you— no need for the Department of Agriculture. A government that approves the drugs you need to beat disease, to heal your child, to keep yourself alive, apparently it's of no use to you. No need for the Food and Drug Administration.

A government that monitors the markets to make sure that swindlers and cheats don't defraud the old, infirm, busy, or preoccupied—there's no need for it. So much for the Securities and Exchange Commission. A government that runs the systems that allow thousands of flights to take off and land safely every year, making air travel safer than driving—no need. Shut down the Federal Aviation Administration.

Government's always the problem, they say. Shutter the Internal Revenue Service; the rich will always manage to hide their money, so it's useless to try and tax them. Convenience is more important than fairness, multimillionaires like Steve Forbes say, once again trying to get you to pay his share of taxes for him as he pushes, yet again, his flat-tax plan. When asked if he won't do better than anyone else under a flat tax, Forbes demurs by saying he'll "do OK either way."

What use to the wealthy, to the conservative, to the powerful is government? None, even when what may end up being the largest natural disaster in U.S. history lands on the shores of one of America's poorer major cities?

While the rest of America was pouring out its heart while watching the devastation of New Orleans and the Gulf Coast of Alabama and Mississippi, the programmers at Fox News found the time to find an economist who argued that "the Founding Fathers never intended—Article 1, Section 8 of the Constitution—never intended to provide one dollar of taxpayer dollars to pay for any disaster or anything that we might call charity." Fox found one Jack Chambless, an economics professor at Orlando, Fla.'s Valencia Community College—I'm guessing this is the network's way of thumbing their nose at those elitists in the Ivy League universities who might be, as Karl Rove puts it, "too educated"—to say that every time the federal government comes in after a disaster and fixes up the area, the people "have no incentive to leave."

Because, of course, the only people who ought to be allowed to live in New Orleans—or near the beach in Florida or enjoy an ocean view anywhere a hurricane might strike—are the wealthy, who can afford to pack up and leave and fix their vacation homes all by themselves with no government assistance. Like the story of the Illinois family profiled in the *Chicago Tribune* who spent

$3,700 to leave New Orleans by limousine, while their Tulane University freshman son watched movies on his laptop in the back.

Predictably, the right wing will holler in outrage that liberals want to "politicize the disaster." But in reality, politics affects everything. As *Editor and Publisher* reported Aug. 30, "On June 8, 2004, Walter Maestri, emergency management chief for Jefferson Parish, Louisiana, told the [New Orleans] *Times-Picayune*: 'It appears that the money has been moved in the president's budget to handle homeland security and the war in Iraq, and I suppose that's the price we pay. Nobody locally is happy that the levees can't be finished, and we are doing everything we can to make the case that this is a security issue for us.'"

Many people in New Orleans didn't have the money to rent a truck, rent a car, charter a bus. The median household income in Orleans Parish, according to 2003 U.S. Census data, is $28,645. Just for comparison, in Baltimore City it's $32,452, and there but for the grace of your god go you. As one anguished woman wrote in her blog while watching the devastation, "They stayed because they could not run, and now they might die because they cannot swim."

But government, no matter how badly it's needed, no matter how awful the tragedy, is never the answer. The old, the infirm, and the poor, they always get what's coming to them. As it was said a long time ago, everyone gets the same amount of ice in this life—the rich get theirs in the summer, and the poor get theirs in the winter. Those are your "compassionate conservatives" for you.

Plan C
November 30, 2005

Perhaps we rejoiced too soon when the nondrinking, nondancing hypermoralist Pentecostal fundie John Ashcroft gave up his spot as the Bush administration's head Puritan in charge. At that point, we pulled the blue drape off the statue of Justice in the lobby of the Robert F. Kennedy Building and cheered in the notion that we rejoined the rest of the human race in something resembling the 21st century.

We were mistaken.

Perhaps I dwell a bit too long on the issues of how minorities are treated under the Bush administration—after all, while Republicans tell us they respect our numbers, truly want us to look at their "new" party, and say Democrats don't respect us, at every opportunity they crap on our heads. But African-Americans, just as an example, are at best only 12 percent to 14 percent of the population. If you want to look at us from a purely business standpoint (and what modern compassionate conservative doesn't, right?), go ahead and write us off. No really, go ahead—we know you will anyway.

But it's hard to understand why Republicans have chosen to piss off 51 percent of the human population. It all revolves around a pill dubbed "Plan B," an emergency contraceptive that has been available by prescription since the year before the Bushies took charge.

Let's understand where we are politically: Right now, religious fundamentalists are trying to relive the Scopes Monkey Trial all over the United States, from Kansas to Pennsylvania. Science is on the chopping block and empirical knowledge is giving way to political viewpoints. The president has no problem telling his rabble-rousing supporters that he supports the teaching of supernatural explanations for natural phenomena in classrooms.

And the U.S. Food and Drug Administration—the regulatory agency responsible for making our drugs safer and more effective than those of nearly every other nation—has been handed over to the politicos who care less about what works than what pleases the yokels who put this administration in charge of things.

Six months ago, the FDA rejected over-the-counter sales of Plan B, also known as the "morning-after pill." As a Government Accounting Office report showed, top Bush administration officials jumped into the decision-making process, something the GAO report noted was "very very rare," and then they ignored both the advice of an independent advisory committee and the FDA's scientific review staff. The GAO report concluded that a top FDA official created a "novel" rationale for rejecting Plan B's over-the-counter status, even making the decision before the review process was concluded.

If there is one issue that drives the far right as crazy as abortion, it's contraception. With regard to the Bush administration's recent high-court nominees, right-wingers have revisited, in terms of right to privacy, the 1965 Supreme Court decision that legalized birth control, *Griswold v. Connecticut.* To the Right, tying contraception to abortion is like nailing two birds with one big rock, and Plan B is the string.

The hard right is all about using unfounded fears to keep helpful contraceptives off the market no matter how effective the science—to this end, they wield confusion as much as possible, similar to the tactics of the proponents of "intelligent design." As the *Boston Globe*'s Ellen Goodman put it in her Nov. 12 column, "Fear of pregnancy is almost as useful in their kit bag as fear of cancer."

Senior members of the FDA quit in protest over how the drug was used as a political football during the approval process. Dr. Susan Wood, who quit her job as the head of the FDA's Office of Women's Health in August, said in a Nov. 15 *New York Times* article that the politics and the FDA's new directors' desire to brush aside science in favor of the right-wing agenda has "only gotten worse" since the agency found yet another reason to delay a decision on Plan B.

As an Aug. 11 article by Susan Yudt of Planned Parenthood noted, the government has no problems with gaming the descriptions of emergency contraceptives like Plan B in order to slide the new rules through the system: "The federal government even went so far as to change the definition of pregnancy in the Department of Health and Human Services' Code of Regulations in order to position [emergency contraception] as a cause of abortion, rather than as a means of *preventing* pregnancy."

Come January, when Supreme Court nominee Samuel Alito comes before the U.S. Senate, it will be interesting to see where he comes down on an issue that pits scientific efficacy against political expediency. The part of the citizenry that can bear children might find it worth their attention.

A Different Kind of Year
December 28, 2005

A few months back, I was invited to speak to the Maryland Writers' Association. After the talk, one of the members of the audience asked a standard question: "Where do you get your ideas?"

In some ways, writing a column such as this is limiting, in that I have to stick to a particular topic: "politics." But since this topic is so broad and all-encompassing, there's no shortage of things to write about. This is even truer thanks to the current administrations we have in Annapolis and in Washington, so the answer to the question was simple enough: "I keep a file, plus I have a limitless well of outrage and a pretty long memory."

The memory comes and goes, but I do keep a file titled "Outrages," and shall we say that the year 2005 provided what they termed in the movie *Top Gun* a "target-rich environment."

Friends tell me, "Well, you must be happy you have so much to write about," and I answer them in all honesty, "I'd much rather have a better country." Because deep inside any political columnist, Left or Right, lurks an idealist who only wants things to be better—"better" meaning, of course, the way they'd like them to be. When things don't work out this way, the columnist is left with either cynicism or righteous anger.

Hence, my file. The first news story of this past year that stands out, from the Jan. 7 *New York Times*, is about the CIA inspector general's conclusion in a report that the people who served at the highest levels of the agency should have been held accountable, but weren't, for the intelligence lapses leading up to Sept. 11. This story came out the month after CIA chief George Tenet was awarded the Medal of Freedom by President Bush.

Come Jan. 11, *The Washington Post* wrote about the District of Columbia protesting the Bush inaugural committee's refusal to reimburse the $11.9 million the event cost the city. Pretty much immediately, the administration told the city to just take the money out of the grants it gets for Homeland Security projects.

In February, tapes and transcripts from phone calls made by traders at Enron were released. The *Los Angeles Times* noted that "traders conspired to shut down a healthy power plant as blackouts rolled across California in early 2001." Gloating traders chanted "Burn, baby, burn!" on the tapes, and bragged about inflating energy costs for "Grandma Millie," as a way to run up power charges in the state.

Also in February, more signs emerged of one of the most disturbing trends under the Bush administration: officials coming to policy via predetermined conclusions. *The New York Times* pointed out that the Environmental Protection Agency's political leadership "instructed staff members to arrive at a predetermined conclusion favoring industry when they prepared a proposed rule last year to reduce the amount of mercury emitted from coal-fired power plants." At the state level, this is similar to the Dec. 18 story from *The Sun* that noted the Maryland Department of the Environment, when blocking stricter anti-pollution standards, used language that was cut-and-pasted straight out of an e-mail from a lobbyist for Constellation Energy, BGE's parent company and the state's largest producer of electricity.

Obfuscation and deceit were big themes in 2005. *The New York Times* reported in February that the administration blocked a report for five full months—which would have placed the real release date square in the middle of the 2004 election campaign— showing that the Federal Aviation Administration had warned in spring 2001, well into Bush's watch, that Osama bin Laden and al-Qaida might try airline hijackings and suicide operations.

Some of the first reports of torture of war detainees came to light in March. Dana Priest of *The Washington Post* wrote of CIA-paid guards in Afghanistan dragging "their captive around on the concrete floor, bruising and scraping his skin, before putting him in his cell." That same month, the Republican head of the Senate Intelligence Committee opposed requests to open broader investigations into misconduct by the CIA and abuse of terrorism suspects.

The year continued with pharmacists refusing legitimate requests for birth control pills; Wal-Mart being accused of using illegal aliens to clean their stores; no right-wing groups on the list of domestic terrorism suspects (worth noting now that we know the feds are spying on Greenpeace, PETA, and Catholic Workers). And of course, in boom or bust, under high inflation or low, there are always tax cuts and rising executive salaries. These stories are in my file, too. They always are.

Since Sept. 11, the Bushies constantly remind us that we are fighting a "different kind of war," when trying to explain why things cannot be as they were before. Well, we certainly are becoming a different kind of country. I'm hoping 2006 proves me wrong.

As They See It
March 1, 2006

Many, many years ago, your humble Political Animal toiled in a boring job entailing working ridiculous hours for a nebbishy boss whose supervisors walked all over him (and, by extension, us). We took out our frustrations the only way we knew how—by tormenting the nebbish ourselves.

My apartment building was only a three-minute drive from the office. So I called one day five minutes before my shift started. "Jim," I said, "I can't make it in to work today."

"What's the matter?" he asked.

"I have a vision problem."

"What do you mean, a 'vision problem'? Is there something wrong with your eyesight?"

"Yeah—I can't see coming in to work." And then, after some squealing of tires, I'd walk in two minutes before the shift began.

Bush administration officials have begun using my little joke in earnest now. Anything that doesn't fit their standard worldview is something they just cannot see, often on purpose. *The Washington Post*'s Dana Milbank pointed out how, during Senate testimony last week, the administration officials sent to Capitol Hill to explain their recent actions concerning the sale of the administration of six U.S. ports, including Baltimore's, had developed a sudden case of selective myopia.

In his Feb. 24 column, Milbank cited the 14-year-old law that requires all sales to state-owned companies, such as the one to Dubai Ports World, that may affect U.S. national security to undergo a 45-day review process. The review, of course, was never done.

Milbank picks up the testimony from there:

> Sen. Robert Byrd (D-W.Va.), who wrote the 1992 law, demanded to know "why that investigation was not carried out."
>
> [Sen. John] Warner [R-Va.] asked Deputy Treasury Secretary Robert Kimmitt to "clarify."
>
> *"Senator,"* Kimmitt told Byrd, *"we have a difference of opinion on the interpretation of your amendment."* The

administration, he said, views it "as being discretionary."

Sen. Hillary Rodham Clinton (D-N.Y.), reading the statute to Kimmitt, said the law *"requires—requires—an investigation."*

"We do not see it as mandatory," Kimmitt repeated.

Sen. Carl Levin (D-Mich.) grew irritated. *"If you want the law changed,"* he told Kimmitt, *"come to Congress and change it. But don't ignore it."*

"We didn't ignore the law," Kimmitt again maintained. *"We might interpret it differently."*

"We do not see it as mandatory"? That's as close to my "vision problem" as you can get, except it's not usually advisable to tell a U.S. senator that "we just couldn't see following your silly little law."

How, one wonders, does the executive branch of a constitutional democracy get away with telling lawmakers that it doesn't feel like being bound by duly enacted and fairly easy to understand laws? It is an act of breathtaking arrogance and gall from an administration that has frankly displayed no shortage of either commodity since George W. Bush first came into office in 2001 claiming that "we will show purpose without arrogance."

On Feb. 23, Milbank examined the former Justice Department attorney-turned-college professor John Yoo, who authored some of the Bush administration's most controversial legal opinions.

It was Yoo whose writings said that the administration could mistreat foreign prisoners up to the point of death and not call it torture. Yoo was the one who argued that the administration could conduct domestic wiretapping via mass data gathering from the National Security Agency, and last week, at the Heritage Foundation, it was Yoo who stated the mind-blowing belief that

Congress' sole ability to declare war under the Constitution was some creation of the "popular imagination."

This is pretty stunning, especially since it's pretty easy to look up the text of the Constitution, and there it is, in plain English, 11 clauses into Section 8 of Article I: "The Congress shall have the power . . . to declare War."

But Yoo once again parses words within an inch of their lives, saying, as quoted by Milbank, "Note that the declare-war clause uses the word 'declare.' It doesn't use the word 'begin,' 'make,' 'authorize,' 'wage' or 'commence' war." These are the ideas of someone who believes that because the president is the "commander in chief," then the president suddenly has the powers of a king in wartime and that the other two branches of government are subservient. And why is this? Because they see it that way.

The sad part about all of this is that the only reason Bush gets away with these awe-inspiring leaps of fancy into a world where the Constitution means whatever he feels it means is because Congress has simply abrogated its power of oversight of the executive branch.

And if the Dubai port deal goes through as scheduled, there's a pretty good chance that once again it will be because the Congress just couldn't see doing its job.

No Sex, Please
March 29, 2006

Back in 2003, before the invasion of Iraq, a senior Bush administration official told *Newsweek*, "Anybody can go to Baghdad. Real men want to go to Tehran." The phrase summed up chickenhawk conservatives' overweening bravado when it came to remaking the world in the image they wished, sort of like the comment from another senior Bushie, as told to journalist Ron Suskind: "We're an empire now, and when we act, we create our own reality."

In terms of women's reproductive rights, the viewpoint from the Right must be: "Anybody can overturn *Roe v. Wade*. Real men want to overturn *Griswold v. Connecticut.*"

By now you've probably heard that South Dakota is making a concerted effort to be the state that overturns *Roe*, the 33-year-old Supreme Court decision legalizing abortion. But it's becoming clear that many of the anti-choice warriors on the Right don't want to stop there—now it looks like they're pushing to find ways to make contraception as difficult as possible as well.

As usual, the battle begins in an intolerant Midwestern state with a strong fundamentalist streak; in this case, Missouri, the state that gave us Rush Limbaugh and John Ashcroft. On March 15, the Missouri House of Representatives voted to ban using state money for contraceptives for low-income women, and, on top of that, the measure would prohibit state-funded programs from referring women to other sources that might provide contraceptives.

A year ago we learned that many pharmacists were flat-out refusing to fill birth control prescriptions or to issue "morning after" pills by claiming that, by filling those orders, their moral or religious beliefs were being violated.

We here at Animal Control remember reading about this at the time and thinking, *There's a simple answer to this: DON'T WORK THERE.* If you want to be in control of other creatures' reproductive systems, don't decide you want to be a pharmacist when you grow up—maybe you should become a veterinarian.

A March 28, 2005, story in *The Washington Post* quotes Adam Sonfield of the Alan Guttmacher Institute in New York, which tracks reproductive issues:

> There are pharmacists who will only give birth control pills to a woman if she's married. There are pharmacists who mistakenly believe contraception is a form of abortion and refuse to prescribe it to anyone . . . There are even cases of pharmacists holding prescriptions hostage, where they won't even transfer it to another pharmacy when time is of the essence.

Lately, the arguments have centered over emergency contraception such as Plan B and RU-486. The religious-right groups pushing the anti-contraception agenda, such as the National Right to Life Committee and Concerned Women for America, deliberately muddy the waters when it comes to both of the drugs, and the Concerned Women for America is very clear about its anti-contraception stance.

The battle over Plan B has even reached the U.S. Senate in the form of a hold placed on the new Bush pick to be the head of the Food and Drug Administration. In 2003 the FDA's Nonprescription Drugs Advisory Committee and the Advisory Committee for Reproductive Health recommended making Plan B an over-the-counter medication. The FDA since then has stalled on the matter. When Bush nominated Lester Crawford to head the FDA in February 2005, Senators Hillary Clinton of New York and Patty Murray of Washington blocked the nomination, saying they would do so until the FDA made a decision on the issue. Health and Human Services Secretary Mike Leavitt, whose cabinet agency oversees the FDA, told the senators that the FDA would make the decision by last September, and so Clinton and Murray released the hold—after which Leavitt and Crawford reopened the Plan B debate for further public comment, thus creating yet another delay.

Now, after Crawford's resignation back in September, President Bush nominated Andrew von Eschenbach, director of the National Cancer Institute and acting FDA commissioner since September, to be the permanent FDA head. And, steaming over the last trick pulled on them, Clinton and Murray have once again blocked the nomination.

The sad thing is, despite an overwhelming percentage of Americans who favor access to contraceptives, such a small yet powerful lobby is slowly and steadily eroding access to them. The basis of *Roe v. Wade* was built on the 1965 *Griswold v. Connecticut* decision, which first established the "penumbras" in the Bill of Rights that established a right to privacy, forming the core of the decision in *Roe*. At the time, Connecticut had laws that would fine doctors who issued or *even counseled the use* of contraceptives.

So remember, while it's disgusting to think of what has happened to women's right to choose what they can do with their own bodies in the state of South Dakota, for some that's just a way station on a trip back to Connecticut in 1964.

Media

I have had a lifelong interest in the media, and not just because it's where I've made the bulk of my living. What happens in politics is inordinately driven by the media—witness how the environment has changed after Fox News started up in the autumn of 1996. Now there is no "objective" truth any more, because as long as there is an organization with a political agenda from the top-down driving coverage, there will always be someone to deny the existence of obvious facts or to give credence to scurrilous rumors. This wasn't the case when I was younger and thought that television news was the solution to many of the nation's problems, not, as is often the case now, the cause.

For a good time of my career in politics, when I was asked "What do you do," my standard flip answer was "I teach politics to journalists, and journalism to politicians." Politicians, even well-meaning ones (yes, there are some), are naturally skeptical of the press. I used to tell them "Treat the press as you would a pet alligator—you don't have to love it. You don't have to like it. You *do* have to *feed* it."

Nowadays political television journalism news is driven by personality, "gets" and "gotchas"—"get"-ting the interview, and on live TV, the "gotcha" question. Only "personalities" make it far now in TV news, which is why they test them with "Q" ratings and why the big ones have agents negotiating their salaries like Hollywood actors. The rest of television news is populated by young pretty people who have either worked their way up through the minor leagues, bouncing from station to station in the hinterlands until they reach the networks, or otherwise land in whatever Nielsen market they find the most comfortable financially and managerially. Or often some of the ones at the network start out as lowly production assistants and manage to suck down enough stress, caffeine and screaming that they triumph over the system and end up in front of a camera, once all their understanding of the blue-collar world has been completely excised from their memories.

I once worked with a person whose driving goal was (like mine, long ago) to end up as a correspondent at one of the major networks. He spoke in police-scanner speak, words tumbling out of his mouth in a mixture of acronyms and jargon, with a thick layer of affected boredom pasted over all of it. He thought nothing of calling people out of a sound sleep in their homes at five in the morning in December to ask them to stick their heads out the window and describe for listeners what a fire down the street looked like. In the business, this is balls. In the real world, this is an asshole.

When I met acclaimed writer and television journalist Linda Ellerbee at a conference once, I told her this story and one where an editor asked me to do something equally rude to a random person picked out of a phone book due to their address being near to some early morning tragedy *du jour*. My answer to that editor, simply put, was "Fuck no."

She signed my copy of her book, "And So It Goes: Adventures In Television" with the words, "To Brian, here's to doing it the right way."

*   *   *

Tune Out
June 7, 1995

Maybe Newt is right.

Maybe the Progress and Freedom Foundation is too—about the FCC, that is. When it comes to communications technology, and the accumulation of power under single sources, perhaps all the real battles have been fought and lost already, and we're all just keeping a single flag flying before the armies of profit come swooping down on our tents like the Sioux came down on Custer.

Author, academic and former reporter Ben Bagdikian began chronicling back in 1983 in his book *The Media Monopoly* the consolidation of communications power in the hands of a few all-powerful corporations. Since then, many have either died in debt or been eaten, by leveraged buyout, corporate merger or fire sale. ABC became Cap Cities/ABC, Time Inc. and Warner Communications merged to become Time-Warner, netting the creator of the giant, Steve Ross, an obscene mega-sum of money before he too discovered he couldn't take it with him and died of cancer at a relatively young age.

Rupert Murdoch and Ted Turner control international information conglomerates, and with single page memos can decide how people on separate continents will have their news interpreted for them (Turner banned usage of the word "foreign" in CNN news copy, noting that the cable giant had more than an American audience). NBC is no longer just NBC, it is CNBC and NBC NewsChannel, which is also piped overseas for foreign, er, international consumption. And it is all owned by GE, whose old initials comprise the musical notes that are the audio signature of its broadcast enterprise: General Electric Corporation—G-E-C.

But the fairly small and exceedingly overburdened government agency that is tasked to ride herd on all the airwaves—the *public* airwaves, lest we forget—would be demolished under the proposal from the conservative think tank that sponsored the broadcast of Professor Newt Gingrich's college courses.

The plan would be to dismantle the FCC and its 2,200 employees and have a small office under the auspices of the executive branch (i.e. the president runs the show, with no interference from a meddlesome Congress or mid-level bureaucracy). Organizations—hell, let's just call them "goliaths"—already possessing FCC licenses would get what amounts to a free and permanent franchise on the airwaves that most likely could never be revoked.

And make no mistake, having a broadcast license in the modern era is tantamount to a license to print money. The Radio and Television News Directors Foundation and Ball State University published the results of a survey in the RTNDA *Communicator* magazine this past April showing that 83 percent of all TV stations made a profit last year with their news departments, the main revenue (and cost) center of a station. Who owns TV stations? More and more, it is the giant chains—Hearst (WBAL), Group W (Westinghouse, which owns WJZ), and Scripps-Howard (WMAR). And these chains would be granted permanent standing to make their cash by the creation of programming appealing to the lower common denominator and the highest possible number of viewers while taking the least amount of artistic, cultural or legal chances.

Gingrich has been quoted in a May issue of *Broadcasting & Cable* magazine that he would like to see the FCC phased out "in three to five years at the most." In that time, billions of dollars would have changed hands as those who are already in possession of FCC licenses seek to acquire more, and preserve their profit margins.

There was a time ago when communications was about information, about news when it was "news." Bagdikian quotes from a memo sent by Edward Wyllis Scripps, the founder of the chain that bears his name, to the editors of one of its papers:

"A newspaper…must at all times antagonize the selfish interests of that very class which furnishes the larger part of a newspaper's income…The press in this country is now and has always been so thoroughly dominated by the wealthy few of the country that it cannot be depended upon to give the great mass of the people that correct information concerning political, economical and social subjects which it is necessary that the mass of people shall have in order that they shall vote and in all ways act in the best way to protect themselves from the brutal force and chicanery of the ruling and employing classes….

"I have only one principle and that is represented by an effort to make it harder for the rich to grow richer and easier for the poor to keep from growing poorer."

In an era where celebrity interviews are passed off as news, when the murder trial of an ex-football player is rammed down the throats of a public weary of the annoying spectacle by ratings-hungry media managers, when telecommunications lobbyists pay college students thousands of dollars to stand in their places outside congressional hearings as if they were ticket windows for Grateful Dead concerts and "policy foundations" whose funding comes from telecommunications and computer industries promote the dismantling of the last barricade that stands between corporate baronies and multi-billion dollar permanent quasi-monopolies, maybe all is truly lost.

We give up. Sell the airwaves. Kill the FCC. Make your

money.

We'll still have the Internet. Or will we?

We're All Ears
August 9, 1995

As our nation's 39th president used to put it, "There you go again." We recall back in 1979, the chairman of the Federal Reserve Board, the cigar-chomping Paul Volcker, deregulated the money supply and let interest rates float. Later on, the second tumbler in the lock clicked open when the Reagan Administration's *laissez-faire* attitude toward policing the securities industry combined with the deregulation of the bond markets combined to create a hullabaloo of fiscal imprudence that only ended recently with the final closure of the Resolution Trust Corporation. In between those events, of course, was the megamammoth financial disaster known as the savings and loan crisis.

Here we go again.

This time, the financial earthquake will be caused not by a president, but by the House of Representatives, which in a few small masterstrokes may do more to transfer money into the hands of a few giant corporations since the heyday of the robber barons in the early twentieth century. Back then it was coal, oil and transportation. Now it's communications and information. The tectonic plates underneath the information superhighway are about to see some major rearranging.

With last Thursday and Friday's roller-coaster ride leading up to summer recess, the passage of HR1555 may do more toward the creation of a future media juggernaut than anything Disney, Time-Warner or Rupert Murdoch may have thought possible. Let's build the scenario, starting from last Friday:

By a vote of 305-117, the House drastically rewrites telecommunications law for the first time in sixty years. When the proviso allowing local phone companies to enter the long distance market without facing real competition at home remains intact, consumer organizations are grim. Bradley Stillman, director of telecommunications policy at the Consumer Federation of America, tells *The New York Times* that when local phone companies and cable companies are allowed to grow too large, their monopolistic tendencies will show through and the consumer will be the first to pay for it. "Congress has reached deep into consumers' pockets, opened their wallets and taken out their money," Stillman said.

How could he be wrong? Already there is little such thing as a "local" cable company—they tend to be part of large conglomerates such as TCI and Time-Warner. Same for the baby Bells—there may only be seven, but in the areas served by Bell Atlantic, NYNEX, et. al., they are as close to lord and master of the communications world as there is. And by virtue of their monopoly power, they can make it awfully hard for any startup company to challenge them for their turf.

And then, of course, there is the Shadow of The Mouse. The acquisition of CapCities/ABC by Disney is the closest thing to an omen the telecommunications could possibly see except maybe for an un-forecasted midday eclipse over Wall Street. It and the purchase of CBS by Westinghouse were what convinced lawmakers that maybe rampant acquisition of information providers might not be such a grand idea after all, and they revised downward the percentage of American households conglomerates' stations could reach—from 50 percent to 35. Still, the House bill would let newspaper companies—not broadcasters—own local TV and cable franchises.

The question is, in the era of multinational, diversified

corporations, which are broadcasters and which are newspapers? Gannett owns TV stations and newspapers. Time-Warner publishes magazines and owns cable companies. And Disney—well, Disney will own you before long. Don't laugh—it almost happened in Virginia.

Last week, the day after the Disney buyout of CapCities/ABC, Charlie Gibson of ABC's "Good Morning America" had the unfortunate task of interviewing his new boss, Michael Eisner, uberboss of Disney. Suddenly, the tables were turned when Eisner asked Gibson, "wouldn't you be proud to be associated with Disney?"

The mere fact that Eisner had the effrontery to ask a newsman to virtually pledge allegiance to the flag of his new corporate masters shows that the line between information and propaganda has never before been so thin in the modern era of "dispassionate" reporting. The times, they have a-changed.

Thirteen years ago, in his landmark study documenting the wholesale consolidation of media power into the hands of a few companies, Ben Bagdikian wrote, "The arrogance of corporate power has reached levels that leave no doubt that it prefers private greed to public civilization. Corporate power, exercised through the media and government, openly ridicules governmental functions that serve ordinary people, while demanding that government further enriches private fortunes."

"Corporations erect glistening skyscrapers and display lavish private goods—options in a rich country—while sneering at appropriations for public services, food for the poor, and money to educate the nation's children—moral obligations for a rich country."

Are we to see a day when the phone bill, the cable bill, the TV programs, the newspapers and the magazines all come from one giant Time-Warner-Disney-Murdoch-Philip Morris-Kraft? The answer is a House-Senate conference and possibly a veto-override away.

And how did Charlie Gibson answer when his new bosses asked about his pride in the Dinsey name? According to *USA Today*, he said, "Yes, sure—I just never imagined working for Mickey Mouse."

They never do.

Freedom Delenda Est
October 4, 1995

We here at Animal Control have to confess a certain amount of glee at the ire that the opinions in the column provoke. Continuing in the fine tradition of political column-writing under the belief that "to get 'em up, you gotta rile 'em up," we like to think that couching political opinion and theory in less-than-diplomatic prose brings politics to people who normally don't care much for the sport at all. After all, if one is to commit the act of journalism, one might as well go for something in the felony range and not just play around with misdemeanors.

This, however, is being taken to new extremes with the newest columnist at The Other Paper, who, if we were to continue the metaphor, has extended the practice well into the domain of 'capitol offense.' We are all for The Other Paper hiring minority columnists, although it seems to appear that they feel that one sole black man writing about politics and society will do for a city that is better than fifty percent black and contains a substantial population of Asians and Latinos as well.

This new columnist, a Mr. Gregory Kane, has gone on record as calling himself a "fascist" when it comes to crime. He then went on to prove himself worthy of the self-applied label when he advocated "warrantless searches" for drugs and guns in public housing complexes.

Well! If there's anything you have to like about The Other Paper, it's that they have the courage to provide a regular space to someone with opinions so irresponsible. Not that opinions like this should not be expressed; *au contraire, mon ami.* We all need someone to laugh at.

The only theory we can come up with here is that perhaps Mr. Kane descended from those African kings and queens that everyone wearing kente cloth seems to believe they descended from these days. Because it was the actions of an irresponsible monarch that led the founders of the United States to word the Fourth Amendment to the Constitution so strongly.

In case Mr. Kane hasn't read it lately (which appears likely), it goes like this: *The right of the people to be secure in their persons, houses, papers and effects, against unreasonable searches and seizures, shall not be violated, and no warrants shall issue, but upon probable cause, supported by oath or affirmation, and particularly describing the place to be searched, and the persons or things to be seized.*

It is somewhat convenient for Mr. Kane to volunteer the homes of other people for the honor of warrantless searches, especially low-income people who traditionally have the smallest voice in society and receive the least of its rewards. We would suggest that if there were to be police actions without due process, perhaps it would be less disingenuous if Mr. Kane were to volunteer his own neighborhood for a start.

His reasoning behind this belief is that if extreme measures such as the ones he advocates are not taken, the sole alternative will be the citizenry rising up as vigilantes to take matters into their own hands.

For starters, the premise that 'if drastic measures are not taken, there will only be one equally drastic alternative,' is rather unsophisticated analysis. Basically, it shows thought about as deep as an ashtray. Much as pundits love to extol the "either/or" scenario, there are as many alternatives as there are creative minds to come up with them, and usually reality proves us all wrong.

Secondly, any civil libertarian will tell you that sometimes there is nothing wrong with citizenry taking the law into their own hands. When the law was wrong, as it was when Martin Luther King marched on behalf of civil rights, he went to jail, knowing that time and moral outrage would eventually release him and bring the law in line with true justice. If citizens take the law into their own hands, the laws and their peers will decide if their actions were just or not. If we remove the safeguards to our freedom, leaving us unprotected from the armed guardians of the state, then who will guard the guardians? Mr. Kane?

Not to launch into a history lesson here (although it appears some people may need it, judging from how many agreed with Mr. Kane during his appearance on the Marc Steiner radio show last week), Mr. Kane seems to be starting a vocal offensive such as that done by Cato the Elder during the third Punic War. "*Carthago delenda est*," he said, "Carthage must be destroyed." And it was— the city was blockaded, conquered, taken apart brick by brick and eventually ploughed under.

Already Fourth Amendment freedoms have been eroded by a high court enamored of the power of the state, and policies of the George Bush administration such as "zero tolerance" saw the confiscation and seizure of property with little or no due process. When individuals such as Mr. Kane take up the call that our freedoms need to be destroyed brick by brick in order to be saved, that is when thinking citizens need a wake-up call.

If Mr. Kane thinks warrantless searches, caning and the death penalty are suitable and just deterrents to crime, he should move to Singapore. But since he chooses to remain here, at least he is committing journalism rather than politics. Thank goodness.

Fear TV
March 6, 1996

How many products can you name that make their sales appeal based on fear? Think about it—fear of rejection, fear of crime, fear of unemployment, fear of bad breath; boy, there's just no amount of people out there who figure they can scare you into thinking you'll buy what they're selling if they can put the (excuse the expression) fear of God into you.

The latest fear campaign on the market is even more amazing in its audacity than anything the makers of the Door Club or a lawyer with a smoking phone booth can devise. It's the end of "Free TV" as we know it.

WBAL television (Channel 11) has been running editorials, narrated by the station's general manager Phil Stoltz, claiming that, if the federal government auctions off parts of the spectrum as part of a deal to balance the budget, the fate of "free TV" may hang in the balance.

In the script of the editorial, provided by WBAL, Stoltz says somberly that, "for hundreds of millions of Americans, free local television represents such a unique, irreplaceable service that it's tough to imagine life without it.

"But that's exactly what we could be looking at if some members of Congress get their way," he goes on.

The editorial continues, saying that the auction of TV spectrum frequencies "would mean the end of free TV."

Now, whoa there, hoss! For starters, how freakin' free is TV anyway?

Sure, after you've bought the set, you go home, plug the sucker in, turn it on, and wham!—instant lousy entertainment, almost all around the clock. Outside of a free babysitting service guaranteed to let your children see thousands of violent and sexual acts before they reach the age of consent, the only other thing it does is to communicate small bits of actual information in between millions of dollars worth of sales pitches.

And think about this: those sales pitches aren't "free" either. Every Nike ad run on national television costs hundreds of thousands of dollars. Every overpaid athlete endorsing a shoe gets perhaps millions of dollars. All of the money put into the advertising of the shoe and into the media buy gets recouped in the price of the product itself. Sure, TV may be free, but you're paying for it in the price of those stupid sneakers that make your kid think he can dunk a basketball at the age of nine.

On top of that, a license to broadcast on the so-called "public" airwaves is like a license to print money. When was the last time you remember hearing of a station having its broadcast license denied at renewal time? No matter what kind of crap aired today, the people who have those licenses to use the airwaves that theoretically belong to us all will continue to have those licenses in the future.

In addition, there are a limited number of frequencies that can broadcast TV signals, which is why most TV markets have maybe four or five VHF stations, max. With the advent of giant media chains, there is hardly any such thing as "local" TV ownership anymore. WBAL is owned by the Hearst Corporation, a media juggernaut with radio, TV and magazine properties all across the nation.

In the new telecommunications bill recently passed by the Congress and signed by the president, media corporations that own properties that reach a quarter of the nation can now increase their holdings to allow them to reach 35 percent of the country, a consolidation of media power already gone overboard.

To avoid essentially a giveaway of billions of dollars worth of frequencies, members of Congress normally as partisan as Sen. Robert Dole and Rep. Barney Frank have argued for an auction, agreeing that to simply let the broadcasters have the frequencies for free would amount to massive corporate welfare. The media conglomerates say they would use the frequencies for high definition television—although there's nothing in the new law that would specifically direct them to do so.

Broadcasters want an arrangement where if they can convince viewers (that's us) to buy enough newer, more expensive HDTV sets to justify their investment in the new technology, they'll "turn in" the old frequencies. The question is, who will decide when the broadcasters have made enough of a return on their investment?

The whole "Death of Free TV" scenario is being coordinated by the National Association of Broadcasters, which has been lobbying Capitol Hill with full-page newspaper ads asking "Doesn't a free society deserve free TV?" The ad copy is almost word-for-word identical to the script read by WBAL's general manager.

If the people of America decide through their representatives not to let broadcasters have for free something that perhaps they should start paying for in these tough times, it's pretty obvious that Hearst Broadcasting and it's ilk are not going to shut down the transmitters and haul the equipment to Mexico. There are still a whole lot of those shoe ads that need to be aired. And if basketball shoes start getting that much more pricey to support the advent of HDTV, maybe even more people will start buying those cheap canvas hi-top sneakers.

Biblical Knowledge
August 2, 2003

In the beginning, there was Reagan.

And in the days of Reagan, the consolidation began with the $340 million merger, creating the behemoth Gannett, which did swallow many newspapers whole across the land. And Gannett did create McPaper, which didst simplify the news for many.

And the Prophet Moon—he wouldst tell you so himself, that he really is a prophet—begat the *Times of Washington*, to give voice to those in the wilderness.

And Reagan doth anoint his chairman of the Federal Communications Commission, Mark Fowler, and saw that it was good.

Fowler didst see unfairness in the Fairness Doctrine of broadcasting, and in 1987 didst cast it aside, saying that with the Fairness Doctrine came unfairness, and with that unfairness came regulation, and that too much regulation didst bring a lack of competition in the marketplace.

And thus begat the beginnings of the One Voice.

For lo, in those dark days, the media were few and they were liberal. And Reagan did chafe under the relentless eyes of the Eye, the Alphabet and the Peacock.

But under Fowler, there begat competition in the form of the Fox, which was brought forth by the Great Aussie Emancipator Murdoch. And Reagan didst make Murdoch a citizen for his service to the true cause.

In their midst did Fowler enable more competition by relaxing the rules, thus allowing bigger companies to own more media.

And then those companies bought up more media, creating less competition. And those media didst promise that they would create more and serious public-affairs programming and they didst say that they chafed under the unfairness of the Fairness Doctrine.

And in those dark days, there were only 50 controlling corporations in the media.

Meanwhile, in the Holy Lands, our Enemy Iran did do battle mightily with the Enemy of Our Enemy Iraq, and the intelligence procured then didst show that Iraq did use chemical weapons upon their foe.

During these days, the Prophet Rumsfeld was dispatched to the Holy Lands, the cradle of civilization, to deal with the enemy of our enemy to make him a friend. And thus didst Rumsfeld meet on the 20th of December in the Year of Our Lord 1983 with the Beast of Baghdad, to encourage his war against the enemy, the Ayatollah. Yet in the documents from this meeting, the Prophet Rumsfeld didst not mention the dreadful weaponry.

But I digresseth.

Years passed, and time marcheth on.

And after the work of Fowler, Cap Cities begat Cap Cities/ABC, which begat the reign of the behemoth of the Mouse of Disney. And Time-Life begat Time-Warner, which begat AOL Time Warner. And RCA begat General Electric, which begat NBC. And CBS was swallowed by Tisch, who sold to Westinghouse, which sold to Viacom. And that which was not swallowed by the former was swallowed by the distant giant of Sony.

And it was thus that the 50 corporations of 1984 begat the 26 corporations of 1987, which begat the 23 in 1990, which begat the 10 in 1996. And it was thus that today the media are almost wholly owned by Time-Warner, Sony, Disney, News Corp.,

Gannett, GE, Viacom and Clear Channel.

And they didst see that while news and public affairs was good, what good is it if it doth not turn a profit? And so gradually the goal of journalism became not that it was quality but in that how many eyeballs did it draw.

And in these days, when the land is ruled by men of Harken and Halliburton, war rages in the Holy Lands, where the traders in the marketplace shiver over rumors of fire in the fields of oil. And the thus minions of Halliburton hath little competition in their quest to rebuild these lands in the days after the war, for the government hath seen it to be so.

For energy is power in the new age, in that the masters of Enron may gouge the people of the land of California, and that the anointed from Halliburton, who maketh not his fortune from the government (despite all the contracts), may say that the gouging happened not. And the Son of Bush did distance himself from Kenneth Lay, and saw that it was good, for the media would not remind the people of those days.

And the owners of Clear Channel, who cometh from Texas, and the Aussie Emancipator Murdoch and the Prophet Moon (still shall he tell you he is such) shall smite mightily those who have quarrel with the Son of Bush.

For these are the days where the rich are taxed too much and the poor too little, sayeth the *Journal of Wall Street*. The taxes must be lowered, sayeth the leadership, to maketh a strong economy for those fighting overseas for the freedom of the company to incorporate in foreign lands and avoid paying those taxes forthwith.

The taxes must be lowered, sayeth the leadership, because we shall not passeth on our burdens to our children, and our children's children, sayeth the Son of Bush. The deficit it doth riseth, but it is not important.

So sayest the media. And it was good.

These Honored Dead
May 5, 2004

It's stunning that here in Baltimore—a city awash in patriotic icons, the town that gave the United States both its national anthem and its Pledge of Allegiance—honoring the war dead is seen as something to avoid.

By now you've probably heard about Hunt Valley-based Sinclair Broadcast Group's decision to pre-empt last Friday's *Nightline* on the seven ABC affiliates it owns for the sole reason that the program and anchor Ted Koppel decided to read the names of the 721 military men and women who have died in the war on Iraq and its aftermath. Sinclair, as noted in this space before, has taken upon itself as the country's largest owner of TV stations to pump in news to all its stations from an operation it calls "News Central" up at its headquarters in Baltimore County. Through News Central, the broadcast company pumps out right-wing opinion and puts its own spin on affiliates' newscasts—in some cases, over the wishes of the local reporters and editors on the scene. Back when the war was gearing up, Sinclair reportedly told its staffers here at Fox 45 to read pro-administration messages in support of the war on terrorism. In itself this is only slightly odious, but when you realize that Sinclair reaches almost 25 percent of the country through its 62 TV stations in 39 markets, you can see how insidious this ham-handed attempt at bias actually is.

Sinclair vice president Mark Hyman, who also doubles as News Central's right-wing commentator, has fired off his response to critics of the company's decision. Hyman was quoted in the *Los*

Angeles Times as saying, "We have a principled view that we don't want to see the memories [of those who have given their lives] tarnished," as part of what Sinclair calls a political statement. In any number of other interviews, Hyman has said that he feels *Nightline*'s reading of the names is not "proportional" to the war effort. Like the Bush administration does all the time, his arguments attempt to tie Iraq to Sept. 11, 2001, noting that *Nightline* isn't listing all the names of the people who died then.

For once and for all, can we say this clearly to those who would keep peddling this malarkey? *There were no ties between Iraq and Sept. 11!* None! There were no Iraqis on those planes, no meetings between Saddam Hussein's people and al-Qaida, no link between a secular regime and the minions of a religious fanatic. To keep bringing up that canard insults the intelligence of every person who makes the sad mistake of watching one of Hyman's "The Point" commentaries through to its finish.

It is sad that the parents and families of these young men and women have to bear the burden of such a clueless media operation. Photos themselves carry no context—they are what you bring to them. Many parents who might have wanted the small honor of seeing the picture of their son or daughter on national television, fresh-faced and serious decked out in military dress uniform, were denied that miniscule bit of pride. Interestingly enough, last Friday *USA Today* spread the pictures of all the servicemen and -women who died in April, the deadliest month of engagement in Iraq, across its front page. One wonders if the Sinclair crowd thought that was a political statement as well.

It's no secret that the Sinclair brass are George W. Bush supporters. According to the Center for Responsive Politics, four of Sinclair's top executives have maxed out their allowed political donations to the Bush-Cheney campaign. Not that you need ask, but no, they did not hedge their bets like many corporate types do and give money to Sen. John Kerry or any Democrats.

Sen. John McCain of Arizona, himself a former POW in Vietnam, saw the Sinclair hooey for what it really was—a cheap ploy to ally itself with an administration that has yet to level with Americans about why their sons and daughters were sent to die in Iraq. Last Friday, McCain sent a letter to David Smith, the president and CEO of Sinclair: "Your decision to deny your viewers an opportunity to be reminded of war's terrible costs, in all their heartbreaking detail, is a gross disservice to the public, and to the men and women of the United States Armed Forces. It is, in short, sir, unpatriotic. I hope it meets with the public opprobrium it most certainly deserves."

If it were up to Sinclair, the only news out of Iraq would be happy stories about all the schools and hospitals that have opened since the end of the war. No pictures of flag-draped coffins would see the light of day, no names of soldiers would ever be read to teary families, no solitary sounds of "Taps" would bring a solemn end to a local newscast. Because, of course, that would be unpatriotic.

President Lincoln said it best, and little has changed since then: "It is rather for us the living, we here be dedicated to the great task remaining before us—that from these honored dead we take increased devotion to that cause for which they here gave the last full measure of devotion—that we here highly resolve that these dead shall not have died in vain."

But for Sinclair, perhaps they have.

Triumph of the Bullies
June 4, 2003

Some years ago, long before we emerged from our chrysalis to become the ever-lovin' Political Animal, fearless wielder of the first-person plural (officially used only by kings, editors, pregnant women and people with tapeworm), we were a humble little radio reporter, toiling away in the burrow of a local station's news department.

Across the hall from that news department were the mighty lords of the manor, the radio talk-show hosts, men of bombast and opinion, who thundered about all and sundry with all-knowing certitude.

One day, we came across one of these lords in the hallway, near the studio door. With a smile, we recall saying, "You know, some day I'm gonna have to call in and crush your argument." The lord replied, "It will never happen."

"Why?"

"Because," he said with the grace of a casino owner, "*I control the buttons.*"

In a nutshell, this explains the political climate of today. The game is rigged. Freedom of the press belongs to those who own the media, and the price of ownership has gone up. The big guys will always win. And, as they say in the time-honored parlance of the schoolyard bully: *Quit whining about it.*

Election stolen after your guy got a half-million votes more? You lost. Quit whining about it.

Don't like the fact Congress passed a $1.3 trillion tax cut benefiting the wealthy while you got a measly $300? Why doncha' give back the money then? Quit whining about it.

Or, as one writer (anonymous, of course) e-mailed us after

we mentioned how the Dixie Chicks got penalized by the media oligarchy, "Get a grip, quit whining, and begin to appreciate how fortunate all Americans are to have strong leadership who won't leave us open to more mass murders." History will probably not alert him to the irony of his words.

Far from the humility of which our new commander in chief spoke back in January 2001, or the compassion of which he spoke during the campaign of 2000, we are now fully in the Era of the Bully, where it is fine for the strong to prey on the weak, as long as there is an adequate (not plausible, just adequate) rationale.

Back in March, U.S. foreign policy over the invasion of Iraq left us wide open to the charge of bullying. *Washington Post* columnist Dana Milbank listed a travelogue of nations slinging the term: "arrogant bully" (Britain), "bully boys" (Australia), "big bully" (Russia), "bully Bush" (Kenya), "arrogant" (Turkey) and "capricious" (Canada). Diplomats have accused the administration of "hardball" tactics, "jungle justice," and acting "like thugs."

And don't forget the famous term for the poor used by the editorial page of *The Wall Street Journal*, the favorite print echo chamber of the right: "lucky duckies" who pay no taxes. Not a day after this president signed a so-called $300 billion tax cut into law (it really will come out closer to $800 million), the paper was defending cutting millions of families out of the child tax credit in the bill. Official prevaricator Ari Fleischer, the president's spokesman, said, "There's a whole other, larger group of Americans, tens of millions, who still pay income taxes, who now will pay less income taxes, as a result of this tax relief. And that's why, in the president's judgment, this is fair to all Americans."

If that statement were rendered in 1970s *New York Post*-speak, it would read, "Bush to Poor: Drop Dead."

It's good to be a bully in 2003. All you need is a lot of money and a lot of power. Movies stink because Hollywood bean counters bully studios for moneymakers to pay off the debt incurred by gobbling up more studios in megamergers. Television stinks because programmers seek the lowest common denominator in ideas, reality TV, in order to grab the most eyeballs for the cheapest prices in order to charge the most money for advertising. The programmers, of course, are bullied again by the network bean counters who require 35 percent-plus profit margins.

Newspapers are run by conglomerates bullied by the bottom line and held hostage to competition from TV and cable news outlets that almost never bother to run corrections when they are wrong, much less acknowledge that they *can* be wrong.

Over the past few weeks, a drama played out in Texas, where a group of renegade Democratic lawmakers left the state in order to prevent a quorum, to stop a Republican majority from eviscerating precedent and the state's congressional districts in a plan designed by über-bully, House Majority Leader Tom DeLay, to increase his party's seats in Congress.

In the course of this sorry little playlet, state GOP leaders apparently snookered the Department of Homeland Security's tracking apparatus into looking for the private plane belonging to one of the lawmakers, and then a commander of the Texas Department of Public Safety ordered all records of the search destroyed. Those same Public Safety officials are now demanding the names of the sources a Texas Democratic representative used to find out that there was paper-shredding going on. Just like bullies do.

There's no shame anymore, no humility—just heavy-handed brute power, wielded by the powerful against the poor, the powerless, those in the minority. But why should they care? Quit whining about it. They control the buttons.

Newsman
August 17, 2005

Nowadays, when you go to journalism school, you shouldn't be surprised to find broadcast majors who began that line of education because friends or family told them that they'd "look good on TV." It's not surprising, because when your ever-lovin' Political Animal started out in J-school, that's what they were telling his colleagues.

Cheerleaders, high-school beauty queens, pretty boys not interested in the pain and sweat of varsity athletics (or varsity athletes looking for the fast track to the broadcast booth)—these were the people in the mid-1980s who went into television journalism. People who thought that learning all the technical parts of the equipment was beneath them because, well, their job was to look glamorous and be on television. Boy, were they surprised.

I mention these mist-shrouded memories because of the passing of the last of the real television newsmen—Peter Jennings. Like this writer, Jennings had no college degree; he didn't even graduate from high school. Jennings learned the hard way; after being thrust into a job far above his pay grade and hitting the wall, he took off and did the real work. Jennings went and became an expert in the most convoluted, dangerous, and trouble-stricken part of the world: the Middle East.

You have to understand that nowadays the TV news business will air-drop a "face" correspondent into a scene; his or her job is to pump the local producer dry of every bit of knowledge, and then, like David Brinkley used to tell newbies, "fake sincerity" that they knew all along what was going on. The networks have far too much money invested in their big-shot talent to actually make them real experts by stationing them out in the middle of God-knows-where, learning who really runs the show, why people X hate people Y, and what it all means. We are a country that thinks that "international news" means what's going on with the immigrant population in California, so no one will really know the difference if Our Man in Beirut knows his ass from his elbow.

Nineteen years ago, this writer applied to become a summer desk assistant at ABC News, to fill in for people who handled the phones when havoc broke out all over the planet. This was right about the time that the Reagan administration gutted the Fairness Doctrine and the rest of the communications laws that made possible the rise of advocacy broadcast journalism and the eventual coming of things like the Fox News Channel. In spring of 1986 the United States bombed Libya, and on the day of my interview Dean Norland, the news-desk manager at ABC, let me sit in Ted Koppel's chair on the set of *Nightline* and listen to the bombs drop as Charles Jaco, the network's man on the scene at the time, hung his microphone out of his hotel window to catch the explosions.

At the time, CBS may have been living on its reputation as "the Tiffany network," but ABC was the place to be. By the end of the decade, its promotional spots would declare that "more Americans get their news from ABC News than from any other source." And the face of that network was Peter Jennings.

CBS had Dan Rather, whose corn-pone charm originated covering hurricanes hitting the Texas coast. Tom Brokaw, a son of the Midwest, was considered a lightweight when he first took the NBC anchor desk after spending time on the *Today* show. Only Jennings, inheriting the anchor desk after the collapse of the three-anchor format of ABC's *World News Tonight*, had the gravitas to step up and remind Americans that we were one part of an increasingly complicated world at a time when the Cold War raged, and we had a president who undiplomatically referred to the Soviet Union as the "Evil Empire." When dealing with an overseas correspondent by telephone one time, I recall an operator butting in to the call, only to hear Jennings switch to flawless French and convince the operator to get off the line. Try and imagine any of today's blow-dried mannequins doing that.

Hunter S. Thompson saved choice words for the practice of journalism, and the recently deceased writer had hardly anything but contempt for the TV version of his chosen profession. Outside of sports, he had little use for it—and watching so-called news anchors on cable like Bill O'Reilly, Shepard Smith, John Gibson, or vapid newsreaders like Stone Phillips or Ashleigh Banfield, makes one wonder about the future of the medium that had so much promise when Edward R. Murrow stood on London rooftops at the end of World War II.

We are as informed as the news we get in this interconnected world, and when we are spoon-fed bits of nonsense about the latest missing white woman, we almost deserve the ugly world we inherit, terrorism and all. Ben Franklin predicted the end of liberty if we weren't able to pay attention, and the simpletons we accept as our news anchors reflect this. We don't have any more men like Peter Jennings, and more's the worse for us because of it. He told us what was really going on, and we were better people because of it.

Funnies No More
December 14, 2005

Politics and funny don't go together as easily as you'd think. Well, not if you earnestly have a love for the process, anyway. You need to have a certain amount of nihilism in your soul to be a political cartoonist—"a pox on both their houses" and all that. Of course, you could be a libertarian, like many (including the excellent Steve Benson of *The Arizona Republic*), which fully allows you to spit a good loogie at the whole endeavor.

This week, editorial cartoonists around the nation—an anarchistic band of individuals if there ever was one—grouped together for "Black Ink Monday," when they used their unique showcase to point out how their numbers are shrinking among the nation's already hard-squeezed newspapers.

You could argue that the op-ed column is not only an original American form (see the book *Poets, Pundits, and Wits* by Karl Meyer) but indispensable as a record of American thought over the course of the republic. Franklin, Twain, Lardner, Rogers, Mencken, Lippman, Alsop, Baker, Trillin, McGrory, Will, Dowd—these are the names that have populated the column across from newspaper editorials. But even more so than the writers, the cartoonists have steered the opinions and conscience of a nation.

It takes a lot to write a column, but it takes more to draw a cartoon. A picture may be worth a thousand words, but an idea, a snapshot of a thought, requires more than 1,000 words to be described adequately. Yet a cartoon can clarify in a single frame what would otherwise require reams of words. A cartoon distills. And better still, it is funny. Or not. It could be wry, ironic, angry, or bitter. But a cartoon pokes delicately into the subconscious of our present-day minds and then jabs until it bleeds. People may ignore the columns—but they *stare* at the cartoons.

It was a political cartoonist, Thomas Nast, who in the late 1800s gave us the symbols for the two dominant political parties in America: the elephant and the donkey. Nast caused the leader of the predominant urban political machine in America to go into fits: William Marcy "Boss" Tweed of New York's Tammany Hall machine went apoplectic because, while his constituents may not have understood the sentiments in the op-ed columns, he knew they sure as hell understood the pictures in Nast's cartoons.

But the art form in America is dying, and it has as much to do with the current political climate as it does the economics of the newspaper business. The bean counter's scythe has, over the last few years, taken the heads of Republican-leaning cartoonists—Michael Ramirez of the Los Angeles Times—and liberal leaners such as *The Sun*'s Kevin "KAL" Kallaugher, who recently took a buyout. It's clear to all now that it has nothing to do with ideology and everything to do with money.

Major metropolitan newspapers have ceased having to do with anything concerned with journalism and the public good; those now are by-products. If the remote ideals that originated with the daily newspaper were still inherent, then the political cartoon might not be dying. After all, what's simpler to "get" than a cartoon?

In my college years, as the editorial-page editor for the *Diamondback* at the University of Maryland, nothing was guaranteed to send various interest groups at the school (truth be told, usually the Black Student Union) into apoplexy more than the cartoonists. One half-page cartoon mocking the leader of the BSU on my watch led the group to come storming down to the paper's offices like something out of Mary Shelley's *Frankenstein*, leaving me relieved that pitchforks were not part of the average student's possessions.

I've been a fan of editorial cartoons ever since. The late Herb Block of *The Washington Post* made his mark on America simply by giving Richard Nixon a 5 o'clock shadow, forever marking him as shifty in the eyes of editorial-page readers. Jules Feiffer's delicate strokes adorned the pages of New York's Village Voice for more than 40 years. Paul Conrad was the powerful artistic voice of the Los Angeles Times before Ramirez. While once visiting The Arizona Republic, I saw on the door of the aforementioned Steve Benson a handwritten note: "I have known many nice Bensons in my life. You are not one of them. Barry Goldwater."

There are no wimpy editorial cartoonists—the job requires a strong constitution, strong opinions, and unwavering faith in one's beliefs. These are days when opinions that vary with the prevailing winds are not rewarded. We're headed toward times when if opinions can't be bought they won't be expressed, and cartoonists are far too mercurial to be owned, and the space in which they ply their trade is too valuable to take risks in.

Black Ink Monday signified the death knell for the political cartoonist. If you don't care, then how long will it be before there is one for the newspaper itself?

No News Is Bad News
May 31, 2006

There's a veritable tiki bar of topics to choose from in what otherwise is one of the slowest news weeks of the year—a strawberry margarita in the form of the Enron trial verdict; two or three banana daiquiris worth of stories about the electricity rate hike and the BGE/FPL merger; a champagne cocktail of former state senator Larry Young thinking about running for the General Assembly again; a highball of 26 million U.S. vets' personal data on a Department of Veterans Affairs employee's stolen laptop; the sloe gin fizz of dumb cluck Congressman William Jefferson and his $90,000 safe disguised as a kitchen freezer—and here I am, reaching for the 7-year-old beer in the back of the fridge called the Clinton sex life.

It's not just me: *The New York Times* last week decided, of all things, to front-page a story speculating about how often Bill and Hillary Clinton sleep with each other, because, you know, it's important. Four-dollar-a-gallon gasoline in California, a thousand dead in New Orleans, 2,000 more in Iraq, an administration with polling numbers as low as Dick Nixon's after Alexander Butterfield spilled his guts about the tapes, and the state of the Clinton Penis (or "the Clenis," as it's known in the blogosphere) is serious enough to warrant Page One real estate in the so-called paper of record for the United States of America. God Bless Us, Every One.

Thankfully, we can rely on the "dean" of the Washington press corps, David Broder, to dislodge us from this fitful reverie where we are back in the horrible, horrible days of 1998, when we suffered mightily under the burden of peace and prosperity, when gasoline hovered around a dollar a gallon, the nation's budget was balanced, and we barely missed Osama bin Laden with a cruise-missile strike. As Broder wrote last week in his column about Hillary Clinton's speech at the National Press Club, "But the buzz in the room was not about her speech—or her striking appearance in a lemon-yellow pantsuit—but about the lengthy analysis of the state of her marriage to Bill Clinton that was on the front page of that morning's *New York Times*." How do we manage, I ask you?

When is something news? When the Washington press—unlike any other newspaper or television media in the world, with what wag Bob Somerby calls its "Millionaire Pundit Values"—declares something news. Your average newspaper reporter in your average no-name American town makes less than a car salesman, a real-estate agent, or a grocery store manager. But in Washington, with million-dollar book contracts, insider parties, clubby dinners featuring the President of the United States, "the press" has more in common with Kenneth Lay and Jeffrey Skilling than they do with the mothers and fathers, the PTA members and soccer coaches, who lost everything when Enron went belly-up.

It's *important*. David Broder said so. It's like when all those corporate CEOs sit on all the same boards with each other and decide they all deserve high salaries because, well, they're worth it, no matter what the company does in good times or bad. "But for all the delicacy of the treatment, the very fact that the *Times* had sent a reporter out to interview 50 people about the state of the Clintons' marriage and placed the story on the top of Page One was a clear signal—if any was needed—that the drama of the Clintons' personal life would be a hot topic if she runs for president," Broder wrote.

It's hard to see a clearer tautology in the news business: Their sex life was once news because they were important. Now, because she is important, their sex life is now news. In what universe is it possible that Bill and Hillary Clinton's personal life, under this tortured logic, could not be news?

Stephen Colbert went to D.C. and offended the press corps right to their faces at their annual logrolling dinner and self-congratulatory jamboree by pointing out obvious truths, truths that America found funny (one month later an audio version of the Colbert speech was still topping Apple's iTunes Music Store) but got members of the Washington media all up in full dander. Colbert didn't stop with a president who had so far managed to escape merciless mocking to his face, but hit a press corps who needed it badly as well.

"Here's how it works," Colbert said that night, "the president makes decisions. He's the decider. The press secretary announces those decisions, and you people of the press type those decisions down. Make, announce, type. Just put 'em through a spell check and go home. Get to know your family again. Make love to your wife. Write that novel you got kicking around in your head. You know, the one about the intrepid Washington reporter with the courage to stand up to the administration. You know—fiction!"

Not funny, they said. How very telling that something that the Washington press doesn't find funny still tops the charts a month later in the real world. And now, here we are in 2006, Al Gore's in the news again, the media is back in Bill Clinton's pants, and D.C.'s millionaire pundits find absolutely nothing wrong with that. It's like everything old really is new again.

The Price Is Wrong
February 28, 2007

[cue music and announcer]

"Welcome once again to the hottest game show in the newsfotainment world of cable television! MSNBC brings you the smartest man alive here in studio and ready to challenge all comers—it's DICK CHENEY IS ALWAYS RIGHT! First, please welcome your host, Wolf Blitzer!"

WOLF: Thanks very much, Johnny. This is the game show where contestants put it all on the line to match wits with the smartest man in America, if not in six of the seven continents, the former vice-president of the United States of America; the man who, here in 2009 is revered universally for leaving office with the lowest recorded popularity ratings in the history of modern polling, proving that nobody likes it when you're right—please welcome Dick Cheney!

CHENEY: [Grumpf, snarl] Let's get this crap on the road, Blizer, I've got places to be.

WOLF: Right, Mr. Vice-President. Today's contestant is a former congressional staffer to a west-coast liberal congresswoman...

CHENEY: [snarl]

WOLF: ...who, after leaving the Hill, found work in a small public policy office devoted to environmental concerns. Please welcome David Belcher of Takoma Park, Maryland!

[mild audience applause]

WOLF: Okay, David, you know the rules, right? You put up your entire life savings against the word of Mr. Cheney with the possibility that he might actually not be right. If you, in some unforeseen circumstance, might actually be right, not only do you get to keep your money, but you get to choose from a selection of fabulous prizes!

BELCHER: Look, I had no idea when I signed that loan agreement that this was part of the fine print—the only reason I'm here is that this was the only option you people presented in the arbitration hearing...

WOLF: Next time you'll pay more attention on what goes into the fine print of appropriations bills during the 109th Congress, won't you, Dave? The viewing audience will also get to listen in on our in-studio news commentators, Tim Russert and Chris Matthews of NBC, and Fred Barnes of The Weekly Standard.

BARNES: George W. Bush was the greatest president America ever had. Except for Reagan, who was Jesus in disguise.

MATTHEWS: When do I get to interrupt somebody?

RUSSERT: As my dad, 'Big Russ' used to say...

WOLF: Right! Okay—let's get started! The first question goes to David: What happened after the United States invaded Iraq?

BELCHER: That's easy—to date we've had more than five thousand American casualties, Saddam was hanged, the country exploded in civil war and the Bush administration conducted air strikes on Iran right before the 2008 elections, and gas prices went to five dollars a gallon.

CHENEY: You're wrong.

WOLF: Mr. Cheney is correct!

BELCHER: Hey, wait a minute!

WOLF: Mr. Cheney?

CHENEY: We invaded to bring freedom and democracy, and our troops were greeted as liberators with flowers and candy.

WOLF: David Belcher loses a thousand dollars and half the annuity value of his IRA. Commentators?

RUSSERT: You know, my dad 'Big Russ' used to tell me that

you should always know when to hold 'em and know when to fold 'em…

BELCHER: That was Kenny Rogers' "The Gambler!"

RUSSERT: Yeah, but my dad 'Big Russ'—you know, I've written a book about him—my dad used to say it all the time.

MATTHEWS: You know, Dave might have been right if he wasn't distracted by how terrible it was that the country was wrecked by Bill Clinton's blowjob…

WOLF: Uh, right. Okay, the next question is for Vice-President Cheney.

BARNES: Donald Rumsfeld was the greatest Secretary of Defense the United States ever had.

CHENEY: That's correct.

WOLF: Mr. Cheney is right!

BELCHER: Wait—you didn't even ask a question!

WOLF: It doesn't matter—Mr. Cheney answered, and the answer was correct. David loses his firstborn son's college fund and the keys to his 1993 Honda Civic.

CHENEY: Heh. Shoulda' bought American.

BELCHER: My car was made in *Ohio*, you imbecile!

MATTHEWS: Oooh, this doesn't look good—Belcher's already sounding as crazy as Howard Dean in Iowa. Let's replay that clip again.

DEAN: [on video] YEEEEEEEEEAAAARGH!

MATTHEWS: I never get tired of that.

BARNES: Did you know that if you look at George Bush the right way, you can see a halo?

WOLF: Our next question is for David. David, who is Scooter Libby?

BELCHER: Scooter Libby left the Bush White House in disgrace after being charged with lying to investigators after the administration all acted in concert to expose an American covert intelligence agent in order to smear her husband, an administration critic.

WOLF: Mr. Cheney?

CHENEY: He's wrong.

BELCHER: Why are you asking *him*?

WOLF: He is the smartest man in America, after all. He told us so. Commentators?

RUSSERT: Well, I have video from 2004 where he told me on "Meet The Press" that he's the smartest man in America, so I can't prove otherwise…

MATTHEWS: Nobody got a hummer in the Oval Office when Dick Cheney was there.

BARNES: He might even be smarter than George Bush.

WOLF: Okay, what about Scooter Libby?

RUSSERT: [silence]

MATTHEWS: Who?

BARNES: See—Dick Cheney is right!

WOLF: And David Belcher loses his house and on Monday reports to his new job as a greeter at Wal-Mart! That's all the time we have today, but thanks for watching America's new favorite game show…

BELCHER: This stupid show doesn't even get a .2 rating!

CHENEY: You're out of line.

[trapdoor opens beneath Belcher]

WOLF: …Dick Cheney Is Always Right!

[audience applause]

Drugs and Guns

As if it's not obvious, I'm not a "researcher." I'm not a scholar (go ahead, ask any of my high school teachers). I'm not a politician. (It was a running joke between me and my wife back when I was married that she had my permission to shoot in the head anyone who asked me to run for political office, and my permission to shoot *me* in the head if I accepted.)

I'm just a guy who has been in the wrong places at the right times, who has hung out with a lot of really smart people and seen a lot of really dumb ones say and do a lot of dumb things. I've also met a lot of really nice people who have seen a lot of tragedy in their lives, and a number of nice people who are, sad to say, really misinformed about reality. Some of them are even my friends.

Over the past decade and a half, give or take a year or two, I seem to have been in front lines of two of the most politically divisive, partisan issues in America—the friends you have on one issue are the enemies on another. And as my ex used to say, it's kind of hard to find an American without an opinion on anything, much less the two topics at hand.

Increase that by an order of magnitude, and you've got people in the nation's capital, where the world is so emulsified by party that even dating services there ask for political affiliation as part of their prospective client questionnaires.

When talking to a member of Congress at one reception in the Capitol, I listed for him the various people for whom I had worked and his face alternatively rose and fell and rose again like the baby in that Super Bowl McDonald's commercial whose face smiled every time his rocker allowed him to see the Golden Arches, then grimacing when the chair moved him out of view.

Given the way people are on the politics of guns and drugs, I'm probably not likely to change any minds. That's okay; it also should be listed above that I'm not an evangelist. My point, really, is to show some of the idiocy that gets bandied about either as official policy, or sometimes, as what some people would like to become official policy on either topic.

It's all very nice and good to say that, because seventy-three people in San Francisco "feel better" because they smoke a joint each day to "help their glaucoma," that pot should be legalized, or that because a 67-year-old shopkeeper in Altoona, PA defended his shop from some marauding teenagers with baseball bats by firing off a couple of shots with the .38 behind the counter, that more guns equals less crime—but that's nonsense. Any scientist will tell you the truth. Anecdotes make lousy policy. Great stories, maybe, but lousy policy.

Oh, and not all science is good science, either. If there's anything that's more dangerous than formulating policy without science, it's formulating it by using data that lie because someone has an agenda to push. And it happens all the time. Even by the "good guys."

I'm not even a hard case about either subject: At a personal level, hell, guns are fun. I've squeezed off a few rounds with assorted weaponry at a local target range, and have even been looking into purchasing a matched set of black powder dueling pistols. And if you're circling the drain with Dr. Kevorkian on speed dial, if your life looks like its going to be nothing but pain between now and when you shuffle off this mortal coil, hell, go ahead and open up the whole medicine cabinet—smoke what you want and more power to you. But outside of those personal beliefs, a whole bunch of policy devils lie in the details, and many of them have never gotten a full airing in the marketplace of ideas.

In "Simon Says," I mention how I had to subdue a junkie who broke into my house—while I was convalescing with a herniated disc in my back. In March of 2008, I was stepping out of the bathroom one morning in my underwear and bedroom slippers after a late night editing this text, only to confront yet another burglar intent on walking off with all my valuables. This one was lucky enough to get away with only a few glancing blows, albeit with my voice bellowing in his ear as if I was the second coming of David Simon's drug kingpin Marlo Stansfield from "The Wire" on a really bad day. I was still yelling at him while threatening all manner of bodily harm, hot on his tail, underwear and all, as he almost broke his neck bolting out my front door. But I still think (and experience tells me) that even if you have a gun in the house, if you're on the spot dealing with someone breaking in, the odds are much more likely that you'll be nowhere near it, or won't think (or be able to) to get it when the moment arises.

So let's get down to the serious business of pissing people off. With any luck, you might be one of the small minority who doesn't find something to disagree with in this chapter. If you are, wow. Miracles do happen.

*   *   *

War Movies
Unpublished, February 2002

I'm still waiting for the movie on the "War on Speeding." After all, we have thousands of traffic laws, police use photo radar at stoplights, laser guns and helicopters to try and spot scofflaws, but still people speed. I guess we should just give up. The "War on Speeding" has failed.

I make this point because I'm struck by how many movie critics found it necessary to include the phrase "failed war on drugs" when reviewing "Traffic," the Steven Soderburgh film up for Best Picture. I spent two and a half years as a spokesman for the "drug czar's office"—another picturesque metaphor run amuck. For a work of fiction, the movie hews pretty close to what we saw in the Office of National Drug Control Policy from 1996 to 1999.

Jesus Gutierrez Rebollo, head of the Mexican federal police force, really was elevated to become his country's drug czar. Rebollo then was arrested for being in cahoots with the head of one of the Mexican drug cartels, Amado Carrillo Fuentes, known as the "Lord of the Skies." Fuentes really was using Rebollo to crack down on his rivals, the Arellano Felix brothers of Tijuana. And, in a deviation from the movie, Fuentes really did die on an operating table after a plastic surgeon sucked two liters of fat from his body to alter his appearance.

It starts with the nomination of an Ohio state Supreme Court justice, played by Michael Douglas, to be the next head of ONDCP. The outgoing director, of course, is a white-haired Army general in full uniform, which I'm guessing is supposed to be a thinly-veiled version of Barry McCaffrey, the general named by President Clinton in 1996.

The position of ONDCP director is a civilian job, so a uniformed general is laying it on a bit thick. McCaffrey really did take a tour of the southwest border of the United States twice while I was there. But (before 9/11) a drug czar would never be allowed to fly in a privately chartered jet loaded up with officials before he is confirmed. McCaffrey usually flew coach, and when he flew first-class, it was because the airline upgraded him.

Screenwriter Stephen Gaghan goes awry when he thinks that any state Supreme Court justice wouldn't make his local paper, and then the national papers, when his daughter spends the night in jail. That the daughter would go on to become an addict without the knowledge of her parents may not be that unbelievable, but then to have her important father running around a city slum facing down armed pushers while being lectured on the "drug war" by a prep school boy is surreal. Any father I know would have punched that kid's lights out.

The biggest horselaugh of the film is reserved for Albert Finney's chief of staff telling Douglas that *The Washington Post* would sit on his daughter's story, since it is "a family matter." In what universe would that happen? In reality, the confirmation vetting process would have stopped this before it started. The minute the news hit the paper of the nominee's daughter in jail on a drug case, he would be asked politely to withdraw his name.

"Traffic" points out some realities our nation faces when it comes to drugs—and it ignores several others. We catch less than one percent—not forty, as the movie states—of the drugs coming in over the southwest border. This problem is more like a cancer than it is a "war." For drugs like marijuana and methamphetamines, there is no border; they are grown and made here. And drug addicts don't just exist in urban ghettos; they are the sons and daughters of the middle class and the well-to-do.

But calling it a "war on drugs" is falling for the game of conservatives who want to intrude on the sovereignty of our neighbors while denying realities at home. And it plays into the hand of those liberals who want to legalize drugs altogether, by claiming that the "war," with its win-loss connotation, has failed and it's time to throw the baby out with the bathwater.

So, kids are still flunking school. When do we see the movie on the "failed War on Stupidity?"

Shot Down With Facts
October 23, 2002

"We are all entitled to our own opinions," former U.S. Sen. Daniel Patrick Moynihan (D-N.Y.) once famously opined, "but we are not entitled to our own facts." With that in mind, we will run down a list of facts about the gun debate, nationally and locally, in light of the actions of the sniper stalking the Washington area.

In the interests of full disclosure, Fact: This writer spent two years as a spokesman for Jim and Sarah Brady at the Brady Campaign, and a year on the board of Marylanders Against Handgun Abuse, a position he resigned upon accepting this columnist position. Pro-gun lobby sympathizers may immediately discount anything written hereafter. But facts do not lie.

Fact: Late in the Friday night of March 22, 1996, long after newspaper and TV deadlines had passed, Rep. Robert Ehrlich (R-Md.) and his mentor, Speaker Newt Gingrich (R-Ga.), engineered and passed HR-125, a repeal of the 1994 ban on semiautomatic assault weapons and large-capacity feed devices. This went for naught when the Senate bill died in the Judiciary Committee.

Fact: During John Ashcroft's confirmation hearings, Sen.

Charles Schumer (D-N.Y.) asked Ashcroft about his vote as a senator in 1998 to cut the length of time law enforcement is allowed to keep background-check information. "You have voted to undermine what the FBI maintains is essential to successful operation of the [National Instant Check System]," Schumer said. "How can we be sure that you will work with the FBI to maintain the integrity of the NICS when you have already sided with the gun lobby over the F.B.I.?" Ashcroft's exact answer: "If confirmed, I will be law-oriented."

Fact: May 4, 2001. Attorney General Ashcroft decides to delay for a second time implementation of a Clinton Administration regulation that would keep background-check records for 90 days.

Fact: October 2001. Virginia gubernatorial candidate Mark Earley, in his race against eventual winner Mark Warner, garnered an "A-" grade from the National Rifle Association against Warner's "C." The NRA noted that they would have given him a solid "A" if only he hadn't voted in 1993 for the state's one-gun-a-month law designed to cut down interstate gun trafficking. In the 2000 congressional elections, Maryland representatives Connie Morella and Wayne Gilchrest (both Republicans) got "F" grades from the NRA. Ehrlich received an "A."

Fact: Oct. 30, 2001. Muhammad Navid Asrar, a Pakistani national, pleaded guilty in Texas to immigration charges and to illegal possession of ammunition. The authorities said that in the last seven years, Asrar, an illegal immigrant, had bought several weapons at gun shows, including a Sten submachine gun, a Ruger Mini-14 rifle, two pistols and a hunting rifle.

Fact: Dec. 5, 2001. Ashcroft tells the Senate, "Each action taken by the Department of Justice...is carefully drawn to target a narrow class of individuals: terrorists."

Fact: Dec. 5, 2001. *The New York Times* reports the Justice Department refused to let the FBI check gun records to see if any of the 1,200 people detained after Sept. 11 had bought guns. The Times also reports that the Bureau of Alcohol, Tobacco and Firearms requested in September to check a list of 186 detainees against NICS records. The check recorded two "hits," meaning two detainees had been approved for gun purchases. The day following the Times reports, Justice Department lawyers stopped the practice.

Fact: Dec. 6, 2001. Under questioning about the policy from Sen. Edward Kennedy (D-Mass.), as reported by *Newsweek*'s Jonathan Alter, Ashcroft says, "The answer is simple: The only permissible use for the national check system is to audit the maintenance of that system, and the Department of Justice is committed to following the law in that respect."

Fact: January 2002. Ashcroft announces that due to his acceptance of more than $50,000 from Enron during his 2000 Senate race he will recluse himself from the investigation of the failed Texas energy giant. Despite receiving more than $370,000 from the gun lobby, Ashcroft does not recluse himself from decisions regarding the administration's gun policies.

Fact: Sept. 13, 2002. Ehrlich tells *The Sun* that he would "review" the state's gun laws "to see what's working." The two programs he mentions: the state's new ballistic fingerprinting law and the Handgun Roster Board, which sets the standard for what is considered to be cheap "Saturday Night Specials" and was part of the law that created the state's assault-weapon ban.

Fact: Oct. 2, 2002. A sniper using what police believe to be a semiautomatic assault rifle shooting .223-caliber bullets goes on to shoot 12 people, killing nine, over the course of 20 days (figures as of press time).

Fact: Oct. 8, 2002. *Chicago Sun-Times* columnist Mark Brown points out that the newsletter of the Illinois State Rifle Association states: "Far be it from us to advance conspiracy theories, but the timing of this sniper activity is unsettling.... Maryland has one of the hottest governor's races in the country, certainly hotter than that in Illinois. The central theme of the Maryland race is gun control. Things heat up. There is this off the wall series of sniper killings. Murder made to order for the antigunners. Hmmm, weren't there some other high-profile mass gun killings at strangely convenient times?"

Richard Pearson, the association's president, defends the newsletter's implication to Brown: "There does seem to be some strange correlation. We wonder about these things sometime. We know how unscrupulous the other side can be. There are all kinds of theories like that."

Those are some facts. Make up your own minds.

The Smoke Clears
November 13, 2002

Well, it went up for a vote, and it went down in flames.

Voters in Nevada, a state that already has legalized gambling and prostitution, had the chance last week to go for the trifecta and legalize possession of marijuana for people over the age of 21. The ballot measure, sponsored by the liberal billionaire drug-policy troika of financier George Soros, University of Phoenix founder John Sperling, and Ohio insurance magnate Peter Lewis, failed by a 61 to 39 margin.

In Arizona, a ballot measure to liberalize drug laws, which would have made possession of pot a misdemeanor subject to a $250 fine, failed as well, by a 57 to 47 margin. And in Ohio, voters overwhelmingly rejected an initiative on the ballot that would have mandated treatment instead of prison for first-time drug offenders.

The Ohio measure is an idea that might make sense in the long run. If there's any hope of cleaning up America's drug problem, it's getting more people into treatment. Drug treatment works; some argue that effective treatment plans beat the success rate for cancer treatment.

Treatment, however, has been held up by conservatives as a touchy-feely, lovey-dovey, soft-on-crime social program that does nothing but coddle criminals. Therefore, most of the nation's anti-drug budget gets shoveled into law enforcement and prisons. And if it were up to a simple majority of our nation's lawmakers (and given the way last week's elections went, it soon will be), more of that money will go toward the somewhat ridiculous effort to stop the drug trade by intervening in the affairs of sovereign nations to our south.

But that's just one side of the coin. It is interesting, if not downright amusing, to note that the people of Nevada, a state where you can smoke a cigarette damn near everywhere except perhaps at a gas station while refilling an open tank (and even then, we have our doubts), refused to legalize pot. Whereas, if you walked for a few hours into the desert west of Las Vegas, crossed the California state line, and lit up a cigarette, chances are good that a state employee would stride up, ask you to put it out, and hand you a ticket. Light up a joint, however, and you likely would qualify for health insurance and a pro bono lawyer in San Francisco.

Drug-policy reformers have known for years that if legalizing pot were ever put on the ballot, thumbs up or thumbs down, it would lose. Surveys over the better part of the last decade have shown that Americans don't want to legalize drugs, usually by margins that come close to 80 percent. That pot failed to pass in a libertarian-minded state like Nevada has got to be a cold dash of water in the movement's face.

And all other drugs aside, and no matter what your personal sentiments are about the weed, there are a few things to contemplate about the wholesale legalization of pot.

Let's stipulate that drugs are a public-health problem; that they are readily accessible and addictive puts a tremendous strain on this nation's resources. Then consider that the most dangerous drug in America—alcohol—is already legal. Think of what adding one more psychoactive drug to the mix would do.

Legalizing marijuana would make it more accessible, and more access means more users. More users mean more problems, and more problems mean more stress on the system.

The rising costs of prescription drugs aren't slowing down, the stuttering economy isn't helping the escalating costs of Medicare and Medicaid, and still too many Americans have no health care at all. And many of us think we can afford to legalize another drug?

On top of that, if there's one thing we know, it's that letting Madison Avenue sell addictive and psychoactive substances is something we don't need. Already, the liquor industry has begun violating their decades-old pledge against TV advertising. Why? Because revenues are down—people aren't drinking hard liquor like they used to—and the promises the industry made had an expiration date that came due the minute the profit margins started heading south.

So, combine the marketers' need to find new outlets for an addictive substance, the lack of real answers from both our politicians and our body politic on the coming health care crisis and the fact that we're already drowning, driving, and crashing in booze—why legalize pot?

One thing we do know for certain: The heavyweights of the lobbying industry, the insurance companies, would never allow outright drug legalization. The costs for all the above, plus the increase in accidents due to increased poly-drug abuse, would send their costs skyward. And in the America devoted to the Almighty Dollar, this would not stand.

So Nevada has stopped the train, for now. This doesn't mean that Soros, Sperling and Lewis will halt their campaign to change the whole of America's drug laws. But it's nice to know for once that not everything, including public opinions, can be bought, no matter how alluring it might seem.

Simon Says
November 27, 2002

David Simon (of HBO's "The Wire" and "The Corner" and NBC's "Homicide") and I share a number of similarities.

We both attended the University of Maryland, wrote at the newspaper there and now support the paper in its efforts at stopping the journalism school's Machiavellian efforts to subvert independent student journalism there.

We both live in Baltimore, him for over 20 years, me for about 12.

And we both know a little about the drug trade here from looking at it firsthand: He as a police reporter for *The Sun*, I as a former local radio reporter, a resident of a neighborhood three blocks from "the Corner" and as a spokesman for the nation's drug czar for two and a half years. I've traveled the country, spoken to addicts in treatment centers from Iowa to Los Angeles, seen the drugs and where they come from in Mexico, in Jamaica, in Bolivia. And in 1997, I had to subdue a junkie who broke into my house while I was home with a herniated disc in my back, and ended up overnight in Johns Hopkins with a Keith Richards-sized dose of morphine in me for my trouble. I still find needles and vials behind my house regularly.

I don't agree with every policy this government has made on drugs. I don't believe we can arrest and incarcerate our way out of the problem. I think an entire generation of black men are in jail because of stupid things like the sentencing discrepancies between crack and powdered cocaine, where an anesthesiologist and his snow-bunny girlfriend in Vail, Colorado can get off light for six grams of powder, but the same amount of crack on a street dealer brings in the feds and hard time.

At the same time, I know that decriminalizing drugs, legalizing them and making the government the dealer isn't the answer. We don't solve the problem of addiction by making drugs legal and then turning the government into the pusher (ignoring lotteries, Keno and slots for the moment).

I also think that calling the drug problem a "war" is the stupidest idea that's come down the pike in a long time—right after making a nondrinking, nondancing, Pentecostal hypermoralist our attorney general. I worked for a four-star general who never liked or condoned the term "drug war" because he knew what real war was about.

But I also know that you can't extrapolate the nation's drug problem from a six-square-block part of Baltimore. America's drug problem exists in the suburbs of Cedar Rapids, Iowa, in the quiet cocaine parties of Vail and in the methamphetamine labs of California. In 1997 more than a dozen kids in Plano, Texas, an affluent white suburb of Dallas, died from black tar heroin overdoses. Do we see them portrayed as hopeless criminal losers with characters on HBO? Not likely.

America's drug problem is not predominantly poor, predominantly urban, or predominantly black. On HBO, there are no meth-addicted mothers from Nebraska, there are no white suburban stoners from the San Fernando Valley, there are no coke-sniffing plastic surgeons inches away from losing their licenses in treatment programs at Sloan-Kettering. They simply don't exist. This is partly because society has built a gigantic support mechanism for them, and it is harder to see them fall.

If you are a M.D. addicted to cocaine and painkillers, you likely have a health plan at work that will cover it. You've got a job that pays a six-figure income as incentive not to wreck your life and you've got a whole bunch of money to burn through before you hit bottom. It could take you 10 years before you lose your job, wife, kids, house and/or life or end up in a halfway house somewhere. Given all the factors working against you, odds are it'll never happen.

If you are a clerk in a convenience store making 40 cents an hour above the minimum wage, you are probably living paycheck-to-paycheck, have no savings to speak of and rent a place to live. An addiction will drop you right out of society and into the criminal-justice system in less than a year. The fall is shorter, but the landing is hard.

Here in Baltimore, we've become the national poster child for the crackhead and the junkie, thanks to the Simon-spawned series "The Wire," "The Corner" and "Homicide." And when our lawmakers try to promote a little local civic boosting, they get shut down by a threat to move "The Wire's" whole filming operation to another city, where Simon can continue to run Baltimore down. After all, as our esteemed former governor Spiro Agnew once said,

"You've seen one slum, you've seen 'em all."

I'll never work for Simon, although I'm sure I have friends who do—set dressers, construction people, a few actors. I don't want them to be out of work. But I have to wonder about us as a town where we'll take the cash for something like this.

In an episode of "Sex and the City," Sarah Jessica Parker's character meets a charming Louisiana sailor who's visiting New York for the first time. He is less than impressed and tells her so. She sends him packing, telling the audience at the end that the city is her first love, and "nobody talks shit about my boyfriend."

We sure aren't New York. We aren't the glamorous socialite—we're the cheap hooker. We get crapped on by our boyfriend, and then go crawling back to get paid for it.

Shooting Season
February 12, 2003

Lock and load, people! The General Assembly is in session, so it's time for the annual firefight over Maryland gun laws!

This year's open season promises to be an exciting one, sports fans, with new players and a wackier scorecard. For the first time in years, Annapolis is home to an anti-gun control governor. Most of the same players remain on the same teams, however, so the climate remains about the same.

Gun-shop owner and professional gun-law naysayer Sanford Abrams is back, pooh-poohing the state's new ballistic fingerprinting law. Citing two California studies, Abrams is calling ballistic imaging programs unreliable. And, for once, Abrams may have a sympathetic ear in the State House, seeing as how last fall, while on the campaign trail, Gov. Robert Ehrlich said he would "review" the program "to see what's working."

We here at Animal Control are always happy to hear when pro-gunners are interested in legitimate academic research. After all, when public policy professors Jens Ludwig of Georgetown University and Steven Raphael of University of California, Berkeley, put out a study indicating that Project Exile, Ehrlich's solution to gun violence, was overrated, the National Rifle Association was less than enthused.

When Ludwig and Raphael's study came out, NRA spokesman Andrew Arulanandam told *The Washington Post*, "I would take the words of the men and women who are on the front lines of fighting crime in Richmond [Va.] over the words of a couple stuffed shirts in some ivory tower."

This is not to be construed as an argument against Project Exile, a Virginia program that imposes a minimum prison sentence of five years to prior violent felons convicted of gun crimes; anything that both Charlton Heston and James and Sarah Brady are for can't be all bad. But a hint of the case against Exile could be heard in the words of Ehrlich when he proposed bringing Exile to Maryland. To wit: "They are felons. They carry guns. They are shooting up the streets."

OK, that's fine. But what about those gun-toting people who *aren't* felons? The kid accused of shooting up the Washington suburbs, John Lee Malvo, wasn't a felon—and he still isn't because he hasn't been convicted yet. Under our system of "innocent until proven guilty," he's only *accused* of the crime. So technically, he is a "law-abiding citizen."

Let's go back to the gun lobby on that. Cue NRA spokeswoman Kelly Whitley: "Anti-gun proposals aimed at restricting the rights of law-abiding citizens have never had a record of decreasing crimes."

Nationally, there have been a few amusing developments in

the debate over gun policy. In a California affidavit, Robert Ricker, former director of what used to be the nation's largest gun-industry trade organization, the American Shooting Sports Council, said that gun manufacturers have "long known" that some of their dealers sold guns to criminals but kept among themselves a bond of silence aimed at silencing dissent.

Ricker was sacked after meeting with the Clinton White House following the Columbine high school shootings. He told *The New York Times* last week that someone needed to speak up about the bad dealers because "we've got a bunch of right-wing wackos at the NRA controlling everything."

In Maryland, we wouldn't know anything about that. Except maybe when people like Gus Alzona of the hyperbolically named "Tyranny Response Team" passed out flyers in Annapolis last year featuring the heads of the Montgomery County delegation pasted onto the bodies of Nazi storm troopers and called it "humor."

Alzona ran for state comptroller in last fall's Republican primary election and, despite losing, improbably managed to get 75,000 people to vote for him. This means little, except perhaps for proving that P.T. Barnum's dictum about a fool being born every minute has dated little over the years.

The other gun news of note is that the gun lobby's favorite researcher, John Lott, author of the 1998 book "More Guns, Less Crime," has been accused of fabricating a study to back up his assertion that merely brandishing a gun, rather than firing it, will stave off an attack. This comes on top of his constant assertion that allowing more people to carry concealed weapons will drive the crime rate down.

Now, we won't go into the volumes of research showing what a horselaugh Lott's studies are—Matt Bai of *Newsweek* probably said it best in March 2001 when he wrote that Lott "has been shown the door at some of the nation's finest schools." On top of that, Lott was letting his 13-year-old son write a five-star review of his book for Amazon.com, under the name "Mary Rosh." Lott then used the Rosh *nom de guerre* to sing his own praises on the Internet. In one posting, Rosh/Lott claimed the gun researcher was "the best professor I ever had."

Yes, it's gun season in Annapolis again. If it weren't for the fact that, in the end, there are real lives at stake here, threatened by a product that lets non-felons play God, it might even be amusing for a minute or two.

Put on your vests and let the laughs begin.

Thinking Different
January 11, 2006

I'm starting to wonder if the gun lobby is onto something. For years, the people at the National Rifle Association and the Gun Owners of America—you remember them, the ones who think that Wayne LaPierre, Charlton Heston and the "from my cold dead hands" crowd are too liberal—have argued that the Second Amendment contains within it the right to take up arms against a tyrannical government—the "insurrectionist theory." Dennis Henigan of the Brady Center to Prevent Gun Violence coined the term while discussing an NRA official quoted in *The New York Times* saying, "The Second Amendment is literally a loaded gun in the hands of the people held to the heads of government."

But when a government's leader—the head of a democracy who constantly talks about bringing freedom to foreign dictatorships—makes the order to spy on his own people, in direct contravention to the very Constitution he has sworn to protect and defend, you have to wonder: *Are they right?*

Despite the existence of the Foreign Intelligence Surveillance Court, whose job it is to vet national-security-sensitive wiretap requests, President Bush felt he had to circumvent the court and the law. This despite the fact that since 1978 the court has heard more than 18,000 wiretap requests and rejected only five of them—all during the Bush administration, in 2003 and '04.

According to Bush administration lawyers, the president's commander-in-chief status supersedes all other constitutional checks and balances during wartime. "National security" is a penumbra that elevates the president above the "first among equals" position they feel the executive already enjoys over the courts and the legislature. But we are now mired in a war created under false pretenses on the strength of bad intelligence, and the leader who entered office without a majority and won re-election with a bare majority now wants us to believe that he has the powers of a king. This, to be understated, is troublesome.

Since 2001, the administration has argued that it can declare U.S. citizens "enemy combatants" and hold them without charges, access to the courts, or counsel as a condition of national security. The administration has not just argued in favor of torture, in defiance of international law and treaties to which the United States is a signatory, but has campaigned for it. Why? National security, of course.

As a *Boston Globe* story put it last week, Bush feels he can "waive the restrictions."

"The executive branch shall construe [the law] in a manner consistent with the constitutional authority of the President . . . as Commander in Chief," Bush wrote (in his signing statement allowing the wiretaps), adding that this approach "will assist in achieving the shared objective of the Congress and the President . . . of protecting the American people from further terrorist attacks."

Does anybody else wonder if, since we are in a war against "terror"—a war against an abstract noun that only the president can define—this war only ends when one man says it is done? When does he stop being a "wartime president"? When a government refuses to look into right-wing militias but spies on the Catholic League and vegetarians and animal-rights protesters, when it locks up natural-born citizens and claims they are without rights, then do we start to worry?

For years I mocked the people who loaded up their survival shelters and bought and stored armaments as if every next week were Y2K. The NRA has called itself, with a straight face, "the nation's oldest civil-rights organization." The NRA claims that James Madison, in "The Federalist Papers," argued for the right of the people to arm themselves to overthrow tyranny—in this instance, the U.S. government.

Having read and studied Federalist 46, I've come to believe that the Second Amendment, as the courts have held throughout the years, is incumbent on the clause the gun lobby always wishes to forget—the part about the "well-regulated militia." But now the politicians the gun lobby helped put into power are aiming the awesome might of that government right back at them. Worried about gun registration? Worried about the government taking away your guns? Well, guess what—before they take, they *spy*.

I'm not saying that I agree with the NRA and that crowd. Not yet. But if people like me start to wonder if they're right, what should the Bush administration think their friends are thinking?

Lethal Tautology
April 25, 2007

"Gun control doesn't work," she said.

I was in a polite argument with an off-duty female Baltimore City police officer at a summer street festival. I pointed out reams of facts, made logical arguments, rebutted her points, but in the end, she always came back to stating it over and over again, as if it changed anything: "Gun control doesn't work."

The sad thing is now, years later, she may be right, because the leadership we have, irrespective of party, will never do what it takes to stop preventable gun deaths in the United States. It won't be long before we have another mass shooting in a workplace or school or at a college or restaurant. And the same things will happen again: The pro-gun people will say "don't politicize a tragedy," and there will be memorials and colored ribbons and the president will fly in and say nice things without ever mentioning the word "guns," and things will continue the same way they always have.

The argument goes, "Criminals will always be able to get guns." Which, if you think about it, is true—because the gun lobby has for years done everything possible to make it easier for *anyone* to buy a gun. If Maryland tightens its already fairly stringent gun laws, you can just get in your car and drive to North Carolina or Georgia, where it's easy. Washington has some of the tightest gun laws in the nation, pro-gun advocates say, and it doesn't stop shootings there. Except, of course, the District has the unfortunate problem of being next to Virginia, where even people with mental illness who are a danger to themselves and others can buy a gun with no problem.

Cho Seung-Hui bought one gun in February and another in

March—one from a gun store and one online via a pawn shop. Both times they ran the "instant check" on him, and he came up clean. Except, of course, the whole idea of the "instant check" came from the gun lobby. The core principle of the law Jim and Sarah Brady pushed for more than a decade ago was a background check along with a seven-day waiting period. (Disclosure: I was once deputy communications director for the Brady Campaign.) During those seven days, law enforcement would have to time to perform a full and complete background check, including mental-health records that are often not computerized. The waiting period also would serve as a "cooling off" period, which might give someone in the heat of anger time to rethink the idea of solving their problems with a firearm.

The gun lobby wanted otherwise—its default has always been, "Give 'em the gun," as quickly as possible and with as little trouble for the purchaser as possible. Which is why, even after the Columbine massacre back in 1999, the gun lobby resisted extending background checks to sales at gun shows, a loophole that exists to this day.

The issue of guns goes beyond political party; it links Republicans and rural Democrats, and it makes many moderate Democrats scared. So when the issue of gun control comes up, moderates run for the hills. Thus, "Gun control doesn't work."

As former labor secretary and author Robert Reich pointed out, if you need an anti-depressant like Prozac, you must go through a doctor to get it. Yet if you're mentally ill, in Virginia, all you need is two forms of ID and you can walk into a gun store and buy a gun—no wait, no muss, no fuss. And as Reich notes, even as powerful as the pharmaceutical lobby is—and Big Pharma has more lobbyists than there are members of Congress—even though it can advertise directly at you on TV, in magazines and on every item in the waiting room of your doctor's office, it can't cut the doctor out of the equation. You *have* to get a prescription.

Yet, it remains easy for anyone to buy guns. The gun lobby says all gun control does is persecute the "law-abiding citizen." Unfortunately, Cho Seung-Hui was a law-abiding citizen up until the instant he began pulling the trigger.

The gun lobby has even managed to get something that doctors and Big Pharma would love to have—immunity from lawsuits. If Pfizer or Bristol-Myers Squibb or Eli Lilly accidentally manufactured a bad batch of drugs and it made it out into the general population, you can imagine the lawsuits and the dollar amounts we'd be hearing about in the news. Lawyers everywhere get moist just thinking about it. But if a gun maker started making guns that exploded in your hand when fired, you'd be hard pressed to get a dime out of the company, because George W. Bush signed the law giving gun manufacturers immunity from lawsuits in 2005. Remember, before the 2000 election, a vice president of the National Rifle Association was captured on tape claiming that if Bush were elected, the gun lobby would be working right out of his office. For the most part, he was right.

So that police officer I spoke to was probably right: Gun control doesn't work. And until enough people care, it won't.

Race

When I started writing "Political Animal" back in 1994, my goal was not to be a "black columnist" but rather "a columnist who happened to be black." But they also tell you "write about what you know," and well, every time I look in a mirror to date, I still see more melanin than the next guy (I live in white South Baltimore, where the next guy is likely not going to have as nice a tan as mine).

If there's one issue that really chaps my briefs, it's how the Republican Party always likes to come out and say, "No—we really *do* want black people to vote for us" while at the same time courting every single neo-Confederate, redneck and crypto-racist who ever drove a truck below the Mason-Dixon line. Before, the term was "code words" when they wanted to talk past the national media; now it's "dog whistle politics." Those politicians who want to appeal to the 1948-issue Strom Thurmond voters of the new millennium now couch their language in words that only their supporters can hear, far beyond the ken of the average voter. And in the meantime they are free to prattle on in the mainstream media about how they believe in a "big tent" and how they "want to appeal to all voters." And I say, "Bullshit." My ears are ringing.

Now Paul Krugman of *The New York Times* may be right—the new movement conservatism may not be about race (Krugman says it's a tactic, not a goal), but from where I stand, it seems to be a well to which the right wing (and unfortunately some on the Left, as we've seen recently) seems awful happy to go any time the water starts getting choppy out there in campaign-land. Jesse Helms proved for the better part of a half-century that you can never go wrong pitting poor white folk against black folk; back when he ran against Harvey Gantt, the black mayor of Charlotte in November of 1990, all it took was the infamous "white hands" ad (where white hands crumpled up a letter saying "You needed that job and you were the best qualified. But they had to give it to a minority because of a racial quota") and Helms pulled away for another term.

Part of the problem we still have with race is trust. There's no real way anymore, especially with the aforementioned "dog whistle politics," to know who is being earnest with the black community. Back in the 1950s, the George Wallaces were right out front with their intolerance. In the modern era, those who want to use race as some sort of wedge don't wear their prejudices on their sleeves—they will lie right to your face. As the nation becomes more and more multicultural, this drives the Pat Buchanans and the Tom Tancredos of the Right crazy, and their rhetoric becomes more and more extreme. While the late, brilliant Molly Ivins joked that Buchanan's speech to the Republican National Convention in 1992 "sounded better in the original German," today's Tom Tancredo screeds against immigrants might make Lee Greenwood's "God Bless The USA" sound like a funhouse version of "Deutschland Uber Alles." Richard Pryor once characterized these types of people by saying, "We got us some new niggers now."

The only saving grace for this is that in not too many years, the "brown people," as they call them, will easily be equal if not greater in numbers, and then it will be a jolly good time seeing what The Old Establishment thinks of *that*.

*   *   *

Bitter to Worse
Unpublished, April 1992

And you wonder why black Americans listen to Louis Farrakhan.

America may not make its Farrakhans, but it sure as hell will sustain them. When a Simi Valley, California jury can rule that four white police officers beat the daylights, the stuffing, the *tar* out of Rodney King and did it all as a legitimate part of their jobs, then the mouthy ministers that white America loves to hate have more ammunition to wield against the nation that nourishes them.

President Bush spent less time condemning the miscarriage of justice in his noon speech Thursday than he did emphasizing "law and order," words used since the Nixon days to tilt the scales in favor of authority. But here, authority may have been undermined.

We have all seen the conclusion of jury trials where the exonerated exclaim, "the system works" and "justice has prevailed," as much as we have seen the guilty using the words "travesty" and "inquisition." It is not a stretch of the imagination where, at the conclusion of each trial, a judge could instruct the participants in the use of the proper clichés like veteran catcher Kevin Costner teaches novice pitcher Tim Robbins in the baseball movie "Bull Durham."

But who guards the guardians? And where is the redress for the prisoners of the system, be they in front of or behind bars, when the system itself is a farce? Black America has placed its trust in politicians and in judges and juries since the attempt was made to even the scales through the series of Civil Rights Acts beginning in 1964. But when the nation's elected president, a man who entered office with the help of a campaign based on fear of a convicted black murderer, can't see the cause for the effect, then maybe we *are* lost.

Maybe I'm wrong. Maybe my eyes were fooled. Maybe the 249 million Americans that watched that tape over and over and over and over last year don't know what we saw. After all, it was on *television*. This is the same medium where David Copperfield can fly without camera tricks, where Michael Dukakis is the same height as George Bush and everyone is in living color. It's only television—we could be wrong. But I doubt it.

A juror in the case, interviewed by CBS under the condition of anonymity, said that given the entirety of the circumstances, the officers' use of force was justified. King was "in full control the whole time," she said. She said they watched the whole tape repeatedly, frame by frame, and could not be convinced that King was in any kind of serious pain, that he even laughed as he was being handcuffed. She said the fact that he was traveling over 100 miles an hour when he was stopped by police contributed to her belief that the police were correct in their need to use force.

Did this woman see the same tape that we did? Or did she grow up in a different America?

Chances are the latter is correct. The part of America that is Simi Valley is to the rest of Los Angeles what white Wonder Bread is to pumpernickel or rye. It is a bedroom community of retired firefighters and police officers, where one report told of a sign hanging from the window near the courthouse: "Support Cops, Not Convicts."

And it is in this America that the victim is blamed for his guilt, that his actions alone created his predicament despite the damning testimony of one of the accused, Officer Theodore J. Briseno, who said that he had to put his foot on King's back to keep him down, lest two other officers, Lawrence Powell and Timothy Wind, beat him further. They were "out of control," Briseno testified.

The case for violence in Los Angeles, the rioting, cannot be justified. But the case for anger and disillusionment cannot be ruled out. Neither white liberal guilt nor black conservatives' urgings to forge ahead can change what is now a nationwide watershed feeling among blacks—that something may always be wrong here.

What does it take? Will blacks need body armor at traffic stops? Will phalanxes of video camera-bearing vigilantes have to interview officers at the site of every altercation, with questions relating to state-of-mind, police procedure, motives and intent?

Blacks from all walks of life have had to deal with the fact that every time they deal with the law, there is the intangible there: the scales of justice sway wildly depending on where you are. Being a "Number Two Male" means never traveling without identification, being lumped in categorically with alleged wrongdoers for the simple crime of walking to the corner. Question authority and the authorities will question you. This writer was stopped four times a year during his college years because of a perpetrator profile that could fit 90% of the receiver corps of the NFL.

No, if there is a bitterness there, it is hard earned. And a jury of twelve, empanelled without a single black, found against their own eyes and for authority, and reinforced that feeling that many, if not most, people of color know deep in their hearts.

Soon the Al Sharptons, the Gus Savages, the Stokely Carmichaels and the Louis Farrakhans will again be blaming white America. Violence may not be overtly called for, but its use will not be decried, either. And people will be listening.

Sadly, shamefully, who can blame them?

Everything Old is New Again
November 9, 1994

It was a year ago today—November 9, 1993, when Republican political strategist Ed Rollins made the claim that his campaign operation for then-challenger and current New Jersey governor Christine Todd Whitman had paid black ministers $500,000 to keep the vote tally light in black precincts.

Nobody now really knows if he was or was not true to his boast, but history shows the black vote was actually lighter that election day. Black turnout in the '93 election was at 8 percent, down from 12 percent four years before, according to *The Wall Street Journal*.

Whitman won that election in a Crisco squeaker—by only one percent. After Rollins' assertions, an outcry went up, but in some political circles people were marveling. "Pay people to *stay home*," they said, stunned. What a twist!

It was ingenious, even if it didn't happen (one black minister in the city of Camden claimed it did, but never produced any corroborating statements or evidence), simply because of the divisive effects of the statement on its face. Politically, it makes the enemy its own fifth columnists, with the ranks of discord being sown among its own ranks. Ministers would look at each other warily, claiming never to have taken a cent, while each proclaiming a little too loudly of their own innocence.

It was probably the newest wrinkle in the cause of "ballot security" that had been heard of in years. In the height of the post-election fallout, and after Rollins had taken a good drubbing from members of his own party, the person he elected and the press, one GOP political operative and ex-George Bush advisor told the *Boston Globe* that he doubted that Rollins "is ever going to be managing any more campaigns."

Fast forward to 1994: Rollins is in the employ of Michael Huffington, who ran a close race against Dianne Feinstein for California's senate seat all the way to the end. Minority turnout plays yet another part in a closely contested gubernatorial election in an eastern seaboard state. And once again crops up the term "ballot security."

Ballot security, plain and simple, is a euphemism for trying to harrass, coerce, frighten or intimidate your opponent's voters and supporters to keep them away from the polls. It has its roots in southern Jim Crow tactics to keep minorities and newly nationalized immigrants from exercising their voting franchise and taking power away from the good ol' boy status quo. It has been used in many ways: large, officially dressed men with large dogs hang around polling places and question voters, people with badges stopping voters and asking them questions about their registration or nationality, even parking official-looking trucks near polls in Hispanic neighborhood with signs reading "Immigration."

Where the Democrats have been famous over the years for doing everything they can to get people to vote ("walking around money" is a staple of the Democrats' arsenal, especially in old-line political machine cities like Baltimore), the GOP has been the prime practitioner of ballot security. This reporter has seen efforts at the national level by the GOP, in which they send out fundraising letters that have boxes for the donor to check what program they wish to fund. Ballot security was one of the choices.

In 1991, again in New Jersey, incumbent Democratic governor Jim Florio lost to Thomas Kean by 1,797 votes. *The New York Times* reported the New Jersey state GOP, aided by the national Republican Party, formed task forces to patrol urban voting precincts carrying signs that said vote fraud could lead to prison. The task force, according to the Times, included off-duty police officers who carried weapons in plain sight.

After that election, the Democrats won a consent agreement from the GOP promising to refrain from future ballot security initiatives aimed at turning away minority voters. Until the Rollins statements came out, many thought ballot security was a fairly dead issue, although in all big-city elections, democratic field operatives school all get-out-the-vote workers in recognizing ballot security tactics in case they crop up again in close races where an urban vote can make all the difference. Sort of like the one yesterday.

The Maryland Republican Party has condemned and distanced itself from the actions of Ross Pierpont, the perennial also-ran candidate who spends large sums of his money each election season in attempts to unseat Democratic incumbents. Pierpont's announcement that his group, the Knights and Dames of Maryland, would patrol the urban precincts of Baltimore (and nowhere else, as if Baltimore is the only place it occurs) hunting out vote fraud may just be the latest effort to make Maryland a little bit more like New Jersey every day. But the most unfortunate part is, with a continuing trend of lower and lower turnouts, unless Marylanders realize that voting is a civic responsibility and begin showing up to the polls, all the ballot security programs in the bag of dirty tricks will not be necessary—because the battle has been won before the votes were tallied.

The Pathetic But Funny Politics of Hate
November 30, 1994

You knew it had to happen: our first piece of hate mail arrived last week here at Animal Control. Actually, it was addressed jointly to this columnist and to Queer Culture columnist Mark Shaw, but here on the political beat we claim eminent domain, and so we get the chance to have our laughs first.

Hate mail is such a sad thing. The usual response, the usual rule is "don't acknowledge them." But a few rules are made to be bent slightly to one side before allowing them to spring back into place, and maybe this is one of them. Hate mail pours into congressional offices and the White House at prodigious rates, especially over the past two years. This reporter got to see a good amount of it in offices of members of the Congressional Black Caucus. It gets categorized and filed, with referral to the Capitol Police or the FBI if it is particularly vicious. Otherwise, it sees the back of a filing cabinet with the rest of the mail.

Most of the hate mail this writer has seen comes from the conservative end of the political spectrum. It uniformly comes with the various Xeroxed articles from "offending" writers, usually with some sort of slurs or exclamations written in the margin with red pen, usually felt tip marker. Why this is, we don't know—it's never blue pen or black pen or green pen, always red. Maybe it's part of the course taken by hate mail writers, a sort of correspondence course deep in the woods of Idaho (home of the hate group with the catchiest name, "The Covenant, The Sword and The Arm of the Lord"). There, with hourly breaks to chant a corrected version of the Pledge of Allegiance, prospective poison-pen writers can learn the Top Ten Epithets to call blacks and Jews, take refresher courses in combating the ZOG (Zionist Occupational Government, a favorite acronym in hate letters) and catch up on trading the latest addresses of commie-pinko, liberal, nigger-and-faggot-loving newspaper columnists.

Much of this hatred can obviously been seen as due to the constant societal threat to the decline in the care and feeding of the heterosexual white male in today's society. With the only political sustenance before this last election coming from Rush Limbaugh, Jesse Helms' fundraising letters and repeated reading of "The Bell Curve," what's a heterosexual white male to do with himself these days? According to talk radio, "the women and the blacks are taking our jobs away" (actually heard from a caller to Allan Prell's program on WBAL), and welfare has apparently eroded away the family structure of the underclass, so the heterosexual white male feels that if there's going to be a campaign, nay, crusade to fix all that ails his world, then by gum, he'd better get cracking.

And the first step is to fire off a photocopied letter, filled to the margins with the painfully creaky, blocky handwriting (also taught in Hate School; bring your own notebook), to your local Jewish or African-American politicians or columnist.

Hate mail genuinely disturbs many people in Congress. They handle it like one would feces from a snake—not only is it foul, but what created it might be lurking around somewhere. A few treat it like this writer feels it should: They note it for the sad commentary it makes on a certain segment of society (and the declining art of polite correspondence), and then they laugh at it.

And then, unless it makes specific and actual threats (which should then warrant its dispatch to the police or FBI), it should either be tacked to an appropriate wall for the bemusement of all, or thrown away.

But, just to assuage the embittered, embattled heterosexual white males, a few facts:

Statistically, more upper level jobs are held by heterosexual white males than by any other group.

The lists of the top CEOs and the wealthiest Americans are both predominantly stacked with heterosexual white males (and attention haters: Armand Hammer was gay, and he's dead).

An analysis, done by Prof. Andrew A. Beveridge of Queens College, NY, looked at 30 cities and 31 suburbs around that state and found that black homeowners are taxed more than whites on comparable homes in 58 percent of the suburban regions and 30 percent of the cities.

Mortgage lenders continued to reject home loan applications from blacks at more than twice the rate of those for whites over the past four years, according to government data. Thirty-four percent of black applicants for conventional home mortgages nationwide were denied credit in 1993 versus 15.3 percent of white applicants. Also, 25.1 percent of Hispanic home-buyers were denied home loans along with 14.6 percent of Asians according to the Federal Financial Institutions Examination Council.

Aid to Families With Dependent Children, better known as welfare, provides $22.5 billion to 14 million people, nearly 10 million of them children. Eighty-six percent of families on AFDC also get food stamps. That's only less than five percent of the population, and soon a Republican Congress will be able to cut the funds to feed the little bloodsuckers.

Anti-egalitarianism academics such as Leo Strauss, Allan Bloom and the writers of "The Bell Curve" are all the fashion nowadays.

And this writer still can't get a cab in downtown Baltimore at night.

So as bad as things look for the heterosexual white male, remember—it could be worse.

Hate letter writers, buck up! Put down your pens! Things aren't as bad as they look.

Deeds, Dammit, Not Words
February 22, 1995

The motto of the state of Maryland is pretty simple. Simple, elegant, clear-cut and offensive. It makes its point in a metaphor that might have been civilized three centuries ago when it was coined, but in today's enlightened society, it draws inferences that we know are not only untrue, but insulting.

Fatti maschii, parole femine, written by John Davies in 1610 and adopted by the first Baron Baltimore and eventually chosen as the motto of the state of Maryland, literally reads, "Deeds are males, words females are."

In other words, women talk, men do. Riiiight. Turn on C-SPAN and see if you still think that's the truth.

There's been a movement for years now to change the state motto; it usually goes down to defeat or gets ignored into submission. It's a worthy cause, but it may not necessarily mean anything. It is an example of symbol rather than substance.

Another example of words exemplifying attitudes centuries-old and equally offensive might be these:

"Let's look at the SATs. The average SAT for African-Americans is 750. Do we set standards in the future so that we don't admit anybody with the national test? Or do we deal with a disadvantaged population that doesn't have that genetic hereditary background to have a higher average?"

Those are the comments, word for word, made by Rutgers University president Francis Lawrence last November 11, taped by faculty members and reported by the Newark Star-Ledger and the Associated Press.

The opinion expressed by Lawrence might jibe with the authors of "The Bell Curve," the book that tries to express the theory that this writer and others of his ilk (you know, the "melanin-enhanced" ilk), suffer from a genetic background that leaves us lacking in the mental candlepower section. Lawrence has since come out and apologized for the statement, categorically retracted it, and unlike many who might have found themselves in the same situation, never backed away by saying he was misquoted.

"In spite of the fact that I did use those words, they are opposed to my beliefs," he said at a news conference. "I regret it, I do regret it, I certainly regret those comments."

Let's look at the words themselves, and what they *mean*. Specifically, the last two sentences, the questions: "Do we set standards in the future so that we don't admit anybody with the national test? Or do we deal with a disadvantaged population that doesn't have that genetic hereditary background to have a higher average?"

"Or do we deal with ..." Lawrence here is asking a question based as the second half of an either/or proposition. "Do we hurt, or do we help," is what a shortened phrase might read when distilled down to its motive. Indeed, this is what Lawrence said he meant to say when he apologized: "What I intended to say was that standardized tests should not be used to exclude disadvantaged students on the trumped-up grounds that such tests measure inherent ability, because I believe that they do not."

Lawrence may have made a number of political mistakes in his term at Rutgers, only the largest of which was the Nov. 11 gaffe. Academia is a harsh environment; the infighting is so vicious because the stakes are so small. Tenured faculty are quick to feel an affront, and Lawrence was criticized for being aloof and uncaring. Students complained they never saw the man.

With this as a foundation, it is no wonder Lawrence was quick to see the tidal wave of resentment after his remarks were publicized. Nevertheless, both his stated and accomplished goals were in direct contrast to what he said at the ill-fated faculty meeting. In his previous job as president of Tulane University, he took a school whose minority population hovered at one percent of the school enrollment and pushed it into double digits. He was well on his was to similar success at Rutgers. Are these the actions of an unthinking racist?

The Al Campanises and the Marge Schotts of the world are the ones who deserve the sort of treatment the students of Rutgers wish to inflict upon Lawrence. Campanis, a top L.A. Dodgers executive fired several years back for saying minorities "lack the necessities" to manage a major league baseball team, was a textbook example of a man in need of a pink slip. During his tenure, he had the power to hire and fire, and yet under his management, the Dodgers never had a black manager. Words, 0; Deeds 0. Not only didn't he mouth the platitudes, but he didn't back it up by actions, either. Unrepentant ignorance deserves time off for contemplation of sins. Al, meet the real world.

There needs to be some sort of check to realize the difference between misstatements (no matter how grotesquely stupid at the time) and genuinely racist behavior. The closest we can come to this is by examining the actions against the record.

Francis L. Lawrence made a mistake. A way to compound that mistake would be to fire him and bring in someone whose actions at minority recruitment and retention would be less than stellar, less than say, those of Lawrence. Do not confuse symbol with substance. *Fatti maschii, parole femine* is symbol. "Deeds, not words" is substance.

Affirmative Contraction
April 5, 1995

Years ago, the University of Maryland sealed a bit of its fate in infamy by turning away a student who wished to attend its law school. That student, who instead went on to Howard University law school, came back and forced the University to open the doors of its law school to all, regardless of color.

That student, as we should all know by now, was Baltimore native Thurgood Marshall, who went on to argue more cases before the Supreme Court than any other man—and to win a larger number of them as well. Marshall then went on to serve on the Court, leaving a lasting legacy to the principles of equality. The University, however, had to take a number of years to finally attempt to live down its part in the affair. In the last decade, the school has made remarkable strides in its quest for redemption.

Today there is another student already in the University of Maryland law school. He too is filing suit. Daniel J. Podberesky, a former undergraduate at the University of Maryland at College Park, is trying to shut down the school's Benjamin Banneker merit scholarship program for black undergraduates, a program created by the university to rectify its historic legacy of discrimination.

Mr. Podberesky, it seems, feels the university is discriminating, all right—against him. In 1990, he filed his original lawsuit against the school, saying he had a better academic record than many of the scholarship recipients of the Banneker program, yet he was not eligible for the full four-year scholarship, because he is not black.

Since then, the case has gone the full route through the court system; like a steel ball in the game of Pachinko, it has bounced back and forth as each court has issued rulings for and against the scholarship program. Currently, Mr. Podberesky has the lead, as last October a three-judge panel ruled the program was unconstitutional because it was a race-based specific state policy. Following that, the 4th U.S. Circuit Court of Appeals in December denied the university's appeal to the full 13-member panel to hear the case.

Last week, the university went for the whole ball of wax and filed an appeal with the Supreme Court. At risk is not only the Banneker program, but some legal scholars say affirmative action programs on college campuses all over the country could be affected by any new precedent.

Some might say, "All Podberesky wants is equality. It's not fair that he is denied a scholarship because of the color of his skin. Isn't that what we were trying to eliminate in the first place?"

Perhaps this is true, but we don't exist in a vacuum, either. Would it be that we could suddenly say that all is equal between the races, that the affirmative action programs instituted at the start of Lyndon Johnson's Great Society had rectified all that is unequal between the races, or the sexes, for that matter?

If anything, we are perhaps even further from the mark than the angry America that voted at the polls feels we are. Although some might feel that affirmative action has gone far enough, the Glass Ceiling Report, put out by a bipartisan federal commission from 1990 Census data, and led by former Labor Secretary Elizabeth Dole, shows that white men, while constituting about 29 percent of the workforce, hold about 95 of every 100 senior management positions, defined as vice president and above.

In addition, according to the report, top managers, when questioned, still revert back to the same excuse when queried about their low rates of diversity in hiring. "Demand is high, but supply is low." This despite figures that show between 1982 and 1991 there was a 36 percent increase in the number of blacks, ages

20 to 44, with a college degree or more. It's not too far a stretch to say these are the kind of numbers the University of Maryland is bent on increasing with its Banneker program.

The part about this whole affair that is so mind-boggling, so absurd, is that the University is *owning up* to its sad part in history. How often do you hear that from a major institution? "Your Honor, we screwed up bigtime years ago, we're not going to do it again, and we'll even start a program to make good on our debt to society." Judges would faint dead away if they found criminals this contrite.

At the start of America's second rollback of affirmative action programs (the first was when the Supreme Court handed down *Plessy v. Ferguson* after Reconstruction), Justice Marshall wrote in dissent of *University of California v. Bakke* in 1978, "It is because of a legacy of unequal treatment that we now must permit the institutions of this society to give consideration to race in making decisions about who will hold the positions of influence, affluence and prestige in America...I do not believe that anyone can truly look into America's past and still find that a remedy for the effects of that past is impermissible."

If the Supreme Court finds in favor of Daniel Podberesky, it means that the history books can be erased, and we apparently are all truly equal. Good luck in your legal career, Mr. P—you'll find plenty of your own kind there in the executive suites.

The Long Hot Summer of 2000
July 19, 1995

It's being called "The End Of Reconstruction." And former vice-president and governor Elbridge Gerry, who is probably somewhere in a Massachusetts grave with an ornate marble headstone, got his name back. This all comes courtesy of the 1995 United States Supreme Court, which apparently has lost the meaning of the term "gerrymander."

For over 190 years in this country, voting districts have been tailored and torn over the whims of the majority party's right to draw regions favorable to themselves. And the saddest dual masterstroke of them all came after the 1990 census, when the majority party then, the Democrats, created a number of congressional districts designed to bring the largest contingent of black representation into the halls of Congress since Reconstruction. Sad, because at the same time, they sowed the seeds of destruction for that very same group.

They should have known. "Be careful what you ask for…," it has been said.

Now, because of a conservative Court's retreat from the gains of the Voting Rights Act of 1965, not only may the 40-member Congressional Black Caucus of the 103rd Congress be a high-water mark, but the apparatus that created it may never be recreated. Each time a district with a majority of black voters was created, it also packed white, more conservative voters into districts. This helped to create the Republican landslide of 1994. Now that there is a GOP majority and a conservative Supreme Court, the workings are under way to slash the precedents which led to the minority districts. Never before was a petard hoisted so high.

Like in many cases involving the history of blacks in America, is that some of the more important issues tend to be forgotten by the people in power. In this case, it is the very real fact that blacks in this country had never been allowed to simply live where they wanted. Segregation pushed blacks to the outskirts of town, across the tracks and alongside major roadways and thoroughfares—the least desirable real estate—and for years, that was where black communities remained. The irritating facet of the 1995 Miller v. Johnson ruling authored by Justice Anthony Kennedy is its refusal to acknowledge historical precedent for the creation of districts where blacks were, in essence, forced to live.

In "gerrymandering" districts like the most disputed one, Georgia's "I-85" 11th congressional district, the map was simply tailored to reach blacks who had been shoved out of town and along a roadway that stretched to the Atlantic. In doing so, they also helped compact more conservative white voters into Georgia's 6th district, the district of Speaker Newt Gingrich, where both the percentage of blacks and the percentage of blacks voting is a meager 6 percent.

Black America is currently in a disjointed state—the NAACP is on the ropes after weathering too many internal crises, conservatives are all but linking the words "welfare" and "minorities" and the chance to hold the line through both the Congress and the courts is eroding like a sand bar during a hurricane. And the hurricane hasn't passed over just yet.

Now that the voting rights issue has virtually played out (virtually, because Justice O'Connor's concurrent opinion leaves room that the court's final say on the issue has yet been made), the next battleground is the last gasp of affirmative action, and some have already conceded that the death knell will soon be sounded. Court rulings have already made it clear that any kind of preference to make up for past discrimination will be under "strict scrutiny" and more than one presidential candidate has said that affirmative action will be in the sights.

It seems there are two choices: Fight the old battles, or try and find new strategies. One political theorist has said that there may be an opening in that the political right may be depleting its ammo once affirmative action has been disposed of. "What does it mean for conservative forces that have used these policies for 25 to 30 years to run against—what will they be left with?" asks Raphael Sonenshein, a professor of political science at California State University at Fullerton, as quoted in *The New York Times*. "It is like the end of the cold war for the conservatives."

Indeed, as the end of the cold war brought on George Bush's "New World Order," a new world is being forged in race relations where districts can be drawn in any weird shape possible unless they are created for reasons of race, and enough politicians feel the playing field has been leveled sufficiently enough that any currently existing racism will not really matter.

How will America react as the rising birth rates of minorities and the encroachment of the rights of legal immigrants by conservatives prompts a backlash at the polls? In 1967, Martin Luther King warned us about the "long hot summer" and the threat of riots as the country's racial situation reached a head.

Our current racial divide may not resemble the parched state of affairs 28 years ago. We may be assured of one thing, however. If the pendulum continues to swing the way it is going, the new millennium may be full of long, hot summers.

Discolored
July 17, 1996

Like in any election year, it seems like sacrilege to deal with hot button issues like affirmative action with any attempt at substantive discussion. Even though California's governor Pete Wilson has retreated from his one-issue attempt at capturing the Republican presidential nomination, his one issue still has a chance at poisoning the atmosphere before November.

Without getting into the arguments for or against affirmative action, one of the problems in dealing with it is the issue of trust. Black Americans would probably be more willing to deal with a frank discussion of whether or not affirmative action is a help or a hindrance if it were not for the fact that the conservatives have been using it as a "wedge issue"—a way to pry liberal politicians from their core group of voters—for years. Presidents Reagan and Bush learned that if you wanted to muddy the rhetorical waters and sow confusion, any bill designed to roll back civil rights gains made over the last twenty years should be called a civil rights bill.

So black America has gotten very distrustful over time at any conservative attempt to "reach out" both across the aisle and the color divide to try and mend fences. Such as it was with the NAACP vs. Bob Dole debacle last week. The civil rights organization makes its standard election year overture to both parties' nominees to speak at the annual convention. Dole, as has been the case with all Republicans invited over the past 16 years, claimed a "scheduling conflict" and instead went to the All-Star game in Philadelphia. And as usual, the consolation prize was Jack Kemp, who, despite his belief in hurt-the-poor, *laissez-faire*, trickle-down economic theories, is the only prominent member of the GOP who has even given the illusion of caring about minority issues.

So when new NAACP President Kweisi Mfume refused to play the business as usual game with Dole/Kemp, Dole cried foul claiming it was a "set up."

Do you really think blacks will find Bob Dole "a new kind of Republican?" Not hardly. Like the new talk show ethic goes: "Talk to the hand, 'cause the face ain't listenin'".

For many years the argument over affirmative action, seen by blacks as a perhaps imperfect method to address past wrongs in hiring and promotion, has been over the issue of quotas. Many feel it becomes reverse discrimination, where previous discrimination against blacks becomes discrimination against whites. After that point is made, you can almost start a countdown clock because someone will always mention "Two wrongs does not equal a right" immediately afterward.

Once again it becomes an issue of trust among parties attempting to seriously address the issue. Real discrimination, real prejudice and real racism against people of color still exist in this country. And if the people so intent upon rolling back gains made in the late sixties and early seventies had been loud and at the forefront in addressing the issue of race, then perhaps they'd have more credibility now when it is becoming more of a flashpoint in the war of partisanship.

Too often conservatives try to kill affirmative action programs without having any solution, or even the glimmerings of one, to the ills affirmative action was created to address. It is as if the entire reverse discrimination argument was created in an historical vacuum, that suddenly white people were being discriminated against and the opportunities were not there for them.

Unfortunately for those who want to inherit the coveted mantle of victimhood, the numbers just don't work out in their favor. There will still be more places where a white person can get hired "without discrimination" than a black, Hispanic, Asian, Native American or a Jew, reverse discrimination or not. No matter how many set-asides, "quotas" or numerical targets assigned to raise the minority representation in places (like Congress, for example) where they have historically been under-represented, there still will be easily twice the number of openings, jobs, seats or otherwise available for the white male.

White women are also taking the back seat. Back in March of 1995, former Secretary of Labor Lynn Martin, commissioned to do a study under the George Bush administration, found that white men, while constituting 29 percent of the workforce, hold 95 percent of the top management jobs. White females, in contrast, hold less than 5 percent.

The study by the Glass Ceiling Commission, pointed out a telling belief held by white male senior executives that has a bitter ring to nearly any minority who finds him or herself alone in an organization woefully short of people of color. Chief executives, the report said according to a story in *The New York Times*, "attribute the scarcity of minority males at the top—who they first think of as African Americans—to a lack of qualified candidates, asserting that demand is high but supply is limited."

As always, you just can't find good help anymore. But without the access to training, colleges and entry-level positions, and in an arena where the deck is already appearing to be stacked except to those doing the stacking, the help just never may be there.

There's a big difference between places that say "we'd like to find minorities" and those who actually go out and do so. Intent means a lot—it goes toward establishing that trust. But too many people in too many places want to tilt the playing field back toward the way it was a long time ago, without wondering why it was being changed in the first place.

Wars of Words
Unpublished, 2001

We are officially in "irony overload."

House Majority Leader Dick Armey met with NAACP President Kweisi Mfume to talk about the supposed "reverse race-baiting" by minorities in the same week former Klansman, now-Senator Robert Byrd felt free to use the "n-word" on national television.

Armey says "it has become an all-too common practice to spread racially charged falsehoods against Republicans for political advantage." Republicans charged the NAACP with "reverse race-baiting" when the civil rights organization ran ads before the November elections in Texas claiming then-Governor Bush was insensitive to the daughter of James Byrd, Jr. during the fight to pass a hate crime law.

To use one of Bush's favorite phrases, guess what? When Renee Mullins, Byrd's daughter, traveled from Hawaii to ask Bush to support the bill, he threw the copy of it she gave him on his desk and told her "no." He was insensitive. There's no room to complain when you bring the wrath upon yourself.

A few years back, Fritz Hollings, the conservative Democratic senator from South Carolina, made a crack about African leaders being cannibals which was flat-out racist. That was years ago; he never apologized for it, and no one has called for his censure on account of it. However, if you're a black leader and you say something nice about the far-out-of-the-mainstream Louis Farrakhan, every white leader in the country will ring you on the phone and demand that you repudiate your statement. Now House Majority Whip Tom DeLay claims if he made the statement Sen. Byrd made, "they wouldn't let me land at National Airport."

Name-calling has gotten ugly in recent years, but don't look to liberals to see who threw the first punch. It was the Newt Gingrich Revolution that advocated calling your political opponents "traitors" instead of the time-honored tradition of seeing the other side of the aisle as the "loyal opposition." As you sow so shall you reap. Robert Michel, the former House Minority Leader who retired in 1994 (leading the way for Gingrich and his slash-and-burn political tactics) was considered to be the last of the real leaders of gentlemen politics on the right on Capitol Hill, and when he left, he bemoaned the coarsening of the atmosphere.

What about former presidential candidate John McCain saying that Chelsea Clinton was so ugly that her father must have been Janet Reno? This happened in the fall of '98; his hometown paper, the *Arizona Republic* (a Quayle family paper), raked him over the coals for it. Who was hitting below the belt then?

It is thigh-slappingly funny that those who were white and on the right—the people who first held the attitudes that minorities, gays and women were being too sensitive and beholden to political correctness when they made their jokes about the supposed laziness of black people, the alleged promiscuity of women and homosexuals in general—now wail about how the jokes made about them consist of "violent speech." Republican TV talking head Ann Coulter prides herself on being the "female conservative pit bull." But when someone barks back in her direction, her particular pack of wolves runs yelping for the hills. As we say in "African-American" circles when someone's just full of it, but we still want to be polite—"oh, PLEASE."

When Florida used a suspect company to "cleanse" its voter rolls of convicted felons that all but targeted black men (without actually checking to see if they were, in fact, felons); when the current Attorney General spoke glowingly to *Southern Partisan*, a magazine that glorifies the Confederate past; when our current president made a campaign trip to suck up to Bob Jones University and its ban on inter-racial dating, aren't black people entitled to wonder about racism in conservative circles?

But Dick Armey complaining about "reverse race-baiting"? It's sort of like the pot calling the kettle…well, you know.

Lott Of Bull
December 18, 2002

If there's anything that has confounded the academicians in the history wing of Animal Control, it's the way the Confederacy is generally viewed in the modern era.

Let's grant that for the short duration of its existence, the Confederacy was a sovereign nation, not a breakaway set of states that seceded from a larger union. It had its own president, its own army, its own currency. And it went to war and lost. It surrendered and once again became part of the union from which it was spawned.

But the primary purpose of that nation, during its existence, was to maintain the way of life that it had claimed was essential to its well-being: that of owning other persons as property. "States rights" meant the right to own slaves. Period. If you don't believe this, go back yourself and read the entirety of the Supreme Court decision in the monumental 1857 case *Dred Scott v. Sandford*, penned by our own not-so-illustrious Maryland native Chief Justice Roger Taney. Everything else that happened after that point can be seen as an effort to preserve the world that Taney affirmed in that one decision—blacks as nonhuman and non-citizens, slavery, then segregation and anti-miscegenation laws, then *de jure* discrimination, then anti-affirmative action and the campaign to de-legitimize the Rev. Martin Luther King Jr. as a civil-rights hero. A led to B, which led to C.

This nation long ago gave up on slavery, but there are large contingents that refuse to give up on any chance to fight back against what they see as the gradual erosion of their old views and that old way of life, no matter how archaic. They stick to the Confederate battle flag, a symbol of a losing and discredited side (do we greet Nazi flags and Japanese battle flags with such reverence?), they publish magazines longing for the "good ol' days" and they sell T-shirts at their conventions and rallies and gun shows featuring Abraham Lincoln's picture and the words *sic semper tyrannis*. (Let us note that legendary "patriot" and executed mass murderer Timothy McVeigh was wearing such a shirt when he was apprehended.)

The subject of this column is Senate Majority Leader Trent Lott, and before those who live to take things out of context start foaming at the mouth complaining that I am comparing Lott to Strom Thurmond, the senior senator from South Carolina, let it be clear that while I am not comparing one to the other, they are both descendants of a similar ideology. One was enamored of the means to return to the "old days" (guns and power), the other is still clearly an adherent to the principles those old days stood for.

In one week alone, we found out that Lott pushed against desegregation of his college fraternity at the national levels back in the 1960s. The outrageous statement he made at Thurmond's 100th birthday party—that the nation would have been better served if Thurmond had been elected in 1948 on the Dixiecrats' blatantly racist platform—is a virtual word-for-word repeat of a statement he made a Jackson, Miss., rally for Ronald Reagan in 1980. In 1998, Lott flat-out lied when he claimed "no firsthand knowledge" of the Council of Conservative Citizens, a racist organization founded, ironically enough, in St. Louis, the birthplace of the Dred Scott decision. (The Conservative Citizens' Web site in the past has called Martin Luther King a "depraved miscreant" and featured articles opining that America was turning into a "slimy brown mass of glop.") Six years previously, Lott had met with the group's members, saying (as was printed in their newsletter), they "stand for the right principles and the right philosophy." When called on the lie, Lott's spokesman conveniently omitted the obvious tense in his statement, "This group harbors views which Senator Lott firmly rejects. He has absolutely no involvement with them either now or in the future."

How much more evidence do we need? How much weight of accumulated actions and words is necessary to show that the leader of the Republican majority in the U.S. Senate is grossly beyond the pale when it comes to race?

He voted against the first black man nominated to the Fourth Circuit of the U.S. Court of Appeals. He voted against the 1982 extension of the Voting Rights Act. He voted against the Martin Luther King holiday.

And the nut doesn't fall far from the tree: *The New York Times* reported last week that when Lott's local newspaper in Mississippi campaigned in 1963 against segregation, his mother, Iona, wrote a letter to the paper's editor saying that it would prove "you are truly an integrationist and I hope you not only get a hole through your office door but through your stupid head."

As it stands, Lott is unapologetically apologetic. At his press conference, when it was mentioned to him that he made virtually the same statements in the 1980s that he did at the Thurmond party, his reply was couched in the passive voice—that those statements "were made." If that's not an avoidance of responsibility, the definition simply must not exist.

Now, he will meet with conservative black apologists, like Roy Innis of CORE and black Republican millionaire Robert Johnson of Black Entertainment Television. The blinds are beginning to be pulled. And the majority of black America can sit back and be sure of one thing: Not one's whit has changed.

Sen. Lott has now told us, "Contrition is bullshit."

Lesser of Evils
October 29, 2003

Any time you hear a comment from a Republican political official at the national level on the subject of race, count on them to discuss the GOP's attempts at making inroads with black voters in glowing terms. If, however, you discuss this with actual groups of black people—regular folk, not ones involved in the political process—you'll see them lower their heads and laugh like Eddie Murphy: "Heh heh heh."

You see, black folk deep down know a few things: There are two choices. Not between voting Democrat or Republican. It's between voting Democrat and staying home. It's a lesson that American liberals learned the hard way back in 1994, when Newt Gingrich and the Angry White Males took the House and the Senate away from the Dems, and it's a lesson that Kathleen Kennedy Townsend learned all too well when she picked a former Republican political nobody to be her running mate over someone like black former Montgomery County Council Chairman Isaiah Leggett. Blacks know that, to quote the father of former Oklahoma Congressman J.C. Watts, to vote Republican is like the chicken voting for Colonel Sanders. So by and large, they'll opt not to participate if the candidate isn't seen to be in their best interest.

This isn't to say that there aren't blacks in the Republican Party—just look at our lieutenant governor. This is to say that every time the Political Animal runs into our good friend, a black female Republican who moved recently from Baltimore to Silver Spring to buy a home and start a family, we jokingly ask her which phone booth her party's black membership are meeting in. They're the exception, not the rule.

Back at the end of April, none other than the sage and prescient

George Will ended a column with the phrase "the successes of African-American Republicans in statewide elections will begin to produce modest—and tremendously consequential—Republican gains among African-Americans in presidential elections."

Unfortunately, until the majority of black America begins to resemble Robert Johnson, the billionaire who built and sold Black Entertainment Television, and Cathy Hughes, who runs Radio One, the nation's largest black radio station chain, it's highly unlikely that Will's prediction will come true. Mainly because most blacks are less well-off, more cynical and more likely to be intimidated, purged from the voter rolls, or turned off by the larger messages sent by Republican political machinations.

For example, down in Mississippi, former Republican National Committee Chairman Haley Barbour is locked in a tight race with incumbent Democratic Gov. Ronnie Musgrove. Barbour recently met with the Council of Conservative Citizens, a crypto-racist adjunct that succeeded the Klan when wearing white sheets no longer held the appropriate cachet to help one be elected to statewide office in the South. When it was pointed out to Barbour that his picture was featured on the CCC's Web site, Barbour told the local paper that he doesn't know anything about the council.

This is after the state's pre-eminent politician, former Senate Majority Leader Trent Lott, had his tenure crash in flames after his indelicate comments about how if Strom Thurmond was elected president back in '48, "we wouldn't have had all these problems." Lott, too, was a speaker before the CCC, and Lott, too, claimed to know nothing about them. For a group that garners so much press (and has an essay on its Web site titled "In Defense of Racism"), it's amazing how little these locally attuned politicians know about the people to whom they are speaking.

In Kentucky, back in July when it began to appear that the state's gubernatorial election might get close, we got to see the old "ballot security trick" pulled out of mothballs again. The first time your humble correspondent heard the term "ballot security" was back in the early '90s, when GOP fund raisers in Illinois sent out literature asking contributors if it was one of the efforts on which local Republicans wanted party funds to be spent. "Ballot security" turned out to be a process in which out-of-county "watchers" were sent into districts with large minority populations in order to "challenge" the identities of voters—usually in districts with no history of voter irregularities. In simpler terms, it was to intimidate black voters—many of them elderly with clear memories of things like poll taxes—and drive down the minority turnout.

Now the *Louisville Courier-Journal* reports a plan concocted by the Jefferson County Republicans that would bring "challengers" into 59 predominantly black precincts—from suburban counties where those challengers have no idea who might be a legitimate area voter or not.

The funny thing is, there's no evidence, anecdotal or otherwise, that shows the whole "show your ID" business deters or reduces voter fraud. But according to a story on ballot security in *American Prospect* magazine, a 1994 Justice Department study showed that blacks in Louisiana were four to five times less likely than whites to have some form of picture identification like a driver's license. As the *Prospect* concluded, challenging people for IDs at the polling place "is a solution in search of a problem. It doesn't make it harder to commit fraud; it just makes it harder to vote."

So remember that look you see the next time a black person is told Republicans really want or care about the African-American vote. "Heh heh heh." Because, to be impolite about it, under their breath, those black people are saying, "N____, *please.*"

Rent-a-Joke
August 11, 2004

Q: What's the difference between Alan Keyes and a parrot?

A: One's loud, annoying, colorful and says a lot of things that don't make sense, and the other's a bird.

So Maryland's own homegrown Harold Stassen is going to throw his hat into the ring to be Illinois' GOP candidate for the U.S. Senate. How lucky for Illinois. Dollar for dollar (which he pays himself), nobody tops Alan Keyes for sheer entertainment value when it comes to running a campaign for elective office.

Back when I was in my final semester as a columnist at the University of Maryland's *Diamondback* newspaper in 1988, Alan Keyes was running for the Senate against Paul Sarbanes. Keyes did a campaign stop on campus, but since he wasn't a household name back then, he brought along Fawn Hall, the leggy blonde secretary famous for shredding Ollie North's documents during the Iran-Contra scandal. The man knows how to campaign, I tell you.

Knock knock! Who's there? Alan Keyes! Alan Keyes who? That's show biz.

Keyes got his clock cleaned in that 1988 campaign. In the general election, Sarbanes brought in almost a million votes from across the state, 62 percent of the ballot. Keyes, with 617,537 votes, garnered 38 percent. Four years later, when Keyes ran against Barbara Mikulski, his totals went even further down. Mikulski tallied 1.3 million votes, or 71 percent, whereas Keyes slid to 533,668, or 29 percent of the vote. Maybe he should have brought along Gennifer Flowers.

In 1996, in the Republican presidential primary in his own state, supposedly as a "favorite son" candidate, Keyes pulled in only 13,718 votes—a meager 5 percent, and less than the total number of registered voters in Kent County that year.

Q: What's the difference between Alan Keyes and the Hindenburg?

A: One's a flaming bag of hot gas, and the other's a dirigible.

According to a report in the *Chicago Sun-Times*, Keyes actually told a member of the Illinois Republican Party establishment that his would-be opponent, rising Democratic Party star Barack Obama, "didn't really represent the views of the people of Illinois." This from a guy who, in his last run at office in his own state, didn't appear to represent more than a handful of percentage points of the voters in his own party.

Q: What does Alan Keyes' ego have in common with the Great Wall of China?

A: Both are man-made creations that can be seen from space.

This isn't the first time Keyes has been sought to leave the Land of Pleasant Living and run against a Democratic Party star. Back in 2000, according to the *Chicago Tribune*, right wingers in New York wanted him to pack up and run for Senate against Hillary Rodham Clinton. Man of principle that he, uh, was, Keyes shot down the idea on the Fox News Channel on March 17, 2000.

"I deeply resent the destruction of federalism represented by Hillary Clinton's willingness to go into a state she doesn't even live in and pretend to represent people there. So I certainly wouldn't imitate it," Keyes said at the time.

It's kind of hard to figure out who comes off looking sadder from this little *pas de deux*: Keyes or the Illinois Republican Party. Here's Keyes, who has failed at his every attempt at elected office, *and* failed at his attempt to host a cable TV talk show on MSNBC, the fourth-rate network famous for finding obscure right-wing nutballs and wackjobs to spew bile in the nether hours. And here's the Illinois GOP, whose first Senate candidate, Jack Ryan, dropped out after it turned out he lied when he said there was nothing embarrassing in his divorce papers. Well, except for that little business about wanting to do the horizontal bop with his wife in public at sex clubs in the United States and in France. For a good Republican, that's gotta be embarrassing. Not the sex clubs, which we're all in favor of here at Animal Control, but that he wanted to do her in France.

The U.S. Census Bureau says that the state of Illinois is home to some 12.6 million citizens. Maryland has less than half that: 5.5 million. Yet the Land of Lincoln needs to come out here to lure away our homegrown failures to run for office? What is this nation coming to? The *Chicago Tribune* probably said it best in an editorial that ran before Keyes even officially announced he was in the race: "He will run and will lose. And then he will hop on the next flight back to Maryland, and the state's GOP will be left with nothing but the smell of jet fumes."

Q: What's the difference between Alan Keyes and a U-Haul truck?

A: Neither costs that much to rent round-trip.

Blinded Date
August 25, 2004

They love us. They love us not. They love us. They love us not.

Being a black person courted by Republicans during an election year is kind of like having a relationship with an abusive lover. You get all sorts of lovey talk to your face all the time—all the promises, the talk of future gifts, and the wheedling of what it's going to be like in the future. "Yeah, baby, I'm gonna take care of you—I got what you need."

But when you open your eyes and look around, you see that

the sweet talker is drinking all your booze, eating all your food, emptying your bank account, kicking your momma out of the nursing home and not making the payments on the car he bought in your name.

Surrogates and friends of the Bush administration are all out on the hustings, talking about what a great pal the president is to black people. On Aug. 2, a guy named Charles Sahm with the Manhattan Institute, a conservative think tank, penned an op-ed in the *Los Angeles Times* titled "Blacks Have a Compassionate Friend in Bush." Sahm writes, "Despite the criticism he's received on race-related issues from elements of the black leadership and from Democrats generally, the reality is that he has consistently championed initiatives focused on economic and social empowerment rather than further dependency on social welfare programs." He goes on to cite the standard litany of things George W. Bush has done to "help" African-Americans: the No Child Left Behind act, voucher programs, his faith-based initiative and promises of more AIDS funding for Africa.

Wow. They love us!

But Terry Neal of *The Washington Post* pointed out May 20 that the unemployment rate for African-Americans back in April was at 9.3 percent—almost double the rate for white people that same month, and up almost three full percentage points since the final months of the Clinton administration.

Neal cites the work of Washington-based black pollster Cornell Belcher, who has been surveying black people in six battleground states: Ohio, Pennsylvania, Missouri, Florida, Michigan and Nevada. Belcher found that while white people may be starting to have misgivings about the war in Iraq, African-Americans have taken those feelings and run with them. Belcher pointed out to Neal that "[s]eventy-three percent of African Americans in those states disagree that the war in Iraq is worth the U.S. casualties there because the country is safer. Sixty-three percent agree that America should cut its losses and pull out of Iraq right now. And... on the question of whether Bush intentionally misled the country, seventy-seven percent agree at least somewhat."

But wait—there's Juan Williams of National Public Radio and the Fox News Channel, opining in *The New York Times* back in June that "[w]ith the presidential election only a few months away, it is time for President Bush to unleash his secret weapon— his relationship with black and Hispanic voters." Williams went on to cite the president's so-called "top-selling point[s]," and they are...faith-based initiatives, school vouchers and the black people he has named to his administration.

Williams is a constant (and supposedly impartial) voice proclaiming the love Republicans have for black people—he was at it again on NPR just last week, interviewing the president's svengali, Karl Rove, about the subject. But there are times you don't hear from Williams or Rove—like when reports about black voter intimidation crop up.

When it is pointed out how thousands of black voters were disenfranchised in Florida in 2000, for example, conservatives flatly deny it occurred. Columnist Bob Herbert of *The New York Times* has highlighted, as recently as Aug. 23, new voter intimidation tactics in Florida: State police officers have gone to the homes of black voters alleging an investigation into absentee ballots (whose details they will not divulge). Herbert looked into it and found that the cops—in plain clothes and armed—specifically singled out elderly black voters, and police officials in Florida say the "investigation" could very well continue through the election.

When Republicans are wooing black voters, you don't hear about their support of crypto-Confederates like Mississippi Sen.

Trent Lott, or Mississippi Gov. Haley Barbour, who claimed he never heard of the Council of Conservative Citizens, a neo-Confederate group whose Web site featured a picture of him taken at one of its events. You don't hear about the GOP "ballot security" teams in Kentucky that, during the 2003 midterm elections, sent operatives from outside precincts into predominantly black neighborhoods to challenge the votes there. Or how the Bush administration, last year, filed a brief with the Supreme Court against affirmative action on the day after the Rev. Martin Luther King Jr.'s birthday. It goes on and on.

Yeah, they love us, they really do. But remember—don't call us, we'll call you.

Liberals and Conservatives

I wish I had a dollar for every time I've heard the old saw, "If you're under 25 and a conservative, you have no heart. And if you're 50 and and a liberal, you have no brain." Or its hoary companion, "A conservative is a liberal who's been mugged." I'm on the very near side of 50 and I'm still liberal and I've had my house broken into three times—twice when I was home at the time—and I still believe what I believed at twenty five, albeit a little less sure about some things.

I have come 360 degrees on the death penalty, for instance. In college, I told my then-girlfriend, who now bosses attorneys around at Wilmer Hale, one of DC's biggest powdered-wig lawyer hives, that I opposed capital punishment. After seeing pure evil in the form of John Frederick Thanos, the Maryland murderer who, when asked by a reporter if he was sorry for the lives he took, answered, "It's not my responsibility to be sorry," I had no qualms whatsoever when the state executed him in 1994. Now I'm back to where I started, knowing that the state's apparatus is far more likely to be misused, and there are no do-overs. And I'm far more than comfortable if the Thanoses of the world sit staring at a cinder-block wall for the rest of their days. It's a worthwhile cost to society, and also legal mistakes—which still happen—are reversible.

I do, however, maintain a firm belief in one thing: "Eat, drink and smoke like a Republican, vote like a Democrat." I enjoy red meat, fine wine, Cuban cigars, leather clothing and big cars driven by other people. While believing in licensing and registration of guns and their owners, I still think they're a hoot to shoot, and have never been in favor of a total ban, no matter what words some of the loons of the gun-nut Right have tried to insert in my mouth.

But the problem with the conservatives of the new millennium is that they overreached. They got a taste of power in 1994, and then when George Bush came to power in 2000, they went nuts. *The Wall Street Journal* called poor people "lucky duckies" because they pay so little in taxes, as if scraping by week-to-week for a paycheck and having little to no chance for retirement was such a prize. Barbara Bush said of the people displaced by Hurricane Katrina when she visited the Houston Astrodome, "And so many of the people in the arena here, you know, were underprivileged anyway, so this is working very well for them."

And of course, the liberal thing. If, after the last eight years, conservatives have to apologize every time they mention their political persuasion for the next ten years, all I can say is, "You had it coming." I remember when, among other things, "politics stopped at the water's edge." Maybe I'm young and impressionable in that right, but when Gingrich's lieutenants excoriated Bill Clinton over Kosovo for things that they would label treasonous under Bush and Iraq War II, for me, that's when the gloves came off.

Until blogs came along on the Internet, talk radio was the unchallenged fever swamp of right-wing thinking. The John Birchers, the nutballs of the far right, suddenly became the mainstream, and it dragged the political center way out of whack, where those who used to be moderate conservatives were suddenly liberal and those who were liberal centrists were tarred as the equivalent of Ramsey Clark in love beads. And reporters for *The New York Times*—the freaking New York freaking Times!—were, like Elizabeth Bumiller, their White House correspondent, too intimidated to ask tough questions of the president on national television. No wonder the first order of business was to drive Dan Rather out of mainstream television journalism: This was the guy who, when Nixon asked him at the height of Watergate, "Are you running for something?" had the balls to shoot back, "No, sir. Are you?"

Now the right is scared. Listen to Bill O'Reilly on Fox claim that the liberal fact-checking site Media Matters for America is as bad as the Nazis. MMA is the web operation that actually records for posterity the vile sewage that used to just float off into the ether, ready to be denied when its perpetrators were confronted with their own words. O'Reilly says, "If you look back at what happened in Germany, you cannot escape the similarities between what Hitler and his cutthroats did back then and the hate-filled blogs, what they're doing now." Well, except for the whole gas chambers and Gestapo and such, I guess.

This is what I've been watching and chronicling since 1994. It's nice not to feel alone anymore.

*　　　　　*　　　　　*

Who's Got The Bag
Unpublished, April 1992

The big question is now—who's going to fill the bag?

It was the taxpayer left with the dopey look on his or her collective face after the HUD scandal. It was the taxpayer left soaking in the financial rain and ruin after the S&L fiasco. And after junk bonds and leveraged buyouts precipitated massive bankruptcies and failures, the Republicans' solid belief in trickle-down economics has been vindicated in at least one area: once again it has leaked down on the financial keystone of America, the taxpayer holding the bag.

Now after the savaging of justice and the looting of Los Angeles, who's going to fill the bag?

Already arrests and indictments are being made of looters and rioters. Police have seen to it that those who allegedly dragged 36-year old Reginald Denny out of his vehicle's cab and beat him have been clapped in irons. The president has toured the scene, from smoking remnants of shopping centers to the Mount Zion Missionary Baptist Church, showing his typical concern and promising the obligatory remedies.

And what of those remedies? It is now as if everything old is new again. It is only a conservative Pollyanna who can say that the inner cities have been leading the list on the president's domestic agenda. It has taken a city on fire to get the president and the Congress to just make mewling conciliatory noises at each other that something must be done, and now with a Democratic urban relief package on the table, the White House has finally sat up and taken notice.

One of the main components of the package that all appear to agree upon is the need for urban enterprise zones—areas in the cities to be staked out for reconstruction and seeded with opportunities for new business. Housing secretary Jack Kemp has been pushing the issue around the edges of the administration and now he's getting his day in the sunlight.

Normally, Republican talk of a capital gains tax cut sticks in the craw like a paint can lid, and here it is again, also in Kemp's set of "urban initiatives." But this time, his idea of a zero capital gains tax rate for people who work and invest in the inner cities can be justified as something more than handing more money to the barons who got so much of it in the last decade.

George Bush pushes for a cut in the capital gains tax nearly every time he gets the chance, but Congress repudiates it each time, rightly claiming that it benefits the people in the upper income brackets, people with real estate and stock holdings—you know, that top 1 percent that got richer during the 80s—more than the average American. But this time, if used properly, a capital gains tax cut for *small businesses in urban areas only* would provide a massive incentive to climb back into the cities and give them a tax base again. Offering the cut to large corporations would only cause more displacement, and leave an even greater hole the next time an indecisive or spineless administration guts the program and lets the companies move their operations to or out of the country.

Kemp's ideas are currently the best thing going for what the 80s have done to America's urban core, and he has more empathy for the minority populations of those areas than anyone else in the Bush administration. But the Republican commitment to those ideas should been seen as questionable at best. It was Great Society programs that begat the businesses that burnt in 1968 and those same programs provided the bootstraps for the people who now form much of the black middle class. And yet, it was those programs that President Bush immediately termed a failure when he was looking for a root cause of the smoky Los Angeles skyline.

Back in the mid-70s, the idea of recreating the urban center of many cities came back into vogue; Baltimore was one of them. The corridor leading out West Baltimore Street was ripe for redevelopment after the destruction that followed the assassination of Rev. Martin Luther King.

Tax breaks were granted, businesses began to relocate to the area—and then the program was hacked off at the knees at the start of the anti-spending Reagan revolution. So here we go again.

All this talk of urban enterprise zones and urban renewal (now *there's* some deja vu all over again) still has to pass the president's desk. And if it takes until after the November election to get there, what's to say anything will ever come of it at all? We have a president that doesn't want to tax or spend, a Congress that wants to spend but not to tax, and a public that doesn't want taxes and thinks the Congress overspends—but *still* wants better education, roads and security.

Pray for the cities, because they are in the hands of the people left holding the bag once too often.

Oath of Hypocrisy
January 11, 1995

It didn't take the hypocrisy long to start up last week. Matter of fact, we here mark the occasion at the precise moment Rep. Connie Morella told *The Sun* that things would change from under Democratic rule of the House of Representatives when 80 percent of the bills that made it to the House floor either allowed for one amendment or none at all.

"This is an example of their arrogance of power," she told *The Sun*, "I think there will be less of that."

Hoo Hah! Praise the Lord and pass the claptrap! A Republican vow that lasted less than a day! Welcome to reality, Connie—because you ain't seen nothin' yet.

The rule agreed upon by the GOP called for 20 minutes debate and then a vote, with no chance for amendments. The "rule" is legislative parlance for the terms under which a bill will be debated before a final vote is taken. If there are no amendments to be allowed on the floor, it is said to be a "closed rule." And granted, the Democrats in their time used the closed rule over the GOP like the LAPD used nightsticks on Rodney King.

It's not that turnabout isn't fair play. Face it, we all expected it. But to start out with the full rigmarole about how times will change, that the smell of reform is in the air and a new day is about to dawn starts to wear pretty thin when the new day starts out like the old day, the smell of old tactics is in the air and the only thing that has changed is who's on the ugly end of the stick.

It gets better. One of the reasons for the closed rule on the provisions of the "Contract With America" was so a provision sponsored by the Democrats wouldn't make it to the floor. The provision? A ban on free trips and gift-giving to members of Congress (of the sort that got Agriculture Secretary Mike Espy in enough trouble in the executive branch that he had to resign—old habits die hard).

Funnier still, this ban was brought out during the end of the 103rd Congress—and squelched then by the Republicans, who wanted to deny the Democratic Congress a victory—any victory—by getting something passed.

If anything is proven in the flurry of legislation in the first days of the 104th Congress, it's that running against Washington is good until you get there. At that point, you want the champagne to be cold, and somebody's got to make sure those lobbyists are there to give it to you.

Following the hilarity of the death of the gift ban was the knowledge that in one vote taken last week, the chickens will be coming home to roost. By this we mean the Fair Labor Standards Act of 1938 and the Civil Service Reform Act of 1978 (both passed under Democratic presidents and Congresses). When the GOP made the long overdue move of making the Congress accountable under the laws that govern the rest of society, it probably had no idea that they will be leaping from the Last Plantation full-tilt into the litigational fray of the 1990s, with little grace-period in between. And should a member of Congress be sued by a wronged employee, who pays the legal tab, win or lose? That's right—you do.

Here's the big horselaugh: the bane of Republican existence, collective bargaining, can now come to Capitol Hill. The Civil Service Reform Act of 1978 gives federal employees the right to join labor unions, form bargaining units and negotiate with employers. Under the vote taken by Congress last Wednesday, it extends that privilege to employees on the Hill. Senator Lockjaw, meet Donald Fehr, our labor union negotiator.

All-nighter sessions such as the one that passed much of the Contract With America legislation may also become a thing of the past, say, like "Mr. Smith Goes To Washington." Old movies are getting hip again—first it was "Boys Town," and then the day before The Avalanche of Laws, House Whip Dick Armey was boasting that the opening session would be like the title to the movie, "The Longest Day." As long as we're on our way to Blockbuster, he might want to start thinking about Sally Field in "Norma Rae." The Republicans, after years of three-day work weeks followed by last minute flurries of late-night steamroller panic sessions, claimed that the Hill schedule under their rule would be more "family-friendly." This, of course, didn't last a day either. Two days in session, with the first of them 14 hours long, and then a break.

As Rep. Barney Frank said on the House Floor, "You said it would be family-friendly! You didn't say it was going to be the Addams Family!"

All along, from campaign to post-election, Speaker Newt Gingrich has said the whole basis for the Contract was fiscal, to strip government of its size and cost and make it accountable to the American people. What he is going to find out is that in doing so, he shall discover that the Congress, known in this writer's eyes as The World's Most Expensive Day Care Center ("Here's your dry-cleaning, Senator..."), will have to pay its employees for all that time they spend doing things other than legitimate House and Senate business. In other words, Senator Mikulski will have to start thinking about how much she'll have to pay that staffer in overtime who drives her from Baltimore to Washington and back each day.

Yep, it's a brand new day in Washington, and we won't spoil the view by saying it still looks a lot like the old one in some respects. But hey—we love hypocrisy. We just hate it when it's the other guy who is the hypocrite.

A Tax on All Their Houses
July 5, 1995

And they laugh at the District of Columbia.

This week's exercise in disbelief comes after last week's amazing defeat of a referendum in Orange County, CA, on a proposal to raise their sales tax by one half-cent in order to make up some revenue after declaring bankruptcy. This comes after their elected treasurer, Robert Citron, causes the county to lose some $1.7 *billion* on bad investments.

Then, blaming "the government," a citizens group mounts a valiant effort (on the cheap, of course) to defeat the hated referendum, which goes down in flames and still leaves the county holding the bag on $975 million in IOUs which stand to go into default.

On top of that, a bond issue touted by the county has had about the same amount of success as, let's say, a man would trying to sell shares in Charles Keating's Lincoln Savings and Loan out of the back of a truck in the middle of Hollywood Boulevard. So instead of raising $130 to $140 million dollars a year and allowing the county to instantly borrow $800 million and keep their schools open and their trash collected, they're left celebrating the "will of the people" and probably hoping the Tooth Fairy will leave them a couple of suitcases of gold bullion under their collective pillows.

Let's recap here. The District of Columbia has something on the order of 40 percent of the land under the jurisdiction of the federal government, which does not pay taxes on it. Instead, dependent upon the whims of lawmakers who don't live there yet can step in and veto local government decisions, the city gets a "payment" to allegedly make up for that fact. This does not take into account the people who work in the District, but are not taxed there—they take their salaries home to suburban Maryland or Virginia. This also does not take into account large quasi-government billion-dollar agencies like Fannie Mae, the federal home-mortgage agency, which pays no DC taxes as well.

Orange County, one of the wealthiest subdivisions in the

nation with household incomes in the top 2 percent among all U.S. counties according to a report in the Associated Press, is home to the California Angels, the Walt Disney Co. (both of which supported the increase, according to reports) and a plethora of high-tech industries. It has its own government and answers to no one but its own voters.

Those voters themselves elect a man who loses more than a billion dollars of their money on risky investments, and then they blame the county government *which they elected* for the loss. A story in the Orange County Register the day after the defeat of the referendum had tax protesters celebrating in the parking lot of the county registrar under signs that say "County Government Is Corrupt."

To top that off, they hope to recoup the money in a number of ways that range from the conventional to the ridiculous. Proposals range from the good old Republican belief in privatization (sell off the airport), to the constitutionally shaky (divert money earmarked for highways and transportation), to pie-in-the-sky wishful thinking (reap a huge settlement from brokerage Merrill Lynch, which the county is suing for its role in the investment debacle).

It's understandable why some people dislike taxes so much, but there has to be a limit to the pathological hatred for them espoused by the nation's conservatives. Those with the money to send their children to private schools, to hire their own private security and pay for their own health care may feel that money they pay to the government is being wasted and abused. But the rest of society, who live from paycheck to paycheck on manufacturing jobs that are disappearing from automation or headed overseas, can only hope that the last safety net provided by state and federal government monies won't vanish like yesterday's dreams.

This state nearly elected a woman whose platform rested solely on the plank that state government does nothing for you but spend money uselessly, so your taxes should be cut by 24 percent. Her impetus for this was the plan extolled by Governor Christine Todd Whitman of New Jersey, who in 18 months has cut taxes 30 percent.

The result? *The New York Times* reports the Republican chairman of the state senate's budget committee doubts that there will be enough money to make up for the loss of $247 million in revenues. The state's nonpartisan Office of Legislative Services says the governor's Treasury Department has overstated the upcoming year's projected revenues by $380 million, not to mention Whitman's claims that the state has a $500 million surplus to deal with any surprises should the federal government shut off the flow of money to the states.

So feel free to laugh at the District of Columbia because they've re-elected a convicted druggie to be their mayor. Laugh at Orange County, where Disneyland has gone from being a theme park for kids to a fiscal theme for angry taxpayers without a clue. The wait is still on for the punch line from New Jersey, although it appears they're telegraphing it far before the end of the joke.

But don't laugh for Maryland, because we came *that* close. DC, Orange County and New Jersey will have to live with their mistakes. Ours is now a talk-show host.

Run, Pat, Run!
February 28, 1996

Okay, now—really. Joke's over. Can someone please explain this "Pat Buchanan as serious candidate for president" stuff to us?

What kind of whacky terbacky are they smoking up there in New Hampshire to give this man a serious start at running for president? Trying for 300 years to make a living farming rocks must have done something to their collective psyche if they think ol' bullyboy Pat could really be president.

It *has* to be a joke. For years, an old *Washington Post* editorial from 1988 hung up on the door of the Animal Control Archives and Walk-In Beer Cooler expressing then what we here still think now. It was when Buchanan was making noises about challenging George Bush and Bob Dole in the primaries. The *Post* said that a number of things would happen if Pat went all the way and won, all of them bad: They'd be deprived of all those sulfuric acid-on-asbestos paper op-ed columns, they'd be ashamed of their part in making Pat the big name that he is and of course, he would be president.

They went on to say the only way they could head this ugly scenario off at the pass would be to endorse him. They'd say how he had mellowed over the years. That his opinions had gone mainstream. That (and here's where it galled them) they *like* him. That should do it, they said.

Well, here we are, eight years later and Pat is allegedly fighting for workers' rights (although we note the thunderous silence on his part concerning little things like collective bargaining), while championing his own crusade against affirmative action, abortion, gays and lesbians and immigration.

Funnier still, did you ever think you'd see the day when

Buchanan and Greenpeace lined up on the same side of an issue? Both were against the North American Free Trade Agreement—when NAFTA was being argued on the House floor in 1993, Greenpeace activists flung handfuls of photocopied $50 bills onto the floor from the gallery. The bills were doctored to show U.S. Grant with a smug smile on his face, while in the corner it read "Trading Pork for Poisons." "Bill Clinton" read the signature for the Treasurer of the United States and, on the flip side, it simply stated: "Not This NAFTA!" Our copy is on the beer cooler right next to the *Post* editorial.

The Greenpeace activists were physically ejected. Not exactly what's happening to Pat at the polls, eh?

Back then, the Congressional Black Caucus decided to come out against NAFTA (and a fat lot of good it did them) on the principle that when jobs started flowing out of the United States (as they have), the minorities put out of work by the loss of manufacturing jobs would be hit harder than the rest of the population at large.

Of course, Pat is also against affirmative action in a big way, so we guess he'd rather have the jobs back, but have no black people in them.

Listening to Pat Buchanan is kind of like "Back to the Future," except it should more properly be called "Onward Into The Past." He talks about the Eisenhower 50s like there was no such thing as crime, divorce, abortion or African-Americans. It was when the only hooligans you met looked like, well, they looked like Pat. Not many other candidates brag in their biographies that they got locked up for kicking a cop in the ass while being tossed into a paddy wagon.

Pat's a bully, plain and simple, and he wants America to pull into its shell, lock the doors and go back to knocking the wife and kids around inside the house like a good old-fashioned domestic disturbance, they way they did it back in the 50s.

But what the hell—go, Pat, go. In the belief that nothing exposes foolishness more than its widespread visibility, let us be the first to wish Pat well in his quest for the Presidency. After all, he hails from Chevy Chase originally—that almost makes him a "favorite son." Once removed, of course.

We here at Animal Control have no need to worry about our part in Pat Buchanan's ascent to the Republican nomination. We didn't make him a designated mouthpiece for the alienated white-boy class of the 80s or 90s. We have nothing to lose.

On the other hand, just imagine how much fun it will be to see Pat in prime time at the GOP convention in San Diego! We can't wait; it'll be the Buchanan Beer Hall Putsch, with Pat's boys doing the *putsching* and *tschoving*.

So let's hear it for Pat Buchanan! The line forms here. We're calling it the Volksmarch on Washington. Coming March 5ᵗʰ to a ballot box near you.

Tax The Poor!
December 25, 2002

America, at its best, is compassionate. In the quiet of American conscience, we know that deep, persistent poverty is unworthy of our nation's promise.
—George W. Bush, 2001 inaugural address

Back on Nov. 20, *The Wall Street Journal*'s editorial page, where many conservative ideas are hatched and test-marketed, published a novel thought: The poor pay too little in taxes, and some, horror of horrors, are so poor they don't pay any at all. The Journal, in its paroxysms of compassion, even coined a term for these people: "Lucky duckies."

By last week, the idea had already taken hold in the heart of the administration. On Dec. 16, *The Washington Post* reported that "Economists at the Treasury Department are drafting new ways to calculate the distribution of tax burdens among different income classes, which are expected to highlight what administration officials see as a rising tax burden on the rich and a declining burden on the poor."

In times of riches or recession, the Republican Party loves the tax cuts. When the budget showed a surplus at the end of the 1990s, George W. Bush argued for tax cuts as a way to give people back their money. Despite the oncoming train wreck of Social Security, a health care crisis and a still-sizeable national debt, he said we could afford it.

If gas prices were too high—pass his tax cut. That $300 you got back could go right into your gas tank.

If you couldn't afford prescription drugs—pass his tax cut. That $300 you got back could help ease the high cost of those pills (which are cheaper over the border).

When the bottom fell out of the economy, the president then argued that we needed a stimulus—pass his tax cut. Never mind the fact that he admitted that most of his tax cut benefited the wealthiest 1 percent of Americans, and that $300 payoff is a long-distant memory. It's time to fix the tax system again.

See, it turns out the tax system isn't fair—to rich people. And those allegedly untaxed poor people, those "lucky duckies" in the *Journal's* parlance, aren't sympathetic to the heavy burden the wealthy pay and therefore won't line up in support for more tax cuts. "Workers who pay little or no taxes," the *Journal's* editorial stated, "can hardly be expected to care about tax relief for everybody else. They are also that much more detached from recognizing the costs of government."

Bummer, dude.

Typically enough, whenever the Right starts moaning about how untaxed are the poorer strata of the Great Unwashed, they tend to forget that little behemoth gnawing at the corner of your W-2s—your Social Security payroll taxes. As economist and *New York Times* columnist Paul Krugman points out, the *Journal's* editors whine that someone who makes about 12 grand a year might only pay four percent of his income in taxes—although when you add in those payroll taxes, it comes to more than 20 percent of income.

But according to the *Post*, ousted White House economic advisor Larry Lindsay was telling an American Enterprise Institute tax forum that payroll taxes shouldn't count toward calculating a person's tax burden because we are supposed to be getting that back as a benefit later in life.

Now hold on a minute there, pardner.

They mocked Al Gore's "lockbox" back in 2000, saying we could save Social Security, cut taxes and give each and every one of us back 300 bucks all at once. Now they're dipping into Social Security after having cut taxes for the rich; they're proposing to cut taxes further on the rich by trying to make those tax cuts permanent; and now they're saying that Social Security (whose funds they are dipping into as we speak) payroll taxes shouldn't count toward our tax burden because we'll *get them back*?

Oy.

This is all too funny when you consider the incoming man at the Treasury Department, John Snow, had the third highest compensation package among 37 transportation company executives surveyed recently, while his rail company's stock was falling. At the same time, that rail company paid no income taxes in at least two of the last four years while recording more than a billion dollars in pretax profits at the same time.

So remember, when companies flee to a post office box in the Bahamas in order to evade paying taxes, they're not doing anything illegal. When the Treasury designate can help his company avoid paying taxes for several years and get rewarded with a $2 million annual pension plan, while at the same time cutting back benefits for retired line employees, that's just doing good business by rewarding good managers.

But on $12,000 a year, you lucky duckies, you're just not taxed enough. Now get back to work.

On principle . . . those in the greatest need should receive the greatest help. . . . Now is the time to reform the tax code and share some of the surplus with the people who pay the bills.
—George W. Bush, nomination acceptance speech, 2000

Promises, Promises
April 23, 2003

The next time you're in the grocery store, check the side of the milk cartons for some of the promises and claims Republicans have made over the past decade.

Back in 1995, Newt Gingrich and his merry band of no-compromise conservatives were claiming that the nation needed a balanced-budget amendment to the Constitution, as they felt politicians (a class that, lest we forget, included themselves at the time) were simply unable to stomach the willpower required to balance the budget themselves. Solving the problem of the deficit was paramount, a subject of campaign promises going all the way back to the 1992 election, thanks to Ross Perot and his charts, and the spotlight thrown on it by the bipartisan Concord Coalition. Despite the campaign to tar Bill Clinton in 1993 by accusing him of passing the largest tax increase in U.S. history—which raised taxes on the wealthy and made them squeal like stuck pigs—the last popularly elected president balanced the budget by 1998.

Today? There are deficits as far as the eye can see, which are dismissed by a conservative political class that is still harping on the idea of tax cuts for the wealthy. In 2000, back when there was still a surplus, Bush promised that we could afford his tax cuts without having to dip into Social Security money. Then gas prices went up, and Bush said that passing his tax cuts would give people money to put in their gas tanks. Then the nation got hit by terrorists, and Bush said we needed tax cuts to help stimulate the nation's economy in order to recover. Since then, we've been treated to tax cuts in order to create jobs for the military to return to (they have jobs—they're in the military!) and tax cuts for, well, the need for tax cuts. Beware the politician whose solution remains the same no matter how circumstances change.

At this point, the lie about the president claiming budget deficits were OK in times of national emergency, recession, or war—the subject of the Bush trifecta joke—has been repeated so many times the White House is moving forward as if it were gospel. They're still dragging around the old canard of the "death tax" on the "little guy"—which only kicks in after the first $2 million worth of assets, and the rest can be paid over 20 years.

How about the line-item veto? That was a big priority 10 years ago—until the GOP realized that it could be turned into a political weapon by the man they despised, and so they put it on hold hoping Bob Dole would win in '96. When Clinton won and signed the line-item veto into law, the Right let it quietly be overturned by the Supreme Court, another campaign item consigned to the dustbin.

Term limits? Uh-uh.

Social Security privatization? In Iowa on Jan. 20, 2000, George W. Bush actually even used the word: "What privatization does is allows the individual worker—his or her choice—to set aside money in a managed account with parameters in the marketplace." Since then, of course, the stock market has lost billions of dollars in equity, and GOP candidates have campaigned in many places saying they never were for privatization. The rest, like Sen. Lindsay Graham of South Carolina, accused their opponents of "scare tactics"—Graham responded to ads mentioning Social Security privatization from opponent Alex Sanders by calling the ads "bogus appeals to emotion that are trying to scare us all to death."

Going beyond mere promise breaking, the Bush administration has made it almost policy to kill reports and commissions that might point out embarrassing facts or contradictions to the party line. When in February the nation's governors complained about the amount of money their states were getting from the federal government, the Bush administration killed the report "Budget Information for States," which serves as the primary document showing who gets what. When it started to become obvious how many jobs were not being created under the George W. bunch, last Christmas Eve they killed the Mass Layoff Statistics report, put out each month by the Bureau of Labor Statistics. And the Senate killed a Department of Housing and Human Services plan to consolidate all the department's legislative and public affairs offices into one section reporting to the secretary, after Health and Human Services Secretary Tommy Thompson delayed giving senators a report on human embryo research that was seen as contrary to the administration's stated policy.

So, there you have it: lies, distractions, secrecy and promises with expiration dates. Top it off with all the shifting reasons why the United States went into Iraq in the first place, the no-bid contracts given to administration friends like KBR (a Halliburton subsidiary) and Bechtel (a major Republican campaign donor), and you wonder why there was such hyperbole over Sen. John Kerry's remark that "What we need now is not just a regime change in Saddam Hussein and Iraq, but we need a regime change in the United States."

Where, of course, in the last presidential election, a half-million more people voted for the other guy.

Patriot Games
January 7, 2004

Much is made these days of being a patriot—who is, who isn't and what it means. Many Americans reflexively say that the United States is "the greatest country in the world" without ever having set foot off their native soil; many haven't even made it out of the state of their birth.

This is a very personal subject for me. I grew up traveling all over the globe as a representative of this country, since my parents were career diplomats. We saw exactly how America's actions were perceived, for well or ill, throughout the world.

I remember very clearly reading Johnny Hart's comic strip *B.C.* when I was young. His caveman characters were reading humorous takes on the "Fun With Dick and Jane" children's books. One strip went, "See Dick throw stones. See Jane throw stones. It is fun for Jane and Dick. But not for the embassy people." I never was the target for any rocks thrown because of my country's foreign policy—but the possibility was always there, and I knew it, even as a child.

I say this because some people need to realize that not everybody on the planet wants to move here. Not everybody on the planet thinks that this is the Land of Milk and Honey. There are other nations where the standard of living is just as high; there are countries with just as good (or better) health-care plans and there are places where the rush to earn the filthy lucre is not the mad dash that it is here, a country where lunches and vacations and bereavement leave are for wussies.

I spent the last 10 years of my life with someone who came from one of these countries. In many ways, visiting her country was like being in America in 1970, without the nasty divisiveness of Vietnam but all the technological marvels of today. I went there and saw the happy, friendly folk, the clearer skies, the beautiful scenery, the more relaxed atmosphere. I saw people who quite happily were living their lives without the driving need to go to the United States and become a millionaire.

During my first visit, the Republican-led Congress had shut down the U.S. government. Overnight, once again, I became a junior ambassador for my nation, explaining to her people how the self-proclaimed "greatest country in the world" could shut down its government over a political difference of opinion. I was the constant focal point in bars and at parties, discussing and debating until past midnight how a country could close its embassies and consulates, turn people away from its parks and close its offices because one party wanted to deny the other party's president the chance to steer the nation in the direction to which the electorate told him to go.

I have friends who have moved abroad, not for politics, but for love or work. I know people who advise in Ethiopia, write in

Paris, teach in Kenya and simply live in London. The world is much smaller now than when I grew up in places like Bogotá, Colombia and La Paz, Bolivia—there is the Internet, for one thing, which allows virtually instantaneous worldwide communication to anyone who can manage to peck out words on a keyboard. So those friends can write us here in the States and ask, "What the hell is going on over there?"

All of them love their country, despite having made the choice not to live in it. My father jokingly told me and my brother one time over Thanksgiving dinner that he "had no idea I raised a couple of little super-patriots" when we talked about our arguments with U.K.-born children while living in the former British colony of Jamaica in the early 1970s. We too became adept at the "Well, who saved *your* bacon in two world wars" argument when serenaded with "Britannia Rules the Waves." When you live overseas, you become the most American of Americans, because it simply *is* your country, right or wrong.

So, in these times, it is expressly galling for the expatriates I know to have to come to the defense of the actions of this president and this administration, who launched us almost unilaterally into pre-emptive war on the strength of evidence that it certainly knew to be shoddy if not manufactured or completely nonexistent. And we have seen that, in these times, to air your criticisms of the leadership of this country you love while not standing on your native soil will be portrayed as treason by the jingoistic right-wingers in the government and among its shills in the media (the most virulent outfit, Fox News, being owned by someone who wasn't himself born an American, Australia's Rupert Murdoch).

The person with whom I spent the last 10 years of my life recently became naturalized as a U.S. citizen. She has worked in the halls of Congress; she has seen America, its good and bad, its glories and wonders, its people and places. She knows of its history and its pitfalls better than many here who took their first breath on this soil and have never left it. She can now fulfill the most sacred duty: She can vote.

Maybe it's because for many jobs now in post-Sept. 11 America you have to be a citizen. Maybe it's because the United States doesn't officially allow dual citizenship. Or maybe it's because, despite all our flaws, we might be worth it. I hope so.

We may not be together any more, but I'm proud that she is one of us now. Congratulations, hon. Welcome to America.

Reagan's Legacy
June 9, 2004

For one thing, if there were no Ronald Wilson Reagan, there would be no Political Animal.

Ronald Reagan came to office with his now-legendary sunny optimism, but he also brought with him something else: the beginnings of the end of civility in modern politics. It was Reagan who began the trend of making "liberal" a bad word. And it was Reagan who created the now-snowballing legacy of the freeloader culture: Taxes can always be cut, government can always can be shrunk and there's never any need to worry about who pays the bills—someone will take care of that later.

Even now, it comes out of the mouth of no lesser a light than Vice President Dick Cheney. In his book "The Price of Loyalty," former Treasury Secretary Paul O'Neill quotes Cheney telling him matter-of-factly that "Reagan proved that deficits don't matter." Spend and cut, spend and cut, and let someone else worry about the trillion-dollar deficits.

Twenty years ago, I was just out of the military, a college

freshman at the University of Maryland, and astounded at the die-hard allegiance for Reagan on the College Park campus. Only a few of us, it seemed—mostly minorities, women, gays, and lesbians—saw, through the "Morning in America" haze, what Reagan really wanted to do. If it wasn't trying to push the Social Security benefit age past the average life expectancy of the black male, it was trying to get rid of other New Deal mainstays like Medicare altogether, a goal of the right wing for years. Walter Mondale's great moment in the 1984 debates came when Reagan tried that old "there you go again" line on him.

Mondale: *Mr. President, you said, "There you go again," right? Remember the last time you said that?*

Reagan: *Uh-huh.*

Mondale: *You said it when President Carter said that you were going to cut Medicare. And you said, "Oh no, there you go again," Mr. President. And what did you do right after the election? You went out and tried to cut $20 billion out of Medicare, and so when you say, "There you go again," people remember this, you know. And people remember that you signed the biggest tax increase in the history of California, and the biggest tax increase in the history of the United States, and what are you going to do? You've got a $260 billion deficit. You can't wish it away. You won't slow defense spending—you refuse to do that.*

Reagan's budget director, David Stockman, admitted years later that so-called "supply-side economics" were purely a sop to bring down the top tax rate—the rate paid by the wealthiest

Americans. Does that sound familiar now? What about simple platitudes woven together to create a gauzy archetype of a president or the blatant assertion that a president "won a war"?

If Reagan won the Cold War—an iffy presumption at best— it is only because he spent the Soviet Union to death, and it took almost a decade to climb out of the financial hole he put us in. Even fervent anti-Communist Richard Nixon was skeptical about claims that Reagan won the Cold War; in the 1996 book, "Nixon Off the Record," he told his aide Monica Crowley, "Communism would have collapsed anyway." Yet again, we have another president who is balancing the budget on the backs of the poor and needy, who has cut taxes on the wealthy, who is trying to wrap himself in the mantle of war and whose followers are trying to turn him into a "great man." And once again, like 20 years ago, it is often minorities and women and gays and lesbians who see through the smoke with disgust.

Sadder still, Reagan turned a deaf ear to the scourge of AIDS. Some reports show that as many as 60,000 people died between the discovery of the disease in 1981 and when Reagan first made public mention of it in 1987. In the president's authorized biography by Edmund Morris, 1999's "Dutch," Reagan suggests, "Maybe the Lord brought down this plague" on gays because "illicit sex is against the Ten Commandments."

The lessons the Right learned in the '80s are being put to full use now, only in much more effective ways. There is a full-time cable network (Fox News) devoted to distributing the Republican line; Reagan's imagemaker, Michael Deaver, can only imagine what he would have been able to do with such a tool. Reagan's tendency never to apologize or admit mistakes is an unspoken credo of the 43rd president. And once again, the term "liberal" is something no politician has the nerve to embrace.

So remember you well the 40th president of the United States. When you see the "loyal opposition" called traitors, when you see the rich get richer and the poor poorer, when you see money for guns but not for butter and a man who claims the mantle of a war hero—either in movies or on the deck of an aircraft carrier— think of Ronald Reagan.

The L Word
August 4, 2004

"Liberal" is not a bad word. I've been one my entire life. My parents are liberals and they've served this nation honorably for more than 30 years, complete with military service. Nearly every uncle on my father's side and most of the ones on my mother's all served this nation with distinction—liberals, the lot of them. And not one is ashamed of the term.

Ronald Reagan years ago did a magnificent job making the word something to be avoided. George H.W. Bush, Bob Dole and George W. Bush have done their best to carry on the tradition; the minute any Democrat wins the nomination to become his party's presidential standard-bearer, the entire Republican attack machine gears up to rear back and roar, "Liberal, Liberal, Liberal!"

But what is a liberal? A liberal is someone who believes that there is a place for government, and the Constitution clearly outlines it. A liberal is someone who knows that unchecked private power leads to inequality, corruption, graft and hatred.

Our form of democracy, as Thomas Jefferson once said, "is the worst form of government known to man—excluding all the rest." By no means is it perfect. For the greater part of U.S. history, our government had enshrined the most odious form of political cancer within it: first slavery, then Jim Crow. It took a civil war and massive nonviolent protest, combined with legal action at every level for almost half a century, to get us to this point. And we still haven't solved all the problems stemming from the decision in 1787 to declare black people three-fifths of a person in the eyes of government.

Having said that, African-Americans are still the biggest fans of good, honest government. We, predominantly, are unapologetic liberals.

Liberals know that the only check on the robber barons of Halliburton, the criminals of Adelphia, the stock swindlers and the inside traders is the strong regulatory mechanisms of a diligent government. We know that when government does its job there are no savings-and-loan collapses that cause thousands, if not millions, of honest, hard-working people to lose their life savings while two or three white-collar criminals get away with millions and short stints manicuring the greens at Allenwood federal penitentiary. We know that when a strong and attentive government keeps its eye on the market, there are no predatory energy traders, like the ones at Enron who laughed at the prospect of cheating little old ladies out of their savings while literally stealing millions and millions of dollars from the citizens of California—and in the end, only a handful of people walk away in handcuffs on the evening news.

This is what liberals believe:

We believe in a government that keeps our food safe via the Department of Agriculture, repairs our roads and the interstate highway system via the Department of Transportation, keeps our skies the world's safest through the efforts of the Federal Aviation Administration and dispenses the world's safest and most modern medications under the oversight of the Food and Drug Administration.

By and large, our government provides us on the whole with honest police, safe oceans, clean drinking water and a decent public-education system. If you take these things for granted, feel free to move to some Latin American country where the bribe is still the most efficient method of arranging public services. Move to Africa, where health care is nonexistent. Move to Russia, where years of distrust instilled in the populace from the old Soviet system keeps a population wary and the Communists not too far removed from the seats of power.

But conservatives will tell you that being liberal is something to be ashamed of. These are people who say they want to shrink government down to the size, according to Bush family ally and Republican lobbyist Grover Norquist, "where it can be drowned in the bathtub." They do not see taxes as something that, while never loved, are necessary to keep America the envy of large swaths of the globe. They would tear down mechanisms that keep track of the stock market, keep the air clean, maintain the ecological balance by protecting endangered species and prevent private concerns from reducing our national forests to tinderboxes of empty stumps and asphalt roadways. They'd let shysters sell you patent medicines, contract your children's education out to people who care less about results than the bottom line and give the nation's Social Security fund to stock-market speculators ready to skim billions in fees off what they see as the jackpot of a lifetime.

In their world, the poor are to be derided, the infirm are to be ignored, wealth is valued over work and victims of discrimination are told to "stop whining." To them, workers are costs, not assets, and if you have little or nothing, it's because you don't feel like working to get it.

These are the people who made "liberal" a bad word. These

are the ones who care not to be their brother's keeper, or to be the village that raises the child. They mock the concept of "compassion" by linking it to "conservative." There is no such thing. "Compassionate conservative"? Please.

Because it stands for caring, and hope, and trust in your fellow man, you can call me a liberal any day. I'm proud of it. We've earned it.

Set Up to Fail
December 21, 2005

After five years of the Bush administration and its cronies, it is clear by their words and deeds what they've decided to do. They are creating a construct in which they can assume no blame for any of their actions, but wherein anything bad that happens in or to the United States in the future is the fault of liberals.

This isn't a "bang, pow!" revelation—I mean, come on!—but given that George W. Bush has cited divine providence in his selection as president, and has yet to make any real admission of guilt, fault, or error, we know that's got to be the game plan, right? The giant right-wing Wurlitzer continues to focus on the powerless Democratic Party as the reason why the United States has yet to be turned into the free-market, small-government paradise enveloped by beams of sunshine, as envisioned by Ronald Reagan. Bill O'Reilly has to resort to fulminating about how liberals want to ban Christmas in towns across the Midwest that are stunned to hear they are keeping high-school students from wearing red and green, or something.

It's all the liberals' fault.

Take torture, for example. I'm against it. You, presumably (and isn't it sad I have to qualify that?), are against it. Sen. John

McCain of Arizona is against it, for the forehead-slappingly obvious reason that it was used on him in Vietnam. But this administration keeps saying that "we do not torture" in defiance of all available evidence. I'm reminded of Malcolm X's statement that just because a cat has kittens in the oven doesn't make them biscuits. Just because the Bush administration has redefined the word "torture" to such exacting standards that one couldn't be surprised if it now means "bagels" doesn't mean that the actions it has been defending aren't torture. They are. They always have been and they always will be. Call it "waterboarding" or "stress positions"—call it whatever. It's still torture, and that's why the Geneva Conventions were created.

But noooooo—we call them "enhanced interrogation techniques" in that same sly way that we have decided that janitors are "sanitation engineers" and layoffs are "downsizing" or "rightsizing." And because we—Americans, the people who brought you Freedom™—say it's not torture, then that must be the case. Because we're the Greatest Country in the World™.

Never mind that torture not only doesn't work but also undermines every goal we may ever have of bringing true freedom and democracy around the world. Even if conservatives think hypocrisy is just another word in the dictionary between "hype" and "hysteria," telling the world that you want to bring it freedom while at the same time creating secret gulags in underdeveloped countries does nothing but piss on the Bill of Rights while you wave it in everyone's faces.

If in the future any terrorist act ever occurs on U.S. soil, no matter whether or not it happens during the remaining years of Bush's presidency, it will not be due to the failure of the current administration to enact any meaningful reforms specified by the 9-11 Commission. They will say it is because Democrats are wimps. "We were attacked because liberals coddle terrorists," they'll say. "Americans died because liberals would rather be in league with Osama bin Laden," they'll say.

Mark my words, the Republicans will run on this in the 2006 and '08 elections as if their political lives depend on it—because they do. If the Democrats ever get control of either body of Congress, with it will come subpoena power, and you will see a whirlwind of open government like never before, and all the GOP's secret abuses will spill forth.

As for the economy, any downturn will be blamed on liberals. Let's remember, Bill Clinton, as the Right spent years and millions of dollars telling us ad nauseam, gave us "the biggest tax increase in history" (even if it was primarily on the wealthy). What did we get? Unparalleled growth, low unemployment, an expansion of the middle class and a trillion-dollar surplus. Both Reagan and Bush II cut taxes for the wealthy in the same-old, same-old, trickle-down economics shell game they've been pushing for years, and look what we get: recessions, no real growth, no real expansion of earnings, a stock-market crash, a savings and loan fiasco (under Reagan), Sept. 11, Enron, the loss of virtually all pro-American goodwill across the globe and more than 2,000 dead Americans in a war of convenience waged under false pretenses.

Yup, it's the liberals' fault.

Abroad

Between its start and its finish, this short chapter covers a span of almost exactly fourteen years. It begins with the end of the first year of the Bill Clinton presidency and concludes at the start of the final year of George W. Bush's term in office.

The two scenarios couldn't possibly be more different, having started out so similar.

Bill Clinton came to office following his term as the Ivy League-educated governor of a Southern state. Same with George W. Bush. Except for the occasional trade mission (which many governors outsource to cabinet members), most governors never get to think about foreign policy, and at the time, both men faced general election opponents with sizeable foreign policy backgrounds on their resumes. George H.W. Bush was the Washington insider's insider, having worked his way up through the ranks—congressman, ambassador to the United Nations, CIA director and the vice-presidency, which is often an endless procession of state funeral visits and meet-ups with third-world tinpot dictators and generals with chestfuls of birdshit salad and delusions of grandeur.

Al Gore was little different when he faced George W. Bush—congressman, senator and vice-president, up against a man who had scarcely ventured outside of Texas when he was elected governor. This more than anything lets you know how little the American public regards foreign policy knowledge as a major selling point when they make their decision in presidential elections. My ex-wife, born in New Zealand and now a naturalized American citizen, used to constantly rail about the general disinterest Americans showed for what happens offshore. "To Americans, 'foreign news' means what happened yesterday in California," she would say.

In this instance, I'm not disagreeing with her.

What came out of that, in the case of the Bush years, was a presidency that looked at foreign policy only in terms of what it could achieve for domestic political gain. Bill Clinton believed in engagement, with military force used almost only as a last resort, in line with Carl von Clausewitz's dictum that warfare is only "the continuation of politics by other means." With Bush, it was always either stick or nothing—there was no carrot in the equation. So North Korea was ignored and marginalized (except when taunted in State of the Union messages) and got the bomb, whereas Iraq got the entire stick despite no WMDs at all.

This chapter only has three columns in it, the first of them being previously unpublished (it was rejected as an un-commissioned submission by *The Sun*'s opinion page editor at the end of 1993). Why so short?

Apparently it's what the American people want out of their foreign policy.

*　　　*　　　*

The Glitch in The Machine
Unpublished, December 1993

As pundits and talk-show hosts conclude with their final broadsides against President Clinton's first year in office, that they all manage to score Clinton poorly on foreign policy remains a unifying trend. In many cases this comes more as an example of where Clinton's expectations were set rather than what were the obstacles with which he had to deal.

Bosnia, for instance. It was clearly a hot potato long before William Jefferson Clinton took the oath, yet there it remains, a foreign policy Rubicon he has yet to either cross or run away from citing the coldness of the water.

Somalia was hand-delivered from the Bush administration, along with the slow-leaking wheeze that is U.S. policy toward the support of elected democracy in Haiti. If memory serves us correctly, the policy is Somalia was roundly cheered when first established—more the humanitarians we see ourselves as rather than as the heavy-handed global flatfoot on the beat that much of the globe views us whenever the C-5s begin touching down on their U.S.-subsidized runways.

So what if United States foreign policy under Clinton appears to move at glacial pace? Short of aberrations like instant outbreaks of war or invasions (Iraq) and military response as a reaction to television pictures (Somalia), it has always been so. Multiply legal time by government time, add Clinton Standard Time and you get foreign policy time. And that's never really needed much adjustment over the last 30 years.

In 1963, when economist John Kenneth Galbraith was ambassador to India, he authored a number of short stories under the pseudonym Mark Epernay. Epernay's tales centered around a "psychometricist" named Herschel McLandress, who specialized in the quantification of human behavior.

One of the inventions of the "learned Dr. McLandress" was the Fully Automated Foreign Policy, a room-sized computer that spit out punch cards with the appropriate action to be taken corresponding to each minor crisis, fracas or disturbance around the globe as reported by news services or embassy dispatches.

The big secret, as Galbraith/Epernay/McLandress knew, is that most foreign policy is simply the reiteration of prior foreign policy, with minor variations. Any change from precedent is tantamount to admitting previous error, and thereby losing face and national prestige.

One of the consequences of the fall of the Soviet Union and George Bush's "new world order" is that many of the precedents established over the tenure of the cold war simply do not apply any more. But still, precedent is all we have—that, and caution. President Kennedy, himself a great fan of the Epernay stories, once said that domestic policy can be uncomfortable, but foreign policy can kill you. Marching troops into Bosnia or leaving them in Somalia much longer would not just kill more Americans, but also Bill Clinton's chances at being a two-term president.

In the story, as McLandress's policy machine becomes more adept at synthesizing dry and concise responses to each nation's peccadilloes, it also outputs the equivalent of pink slips for the squadrons of desk officers, functionaries, assistant secretaries and other assorted panjandrums inside the walls of the State Department. The story concludes with the president querying the secretary of state about the efficiency of the new machine, and once satisfied with its success, presenting the secretary himself with the last of the punch card pink slips.

Right now the American people and the punditocracy may be

hammering Clinton over his fully automated foreign policy. The news brings back daily atrocities in Bosnia, in Somalia, in Haiti, in North Korea. With each comes another broadside about the president's amateurism in the global arena.

It is a president's job, however—his real job and not necessarily his political one—to do the right and sensible thing. The road to Bosnia for American troops would only lead to a holding action in a free-fire zone: Lebanon without the sunshine. Invasion of neighboring states, while a favorite of previous administrations, remains a poor alternative in a country such as Haiti, which still harbors a collective bad taste from the last time Marines took up residence there.

If America dislikes the Fully Automated Clinton Policy, remember how it got there. And that computer, no matter how sophisticated the programming, can't give voters the pink slip.

This Is Now
December 20, 2006

The United States built its reputation on valuing freedom and democracy—this is something I grew up not only believing, but having to tell people as a child. I spent the better part of my formative years in Latin America, where dictators were the norm, where every country around had some form of secret police and where military coups were as common as holiday fireworks displays.

I remember in 1974, returning from a family trip to Peru and Machu Picchu—we were part of a large contingent of embassy families on vacation from our home base in La Paz, Bolivia— when a small boy at the Peruvian-Bolivian border informed us of the Aug. 8 "coup." "What's the name of the new president?" my father asked. "Ford," he was told.

When he mused what an odd name that was for a Bolivian president, the child, not much younger than me, told my father, "Not our president—*your* president!" For Bolivians, a non-electoral change in leadership in the States could only be explained as some sort of coup—that was the mind-set then.

Keep this picture in mind when you think of the Dec. 10 death of former Chilean dictator Augusto Pinochet. Because while there is little to mourn about such an all-around bastard, his demise, at 91, was far too late in arriving. And yet the only thing more disgusting than Pinochet's long life may be its treatment by the editorial page of *The Washington Post*.

Where to begin with Pinochet's butchery? Torture? Death squads? State-sponsored terrorism? Political opponents hurled alive out of planes over the ocean? Tens of thousands of people murdered in the name of "anti-communism"? Barring the invocation of Karl Marx's legacy, these are the kinds of arguments the United States made to justify its incursion into Iraq (after the argument for WMDs fell through).

Author, lawyer and blogger Glenn Greenwald used, in a Dec. 12 post to his Unclaimed Territory blog, a Nexis search to look at how the *Post* editorial page viewed Pinochet back in September 1983, when Katharine Graham still published the paper and iron-willed Meg Greenfield was the editorial page editor and conscience of the capital:

> Some tens of thousands of Chileans were killed outside the law, many others were imprisoned and exiled, the natural political tendencies of the country were suppressed and an economic system was imposed that has meant extreme hardship for most of the people.

For turning a national crisis into an excuse for personal dictatorship, Gen. Pinochet will not be forgiven. It explains why most of his countrymen, believing his continuance in power to be a national disgrace, have turned against him now.

Yet the *Post's* editorial page is now run by Fred Hiatt, an unapologetic booster of the Iraq war and a man whose page trumpets the philosophies of former U.N. ambassador and proto-neocon Jeanne Kirkpatrick, who died Dec. 7. She argued in the 1980s that no matter how odious the behavior of right-wing dictators, they aren't as bad as left-wing ones, because she felt that when their rules end, their nations would more likely become liberal democracies.

Do you see any linkage here between then and now? And yet the *Post* concludes its Dec. 12 obituary for Pinochet, who is praised with faint damnation, with a paean to Kirkpatrick, and by proxy the former dictator: "She, too, was vilified by the left. Yet by now it should be obvious: She was right."

It is bullheaded folly like this that lands us where we are. It is the Right's arrogant belief in the steadfastness of their omniscience that ends with thousands dead.

Heaven forbid a nation might have to spy on its own citizens. Perish the thought that a country might have to torture a few to ensure freedom for the many—that we might need to break a few dozen eggs in order to ensure a more perfect omelet. Greenwald points out how a few simple little caveats can allow a free nation built on morals and ideals to dismiss our principles. "Thus," Greenwald says of the *Post* editorial, "a history of state-sponsored torture, murder and tyranny—while undesirable and all—can be dismissed away with a deeply amoral 'however.'" (The

Post's editorialist writes, "It's hard not to notice, however, that the evil dictator leaves behind the most successful country in Latin America.")

You can almost picture this sentence being written by the hagiographers of George W. Bush some decades into the future, after untold lives eventually result in some unsteady calm and civility in the Middle East: "It's hard not to notice that without the bold incursion of the United States into Iraq under Bush's leadership there would be no fragile peace amid the tender roots of democracy like there is today."

Let's remember the long list of brutal right-wing abusers of human rights that have been coddled by the U.S. across the globe for the last quarter-century: Pinochet in Chile, Somoza in Nicaragua and Marcos in the Philippines under Reagan; Saddam Hussein under George H.W. Bush; and Islam Karimov of Uzbekistan under the current president, just to name a few. But none of their abuses will matter in the future if, in the end, somebody can point to their booming capitalist economy and say, "You know what? We were right."

One Less Friend
November 28, 2007

If George W. Bush wants to look at his legacy in the present tense, he might start with observing how his policies have changed the governments of our allies. This past weekend, yet another nation tossed out its leaders, partly as a result of their hewing the Bush line.

Staunch Bush ally John Howard and his Liberal Party suffered their most ignominious defeat in the entire 63 years of the party's existence in Australia's national elections, and the icing on the cake was something that hadn't happened in more than 70 years: Howard himself, the sitting prime minister, lost his seat in Parliament as well.

Reports coming from Australia are pointing to two of Howard's stances that were the biggest contributors to his electoral defeat, and not so coincidentally, both of them are positions the Bush administration has espoused. Under Howard, Australia has been one of the few remaining members of Bush's "Coalition of the Willing," and more importantly, Howard had been an opponent of the Kyoto Protocol and backed Bush's refusal to sign them.

Kevin Rudd, the country's next prime minister, has already stated that he will pull Australia's 550 combat troops out of Iraq. This deals an ugly blow to the Bush administration's dwindling public relations effort to make Iraq appear to be the supposed beneficiary of a group of nations rather than America's unilateral no-carrot-and-plenty-of-stick policy implemented by former Defense Secretary Donald Rumsfeld via the machinations of Vice President Dick Cheney.

If there's one thing that Republican presidential candidates might want to take note of, it's how the climate-change debate arrived in Australia at the same time the country experienced what Australian news services are calling the "worst drought in a thousand years." Under Howard and Bush, the United States and Australia were the only two major industrialized countries not to sign onto the Kyoto Protocol, leading Al Gore to call the two countries the "Bonnie and Clyde" of global warming in a recent visit to Sydney.

Howard's rejection is just the latest in a string of political upsets of leaders perceived to be sympathetic to the Bush agenda. With the sole exception of France's Nicholas Sarkozy, nearly every major head of state of an American ally has been deposed in favor of someone who would stand up to Bush's person-to-person style of international diplomacy. Britain forced out "Bush's poodle," Tony Blair, in favor of the far more muted Gordon Brown. Leftist Romano Prodi ousted Bush ally Silvio Berlusconi in Italy, even though Berlusconi tried at the last minute to salvage his chances by announcing before the April 2006 elections that Italy would withdraw all its troops from Iraq by the end of the year. Before that, in 2004, Jose Maria Aznar of Spain was ousted, right after his government tried to politically manipulate the blame for the Madrid train bombings, whose link to Islamic radicals might have been seen as a result of Spain's involvement in Iraq (a 2003 poll showed 92 percent of Spain's population opposed the invasion).

At almost every turn, Bush's foreign policy is being rejected by the voting population of nearly every major ally in the world, something that likely will have no effect whatsoever on the attitudes held inside the vice president's office where, for all we know, plans are still under way for a campaign to attack Iran. If the vice president gets his way, don't be surprised if we see even more upheaval in the coming months before the U.S. elections in November 2008, as more allies take cautious steps away from us until they see who comes out the winner and takes office in 2009.

Right now in Annapolis, representatives are gathered for a meeting to try and restart the so-called road map to peace that the Bush administration weakly touted as its effort to calm the Israeli-Palestinian turbulence. Except for the fact that it's being held in Annapolis, the whole thing is yet another sign of how flaccid the president's efforts at diplomacy are to the rest of the world. Even Israeli wags are joking how Secretary of State Condoleezza Rice's first name has produced a Hebrew verb, *lecondel*, meaning "to come and go for meetings that produce few results."

With the exception of the 2000 elections, when Al Gore faced then-Texas Gov. Bush, foreign policy has been seen as a strong point for the Republican Party for the last quarter century or more. But with the "grownups" of Bush, Rumsfeld, Cheney and Colin Powell leading to the biggest foreign-policy disaster of the last century, the Republican brand has been permanently soiled for a long time, and the people trying to claim its mantle don't appear to be much better at it.

Until Jan. 20, 2009, don't be too surprised if just about any of our efforts at multilateral peace are taken with a grain of salt by the leaders of most of the world's more important countries. Just because Bush doesn't see himself as a lame duck doesn't mean that the rest of the world hasn't written him off. The voters of Australia said that loud and clear this past weekend.

War

It's small comfort being right, but it is still a comfort nonetheless. I'm not on network television. I don't occupy primo space in the op-ed pages of *The New York Times* or *The Washington Post*—hell, I was turned down by the Baltimore *Sun*. I don't steer mainstream opinion as I might if I wrote for the New Republic or one of the equivalent political magazines on the Right (although at the start of the war, TNR might as well have been one of them, what with its cheerleading for the invasion of Iraq).

But I look back on the columns I wrote at the end of 2002 and the start of 2003, and I can say, dammit, I was right. More so than William Kristol, who now writes for *The New York Times* (and has been wrong more often than any man I have ever seen who doesn't bet the Washington Generals against the Harlem Globetrotters). More so than Richard Cohen of *The Washington Post* (and I would argue that I am funnier too, and I don't need my grade school teacher's endorsement to say so), although I may never get the five grand and the three-word appellation on my obituary that Pulitzer Prize-winner David Halberstam told me is the sole bragging rights one earns when the call comes in.

Because as this book goes to press, the number of American military fatalities in Iraq is a hair's breadth short of four thousand. *Four thousand* Americans who volunteered to serve their country, left its soil and fight for principle only to die for a lie and be shipped back in blank boxes without ceremony in dead of night.

At the same time our government has prosecuted this war, they have shorted the troops on the armor they need to survive it, cut funding for the care of the veterans who fought it, neglected the hospitals that provide for their care and mocked and derided decorated veterans of the military who have questioned them. If this nation was as strong as its ideals and had the courage of its veterans, George W. Bush and Dick Cheney wouldn't qualify to polish the dog tags of Max Cleland and John Kerry and John Murtha.

When this administration started beating the drums for war with Iraq, far before Osama bin Laden was even close to being in the crosshairs, I knew something was wrong. There were reports even before 9/11 that Bush wanted to take out Saddam Hussein, and as we found out later from the "Downing Street Memo," the "facts were being fixed around the policy." So when Colin Powell went and did his song and dance before the United Nations, let some of us remind you that we were not moved.

But we would regret it, they said. We would be frog-marched out of journalism, we would be sorry, we would be ashamed, they said, when it turned out that the WMDs were there. When Americans are greeted as liberators and flowers and candy would litter the streets of Baghdad like Paris after the Nazis, the doubters would never darken the public square again.

Yeah, how did that work out, anyway? Except for the four thousand American dead, that is.

It's very hard not to sound bitter about this, but I find it kind of difficult to turn on the television or read a newspaper and be anything otherwise. War isn't the first option—it should be the last, and we were letting our foreign policy be dictated by shabby little cowards like the *Los Angeles Times*' Jonah Goldberg, who ascribes to what he calls, "The Ledeen Doctrine," where, as he says "Every ten years or so, the United States needs to pick up some small crappy little country and throw it against the wall, just to show the world we mean business."

This is what America's foreign policy and global image have come to: paper machismo and cold coffins. Four thousand of them. And knowing that is where being right is never comfort enough.

*   *   *

Patriotic Sheep
October 2, 2002

The words of a famous American author are suddenly in vogue once again. Mark Twain wrote in his last novel, "The Mysterious Stranger," of the dangers of being led by men with the passion of war in their hearts. In it, Satan tells a young boy, "Oh, it's true. I know your race. It is made up of sheep. It is governed by minorities, seldom or never by majorities. It suppresses its feelings and its beliefs and follows the handful that makes the most noise. Sometimes the noisy handful is right, sometimes wrong; but no matter, the crowd follows it. The vast majority of the race, whether savage or civilized, are secretly kind-hearted and shrink from inflicting pain, but in the presence of the aggressive and pitiless minority they don't dare to assert themselves."

We are barely a year past the days of tears and smoke, when we swore to track down the evil that knocked down our towers and flew planes into our buildings and fields. We sent men and machines to Afghanistan to rout out the people who planned the attack and nurtured the planners. We sent military to nurture the new government that arose there. And then, like the last time we "helped" in that area, we left. Veni, vidi, here's a few dollars in aid, and vici as soon as we can find the road map to Baghdad. We have given the Afghans no Marshall Plan, no infrastructure, no road map to real democracy. But here we are, on the brink of yet another war, while already ensconced in one undeclared war against an abstract noun. And the worst crime of all is to question any of it.

In the last week alone, President Bush asserted that the political opposition "was not interested in the security of the American people." On C-SPAN, South Carolina House freshman

Joe Wilson, a Republican, accused five-term California Democrat Bob Filner of harboring a "hatred for America." The currency of politics has become the questioning of the patriotism of the opponent.

What the hell happened here?

At one moment, we are bombing the bejeezus out of a country, and then the next minute, we are looking across the map to bomb the daylights out of someone who has yet to attack us. Proponents of attacking Iraq rail constantly about the possible nuclear weapons, biological weapons and chemical weapons that Saddam Hussein *may* be building, and the need to strike preemptively before he unloads them on us.

George Santayana was right all along. We have forgotten even the recent past and are now going to repeat it and repeat it and repeat it. We spent 50 years in a Cold War with a nation that had better capability to destroy us on several orders of magnitude— and we survived. We did not "pre-emptively attack." And we used to have a semi-official policy of not attacking nations that did not attack us first.

(We used to use the CIA to destabilize their governments and prop up tyrants that did what we wanted, but that's another story. See, "Pinochet, Augusto, 1973-1990." For dictators we liked until we didn't, see "Hussein, Saddam, 1980-1989.")

We were told that Mohammad Atta met with Saddam's agents—until it turns out that it wasn't true. We are told Iraq has nuclear capability—but given no evidence to support the allegations. We were told the president has full authority to move militarily without the approval of Congress or the United Nations—until the president decided it would be better if he made his case to the Congress and the United Nations. And, despite the fact that at every turn we are given reasons to doubt the veracity and the motives of the politicians in charge, we are told now, as we were last year by our own attorney general, that by questioning the authorities we are virtually giving aid and comfort to the enemy. In short, we are being accused of treasonous thought.

In the coming weeks and months, the drumbeat will continue. It is likely that before the middle of the next year we will be embroiled in an attack that could detonate a three-way war between Iraq, ourselves and Israel, and send our oil-based economy spiraling fully out of control.

It is one thing to repeat constantly that we are "the greatest nation in the world." But to believe this when our leaders suddenly argue that the precedent for the use of force has changed, and we can and should use it whether or not we have allies, or have thought out the full future consequences of our actions, is foolishness. We found this out 30 years ago in Southeast Asia.

Bullies are never heroes, no matter how they justify their actions. And if we let our leaders act in our name, as the international community condemns our actions, we are no better than our representatives.

We become a nation of heavily armed, patriotic sheep.

State of the Truth
February 5, 2003

Every year, by law and by custom, we meet here to consider the state of the union. This year, we gather in this chamber deeply aware of decisive days that lie ahead.

And when Karl Rove has made those decisions, he tells me, and I tell 'em to you.

We will not deny, we will not ignore, we will not pass along our problems to other Congresses, to other presidents, and other generations.

Riiiiight.

To protect our country, we reorganized our government and created the Department of Homeland Security, which is mobilizing against the threats of a new era.

Even though I originally wasn't for it, and we're not gonna fund it.

To bring our economy out of recession, we delivered the largest tax relief in a generation.

And still we lost 2 million jobs.

To insist on integrity in American business we passed tough reforms, and we are holding corporate criminals to account.

(snort)

In the Middle East, we will continue to seek peace between a secure Israel and a democratic Palestine.

By ignoring them.

We have confronted, and will continue to confront, HIV/AIDS in our own country.

By telling gays and teenagers not to have sex.

To date, we have arrested or otherwise dealt with many key commanders of al-Qaida.

Except Osama bin Forgotten.

They include a man who directed logistics and funding for the September the 11th attacks.

Who has nothing to do with Iraq.

The chief of al-Qaida operations in the Persian Gulf who planned the bombings of our embassies in East Africa and the U.S.S. Cole; an al-Qaida operations chief from Southeast Asia; a former director of al-Qaida's training camps in Afghanistan; a key al-Qaida operative in Europe; a major al-Qaida leader in Yemen.

None of whom are from Iraq.

All told, more than 3,000 suspected terrorists have been arrested in many countries. Many others have met a different fate. Let's put it this way--they are no longer a problem to the United States and our friends and allies.

But their children will be.

Tonight, I am instructing the leaders of the FBI, the CIA, the Homeland Security and the Department of Defense to develop a Terrorist Threat Integration Center, to merge and analyze all threat information in a single location. Our government must have the very best information possible, and we will use it to make sure the right people are in the right places to protect all our citizens.

John Ashcroft will start by checking all your bedrooms. Unless you have guns in there. Because that would violate your Second Amendment rights.

Today, the gravest danger in the war on terror, the gravest danger facing America and the world, is outlaw regimes that seek and possess nuclear, chemical and biological weapons. These regimes could use such weapons for blackmail, terror and mass murder.

They rhyme with "Korth Norea."

They could also give or sell those weapons to terrorist allies, who would use them without the least hesitation.

Scary! BOOGA BOOGA BOOGA!

In Iran, we continue to see a government that represses its people, pursues weapons of mass destruction and supports terror. Iranians, like all people, have a right to choose their own government and determine their own destiny, and the United States supports their aspirations to live in freedom.

Which is why my administration is full of people who illegally sold arms to those oppressors and sent a key-shaped cake to the Ayatollah.

On the Korean peninsula, an oppressive regime rules a people living in fear and starvation. Throughout the 1990s, the United States relied on a negotiated framework to keep North Korea from gaining nuclear weapons. We now know that that regime was deceiving the world and developing those weapons all along.

And it's all Bill Clinton's fault.

Our nation and the world must learn the lessons of the Korean peninsula and not allow an even greater threat to rise up in Iraq.

Which, unlike North Korea, has no nukes.

Evidence from intelligence sources, secret communications and statements by people now in custody reveal that Saddam Hussein aids and protects terrorists, including members of al-Qaida.

Even though Saddam is secular and al-Qaida is fundamentalist.

Before September the 11th attacks, many in the world believed that Saddam Hussein could be contained. But chemical agents, lethal viruses and shadowy terrorist networks are not easily contained. Imagine those 19 hijackers with other weapons and other plans—this time armed by Saddam Hussein.

Imagine it? You'll *see* it if we don't fund Homeland Security.

We will consult. But let there be no misunderstanding: If Saddam Hussein does not fully disarm, for the safety of our people and for the peace of the world, we will lead a coalition to disarm him.

A coalition of one.

What's that? OK—sorry, Tony. A coalition of two.

We Americans have faith in ourselves, but not in ourselves alone.

But it's looking like that's the way we're gonna have to play it—alone.

We do not know—we do not claim to know all the ways of Providence, yet we can trust in them, placing our confidence in the loving God behind all of life. And all of history. May He guide us

now. And may God continue to bless the United States of America.
'Cause we're gonna need it.

False Humility
March 12, 2003

In 1983, the biggest threat to sleepy little Incirlik Air Base in southern Turkey came not from Iraq to the south but from the north. The mighty Soviet Union was 20 minutes away by air, and in June of the previous year President Ronald Reagan had termed the communist country bordering the Turks to the northwest the "Evil Empire."

We military personnel stationed in Turkey were issued chemical weapons suits and gas masks (both hilariously antiquated compared to today's equipment) and trained in their use upon arrival. At the sound of the klaxon, we had nine seconds to get the masks out of their hip-strapped satchels and over our faces. We would then hurl ourselves under the nearest embankment or into one of the five-foot-deep gullies that crisscrossed the base to sluice away the almost biblical spring rains.

Despite the Cold War escalation of words, the general mood at Incirlik then was not fear. The klaxons only went off during exercises, and Incirlik was a sleepy little base, where, due to an agreement, no U.S. planes could be stationed longer than 89 days. Once a "broken" F-16 reached the 80-day point—termed a "hangar queen" by maintenance personnel—we had to remove its wings in order to shovel the fighter into the hold of a C-5 cargo plane and ship it out before the 89-day mark. If a plane stayed longer, it became property of the Turks, we were told.

Back then, the Turks were our friends and staunch NATO allies, despite their constant enmity with neighbor Greece, and it reflected in the general comfort the Turks had with Americans there.

How times have changed.

In 2003, the Turkish people have become so anti-American that they forced their parliament to reject the United States' request to use Incirlik as a launching point for a second war in Iraq. Our friends have decided that we have become lousy house guests.

How did we get to this point? In the presidential debate on Oct. 11, 2000, candidate George W. Bush said, "If we're an arrogant nation, they'll view us that way, but if we're a humble nation, they'll respect us."

We are trying to buy off the leadership of Turkey against the will of its people and, in the process, are selling out the Kurds in northern Iraq. As *Washington Post* foreign policy columnist Jim Hoagland put it, "Republican administrations abandoned the Kurds to Baghdad's atrocities three times in three decades: in 1975 at the end of the Kurdish rebellion, in 1987 when Hussein used chemical weapons against them and in 1991 at the end of the Gulf War."

This administration has alienated old allies like Germany and France, and is starting to issue veiled threats to neighbor Mexico, and a total lack of a policy is causing the North Koreans to escalate their brinkmanship almost daily. All this for Iraq.

The administration's reasons for armed incursion of Iraq keep shifting like a weathervane. First, they said Iraq might have nuclear weapons. Then, when it became clear that a nuke program was difficult to build and nearly impossible to hide, it was chemical weapons. Later, we were told that Iraq is in "noncompliance" with U.N. resolutions—yet other nations have ignored U.N. resolutions, and we find no quarrel with them (for instance, Middle East allies whose names begin with the letter "I").

It was for freedom for the Kurds—as already noted, that answer is clearly a prevarication. We've heard talk about the need for "regime change," which could begin a bloom of democracy throughout the Middle East. Not likely—our friends the Saudis have little interest in democracy, nor do the fundamentalists that rankle under their rule.

The administration has said a war in Iraq could lead to peace between Israel and the Palestinians, but that theory bears a disconnect with reality. And so does the explanation that we are attacking Iraq because we were attacked by militant ex-Saudi terrorists based in Afghanistan.

The United States is not a "humble" nation when it systematically alienates its historic allies. It is not a friend when it unsubtly makes threats, saying that Mexico's citizens may see retribution from the administration's corporate and fiscal cronies— because of its vote on the U.N. Security Council—similar to the way the Right has stirred up feelings against the French.

Amid the debate, more than 225,000 troops gather in the Middle East, with the knowledge that this time the goal is not just to repel Iraq from Kuwait but to expel Saddam Hussein from rule, and then to allegedly create a new form of democracy in a region that has never seen such a thing.

If there is one person the amateurs running U.S. foreign policy have deified, it is Reagan. But in their zeal, they should go back and take to heart a phrase he made at the start of his "Evil Empire" speech: "Regimes planted by bayonets do not take root."

The Last Refuge of a Scoundrel
March 26, 2003

This is America today:

Paul Weyrich of the Reaganite conservative Free Congress Foundation, on Natalie Maines of the Dixie Chicks: "The Dixie Chicks may be entitled to their opinion, but for them to give aid and comfort to the enemy when we are on the edge of war is just outrageous. . . . I guess there's no loyalty to this country any more."

House Speaker Dennis Hastert (R-Ill.) on Senate Minority Leader Tom Daschle (D-S.D.)'s critical statement on the Bush administration's failed diplomacy: The remarks "may not give comfort to our adversaries, but they come mighty close."

Columnist Daniel Pipes in the Rupert Murdoch-owned *New York Post*: "Why the Left Loves Saddam (and Osama)."

In the same issue of the *Post*, the newspaper's gossip column, "Page Six," helpfully gives a list of what it calls "appeasement-loving celebs" whose work should be boycotted: Samuel L. Jackson, Janeane Garofalo, Sheryl Crow and, of course, Susan Sarandon.

While Sen. Joseph McCarthy is long gone, blacklisting never goes out of style.

Maines never said a word about the troops. She never said a word about "America." She simply expressed the opinion that she and her band were embarrassed that the president of the United States is from Texas.

For this, she earned the wrath of the nation's conservatives, the enmity of a large segment of country music fans (the Chicks are the No. 1 country music act in America), the burning of their CDs and a demand from the South Carolina House of Representatives that the Chicks perform a free concert for troops from the state and their families.

It's unclear whether pressure from fans, Maines' record label, or conservative media forced her to apologize, even though she really had nothing to apologize for. But you have to wonder what it will do to the Chicks' bottom line when a company that owns 1,233 radio stations in America (including at least two in Baltimore, one being the pop station that used to play the Chicks' song "Landslide" almost interminably) is also financing patriotic rallies where people brought signs blasting the band. (Not that there's any connection, but the aforementioned station conglomerate Clear Channel Communications also syndicates Rush Limbaugh.)

In case you haven't gotten it yet, here it is in a nutshell. Criticizing the president is not the same thing as criticizing the troops. Criticizing the president is not the same as criticizing America. And criticizing the president is not "giving aid and comfort to the enemy," which is the classic definition of treason, a federal crime that earns felons the death penalty.

So here are a few questions. When the Clinton administration sent troops to quell the ethnic cleaning in Kosovo, we can presume Sen. Don Nickles (R-Okla.) was giving "aid and comfort" to mass-murdering tyrant Slobodan Milosevic when he said, "The administration's campaign has been a disaster. . . . [It] escalated guerrilla warfare into a real war, and the real losers are the Kosovars and innocent civilians." What a traitor to America.

When then-House Majority Whip Tom DeLay (R-Texas) said of the intervention that "Clinton's bombing campaign has caused all of these problems to explode," we can presume that his criticism of the president's foreign policy provided clear and forthright evidence that DeLay hates America.

You see, "freedom" is funny like that. Of course DeLay and

Nickles were no more unpatriotic for denouncing administration policies while U.S. troops were in the field back in 1999 any more than Maines or Daschle are today.

There's no shortage of it, and it's not new to this period of conflict, either. Recall White House spokesman Ari Fleischer's veiled warning after colossal boob Bill Maher remarked on the cowardice of U.S. fighter pilots—that Americans need to "watch what they say."

And remember when critics asked Bush spokesman Dan Bartlett exactly what information the government had prior to Sept. 11, 2001. Bartlett said that asking pointed questions like those "are exactly what our opponents, our enemies, want us to do."

Last September, then-Senate Majority Leader Trent Lott (R-Miss.) posed the ludicrous question, "Who is the enemy here? The president of the United States or Saddam Hussein?"

The simpleminded, the Know-Nothings, the John Birch-style über-patriots like to create a "slippery slope"—a classic logical fallacy—to support their contention that the president equals the troops, which equals the flag, which equals the Constitution, which equals freedom. There's no daylight, no wiggle room, between any of them—as long as it's *their* guy in power.

There was no shortage of criticism of Bill Clinton during his presidency, and it hasn't abated since he left. The far Right has tried to draw a metaphor from an act of consensual sex to everything from fiscal policy to the refrain that the Clinton administration somehow bankrupted the U.S. military. Funny how this criticism never was seen as treasonous. I suppose it all depends on whose ox is gored.

When a government seeks to paint any opposition as unpatriotic and any dissent as treason, when it uses its allies in industry and the media to hound skeptics and blacklist celebrities, when it attempts to paint legitimate questions of policy as either a vote for America or a vote for dictatorship, that's not freedom any more.

That's fascism. Smart people know the difference.

War Games
April 19, 2006

In case you haven't been paying attention, no fewer than seven former military commanders of flag rank have called upon our Secretary of Defense, Donald Rumsfeld, to resign. Army Maj. Gen. Charles Swannack, Army Maj. Gen. John Riggs, Army Maj. Gen. John Batiste, Marine Corps Lt. Gen. Greg Newbold, Marine Corps Gen. Anthony Zinni and Army Maj. Gen. Paul Eaton, along with former Army general Wesley Clark, a Democratic candidate for president in 2004, have all publicly said that Rumsfeld ignored advice of commanders on the ground in Iraq and made a mess out of the post-invasion there.

Unfortunately, George W. Bush sees the approbation of press, public, or military as an excuse to dig in further. Once again, recall that this is the administration that, no matter how poorly any operation fares, can find someone else to take the blame. Abu Ghraib? A few bad apples in the lower echelons of the military. Katrina? Poor planning on the part of the locals. When the federal Environmental Protection Agency puts out a 268-page report that blames global warming on the use of fossil fuels, to Bush, it's the fault of "the bureaucracy." This president can never, ever, be wrong.

The terrifying part of this most recent news deals not with the mistakes the administration has made already but the ones it purportedly is planning to make. The nation's premier investigative reporter, Seymour Hersh of *The New Yorker*, recently wrote a story pointing out that the U.S. military has begun drawing up tentative plans to attack Iran due to its recently announced capability to enrich uranium, the forerunner to the creation of an atomic bomb.

We saw this kind of gamesmanship before under this administration. And while the Bushies were intent on convincing Americans that Saddam Hussein was the greatest threat to democracy and freedom in the world, North Korea's Kim Jung Il steadily marched his country toward a nuclear-weapons program as well.

You don't have to be an Army general to see what some of the immediate consequences of a military strike on Iran would be; all you have to do is drive down the street to your local gas station. After a war in one of the world's largest oil-producing nations joined with a hurricane strike on our country's predominant oil-refining regions, gas has risen up to and in some cases over the $3-per-gallon mark. Throw in an attack on yet another oil-producing country, and it wouldn't be too far-fetched to see $4-per-gallon gasoline in the United States. And try as he might to argue that his tax cuts have saved the economy over the last six years, I don't think even George Bush could explain away how another massive gas-price spike could be the fault of something other than a foolish military incursion.

The Iraq war was part of a domestic strategy on the part of the president and his aides to use patriotism and jingoism to paint liberals and opponents as weak or traitorous during an election year—recall the movement inside the administration to wait until the fall of 2002 before pushing for the invasion, as then maximum political advantage could be taken, and the GOP could try—and succeed—to break the 50-50 vote deadlock in the Senate.

Now it is 2006, yet another election year, and the only card the Bushies have ever played that has never failed is the national security one. By starting to pound the nuclear threat from Iran, the administration hopes to once again deflect attention from foreign-policy failures like the Iraq war, and move whatever attention there is to the continuing disaster that is New Orleans, and force the Democratic Party yet again to sign onto another "my country, right or wrong" scenario.

The one fly in this ointment is the fact that everyone, including the U.S. military, has seen this game played before. And already the signs are showing that they won't go along with it again—when was the last time you saw top military brass come out and call for the resignation of the top civilian leader in the Pentagon during a so-called time of war? Approval ratings in the 30s means that the press might even start using the phrase "wag the dog," something we haven't heard since Bill Clinton tried to stop Osama bin Laden during the impeachment hearings in 1998.

George Bush may think a war in Iran may save his presidency. What is scary is that he can't see that it may just put the final nail in his political coffin, and those of more Americans as well.

Ari Saeed al-Sahhaf
May 7, 2003

The brother of your intrepid columnist here at Animal Control, like many Americans, is fascinated with the former Iraqi minister of information, Mohammed Saeed al-Sahhaf, for his masterful prevarication in the face of incontrovertible evidence to the contrary. We have been sent any number of e-mails pointing to the phenomenon of the Cult of al-Sahhaf—Web sites and stories of various and sundry press flacks and public relations professionals marveling at the Iraqi's total and utter commitment to remaining "on message."

Much as we're all for expanding the need for cross-cultural education among our fellow countrymen, we feel that, in the spirit of U.S. Rep. Bob Ney's (R-Ohio) idea to rename french fries "freedom fries," we also need to honor America's own chief dissembler, the president's official bullshit artist, the esteemed Ari Fleischer.

Fleischer is no flamboyant poet, no lyrical liar like al-Sahhaf—the needs are much different when you're the mouthpiece for a Texan with a "gentleman's C" in spoken English. Al-Sahhaf comes from the land of *Arabian Nights*, so phrases like, "We will drag the drunken junkie nose of Bush through Iraq's desert, him and his follower dog Blair," are really of no use in an American policy-making setting.

No, Fleischer is the master of the subtler arts of mendacity: changing the subject, stretching the definitions of words, reclassifying the parameters of debate and, of course, the non-denial denial and the ever-popular flat out untruth.

Newsweek.com made the comparison between Fleischer and al-Sahhaf on April 21, saying, "When it comes to entertainment, Fleischer is on his way to matching the Iraqi information minister." When asked about the president's reaction to the pyrotechnically homophobic remarks made by Sen. Rick Santorum (R-Pa.), who was commenting on a gay-rights case before the U.S. Supreme Court, Fleischer said the president doesn't typically comment on cases before the Supreme Court.

As Newsweek.com put it, "When the reporter pointed out that Bush had spoken out quite a lot about the Michigan affirmative-action case currently before the court, Fleischer said, 'That's why I said, 'typically.'"

Later on, Fleischer added that the president thinks Santorum is "an inclusive man." Your jaw drops in wonder, doesn't it? Santorum is "inclusive" the way Byron De La Beckwith was "tolerant" or Jerry Falwell is "noncontroversial" or Rush Limbaugh is "slim."

On Oct. 11, 2000, during the run-up to the presidential election, George W. Bush said—and you probably remember this—he was no fan of "nation building." His exact words were, in fact, "I think what we need to do is convince people who live in the lands they live in to build the nations. Maybe I'm missing something here. I mean, we're going to have kind of a nation-building corps from America? Absolutely not."

But Fleischer says that never happened. As *The Washington Post*'s Al Kamen wrote Feb. 28, "yesterday White House press secretary Ari Fleischer proved the critics wrong once again. 'During the campaign, the president did not express, as you put it, disdain for nation-building,' he said. So there you have it."

Kamen has become, along with the *Post*'s Dana Milbank, kind of a chronicler of various al-Sahhaf—sorry—Ari-isms (something less polite company might call "lies") from over the years. Take Kamen's report from the beginning of the war. "Reporters also asked about Bush's Sunday statement that aid would begin moving into southern Iraq in 36 hours. Fleischer said, 'We didn't expect the—the Iraqis to cease caring about their own people, to cease feeding their own people, to put up impediments to the humanitarian relief supplies,' such as laying mines."

Kamen writes, "Moments later, a reporter asked [Fleischer] about 'your comment before about how you didn't expect the Iraqis to interfere with humanitarian aid. . . . '"

"'I didn't say that,' Fleischer said."

Milbank raised White House ire last October with a piece titled "For Bush, Facts Are Malleable." In it, Milbank wrote that the White House once admitted the president was "imprecise," while noting the administration still stood by its words—imprecise as they were. Fleischer's take on it, according to Milbank? "'The president's statements are well documented and supported by the facts,' Bush press secretary Ari Fleischer said. 'We reject any allegation to the contrary.'"

After all, later on he can deny the existence or credibility of those "facts" supporting the statements.

So far, Fleischer has managed not to get tied to any one legendary gymnastic phraseology the way famed former Nixon spokesman Ron Ziegler was hoodwinked into saying, "This is the operative statement. The others are inoperative." But the fact remains that this is an administration for whom the press is only useful inasmuch as a lap dog can be trained not to drool while fetching the morning paper. So Fleischer apparently has full approval from his superiors to deny, dissemble, distort, equivocate, exaggerate, evade, invent, fib, prevaricate and pretend to his heart's desire—so the president doesn't have to do it for him.

After all, this White House now knows that it can hold as few news conferences as it wants, allow only its pet reporters to ask questions (calling on the patsies at Fox News!) and no one cares.

So really, al-Sahhaf? He's a piker. All hail our own Minister of Disinformation, Ari Fleischer. After all, he'd only deny it.

Forgotten But Not Gone
July 16, 2003

Remember when the Bush people came into office? They had this grim front of sheer competence, with a stable of old hands going back to the Ford administration—the wall of Old White Guys Ready to Do the Job from Day 1. With Condoleezza Rice and Colin Powell thrown in for a little color and foreign policy heft. Wow. What the hell happened?

The United States goes into its first preemptive war (not like that other little imbroglio in Southeast Asia), and we're getting taken by forged documents from Niger and sandbagged by Iraqi expatriates like Ahmed Chalabi, who wants to be the next Shah of Baghdad. And how about all those weapons of mass destruction that George W. Bush so clearly and vividly detailed in his State of the Union address? (In case you forgot, here's a sample: "U.S. intelligence indicates that Saddam Hussein had upwards of 30,000 munitions capable of delivering chemical agents. Inspectors recently turned up 16 of them, despite Iraq's recent declaration denying their existence. Saddam Hussein has not accounted for the remaining 29,984 of these prohibited munitions." So far, we are still 29,984 short.)

We are constantly bombarded with polls showing the president with approval ratings of 60 percent or so, but behind the numbers there's some serious unease in America on how this war is progressing. Much as this country can suffer from some serious myopia when it comes to even recent foreign policy, many people remember the promises this president and his advisers made about what getting rid of Saddam Hussein would do, and how much safer the world would be.

Well, guess what? As far as anyone can tell, Saddam's not even dead! By our count, that makes it Evil People 2, Bush 0. If Osama bin Laden and Saddam Hussein had nothing in common before, they sure as hell do now.

A recent ABC News-*Washington Post* poll showed slightly more than half the country thinks there has been an unacceptable number of casualties in Iraq. Who can blame them for thinking as such? The military victory the troops achieved happened so fast, and then our president got all tarted up in a Navy flier's outfit and preened on the deck of an aircraft carrier with a mission accomplished sign as his backdrop. Usually, when things like this are done, it gives a signal to the people that, "OK—this one's over. You can go back to watching Laci Petersen stories again." Except, people expect their kids to come home when wars end, not to be stuck in a 110-degree summer camp where people shoot at them.

Foreign policy is not a child's game, but increasingly this president and his advisors are treating it like one. The height of this absurdity came when the president of the United States, the leader of the free world and (as if they've quit belaboring the title) the commander in chief of the mightiest military force the planet has ever known, actually encouraged rebels to try and kill our troops. "Bring 'em on," he said.

Even Lyndon B. Johnson, the original President of the Great State of Machismo, never taunted the North Vietnamese like that. Maybe there's been something in the Texas water since 1967, but for a president to personally invite attacks on troops is truly breathtaking in its irresponsibility.

Of course, official explainer Ari Fleischer was brought out to give the obligatory "he didn't say that, he said this" disclaimer. "I think what the president was expressing there is his confidence in the men and women of the military to handle the military mission they still remain in the middle of," Fleischer spun.

Well, then—and we may be a bit obtuse with this, and you can forgive us for our stupidity—why didn't he just *say that*? From where we stand, there's a huge difference between "Yay, troops—*hoo-ah!*" and "Bring 'em on."

Less than a month ago, Bush wasn't even mentioning Saddam Hussein by name in his speeches—shades of bin Laden, who also got the no-name treatment after Afghanistan was supposedly all wrapped up for the forces of freedom and democracy. In a speech to Northern Virginia Community College down in Annandale on June 17, the president would only refer to Saddam as "that dictator in Iraq." Out of sight, out of speech, out of mind. And now apparently, according to the CIA's analysis of tapes aired on the Arab TV network Al-Jazeera, forgotten but not gone.

Nobody wants Iraq to become a so-called "quagmire." Not the troops, not the parents and families of the troops, and not this administration. But the fact is we were sold a bill of goods to get into this war. We were told expressly and in detail exactly what we were supposed to find, and we were told how the Iraqis would feel about it when we were done. So far, none of it—not one bit—has actually come to pass.

Harry Truman had a famous sign on his desk: "The buck stops here." But our current baseball-loving president maybe ought to have this old quote referring to our national pastime on his desk: "You can win, you can lose, or it can rain." Because, in Iraq, it looks like the rain will be falling, figuratively, for a very long time.

The Trap
August 9, 2006

Last week I had the chance to interview an author who, with his own money and on his own initiative, flew to Iraq to write about the soldiers on the ground there. The author is an historian, his father was active-duty military and he has a long family history of relatives who served in wars such as the ones the U.S. has waged in Korea and Vietnam, and World Wars I and II.

Not being of the military persuasion himself, he had dedicated much of his writing career to telling the tales of the people who served in these times of stress. Soldiers, sailors, spies and Marines—each service faces different challenges in different wars. And with the advent of new technology, every generation's version of a fighting man or woman has to learn to cope with new things. In "Prodigal Soldiers," James Kitfield's book about the retooling of the all-volunteer military in the years between Vietnam and the first Gulf War, one of the Navy pilots about to launch off an aircraft carrier deck into the darkness of the nighttime Baghdad sky says, "Goddamn, sir. I sure hope this stealth shit works."

If there's one thing that hasn't changed over the years, however, it is the political environment back home surrounding a failed foreign policy experiment by an overzealous administration. In the late 1960s and early '70s, it was Vietnam, and it cost Lyndon Johnson his popularity and eventually his presidency. It would be three presidential terms later before the United States would finally pull out of the political miasma of the Far East.

Now here we are again, in an even more deadly and more sectarian part of the world, shoved into a war of convenience by a president who had hoped to invade long before Sept. 11 and simply needed some sort of justification to do so. Without a clear-cut global enemy like communism, conservative Republicans had no political hammer to wield in asserting their belief in themselves as "the daddy party," and so were getting hammered in peacetime by domestic-issues president Bill Clinton.

Under Karl Rove's stewardship, and thanks to the national tragedy that was Sept. 11, George W. Bush, a man who disappeared from his own stateside military service during Vietnam, was transformed into some heroic commander in chief leading a "global war on terror." Conveniently, this phraseology allowed the Right to not only claim Bush's mantle as a wartime president with all the powers it entails, but also to create an open-ended conflict whose definition could only be changed by those who created it. We are at war as long as they say we are at war.

This also allows the hard-core Right to lay claim to a long and useful syllogism that we first saw in the Vietnam years. The president is the commander in chief, who leads the troops, who fight in the war, who protect freedom; therefore, the president is the chief protector of freedom. If you are against one, you are against all. This chain is the trap.

The fact is, it is possible to oppose a president without opposing the troops. It is possible to object to the mission without opposing the troops. And it is possible to believe in freedom while disagreeing with the mission those troops have been sent to conduct. But simple logic and common sense often are not either simple or common in this day and age.

Liberals, in the heat of their dissent to this president and his failed policies, often find it easy to fall into the trap. Mistakes and malfeasance by individuals or units in the military often help. Let us recall that Lynndie England is not the face of the Iraq policy— she's an individual who got caught up in a policy articulated by lawyers like Albert Gonzales, now our attorney general, and former Justice Department official John Yoo, and administrated by Defense Secretary Donald Rumsfeld. In the recent Hamdan decision handed down by the Supreme Court, Rumsfeld was all but in name cited as a war criminal for violations of the Geneva Conventions.

But remember that soldiers are tools—they are the physical arm of an administration's policy, and as Prussian military theorist Carl von Clausewitz wrote, "War is the continuation of politics by other means."

The author I spoke to last week simply wished to tell the stories of the men on the ground, the people our government hires and trains to go out and, under our official imprimatur, take the lives of others. These people come from all walks of life, with their loyalties to each other and their country; it's as simple as that. Their stories have been told in books from "A Bridge Too Far" and "The Longest Day" in World War II, to "Platoon Leader" and "We Were Soldiers Once…and Young" in Vietnam. Every generation that goes to war needs its tales told, and not just political screeds, but stories of the people who hold the guns and see the dying.

It's a mistake to aim our fire at those who would tell those stories. And it's also a mistake to fall into the trap set carefully by those who would use the lives of those military men and women to advance a policy built on a sand castle of lies.

Five Years Later
September 13, 2006

Stepping back from the current political scene to look at our nation and what we have evolved into in the last five years, you have to wonder what the Founding Fathers would think. Five years ago we were attacked by a multinational band of fanatics, members of a radical sect of Islam who wanted to make a statement about Western values and, according to their leader, retaliate for the placing of U.S. troops in Saudi Arabia, home to Islam's two holiest sites, during the first Gulf War back in the early 1990s.

In that time, we've had two national elections and are weeks away from a third, and our leaders' reactions to this catastrophe has been one of polarization, with those in power exercising a strategy of painting the loyal opposition as defeatists, appeasers and fifth columnists. For five years the president, vice president, secretary of defense and attorney general have been the lead culprits in a hard-right scheme to consolidate power and create a kind of conservative hegemony. For the last two elections, it has worked, but the wheels are beginning to come off the bus.

The people in charge of this, a country clearly founded on a set of simple principles—the right to speak out, the right to dissent, the right to confront your accusers and see the evidence against you—have taken these ideas and twisted them all out of proportion while constantly mouthing the words "freedom" and "liberty," as if to divorce them from their real meaning. How can anyone listen to the words of our president or vice president and believe they mean what they say?

On *Meet the Press* Sept. 10, moderator Tim Russert fired a withering round of questioning at Dick Cheney about all the unequivocal, provable mistakes that this administration has made in the last five years, and yet the vice president persisted in his conflation of al-Qaida and Saddam Hussein. Cheney's May 2005 statement that the Iraqi insurgency is in its "last throes" did nothing to deter the veep from his hardheaded belief in throwing more and more American lives into the middle of what is turning into a full-blown civil war. Since that statement of Cheney's, more than 1,000 U.S. troops have died there. How much more wrong can one man possibly be?

Listen to Cheney's response when Russert told the vice president that 54 percent of Americans believe that our involvement in Iraq and Afghanistan is creating more terrorists, rather than the president's stated goal of eliminating them:

> I, I, I can't buy that. I mean, I think you've got to look what's happening in Afghanistan and Iraq in terms of the— where we were five years ago and where we are today. I mean, take Afghanistan. Afghanistan was governed by the

Taliban, one of the worst regimes in modern times, terribly dictatorial, terribly discriminatory towards women. There were training camps in Afghanistan training thousands of al-Qaida terrorists. All of those training camps today are shut down. The Taliban are no longer in power. There's a democratically elected president, a democratically elected parliament and a new constitution and American-trained Afghan security forces, and NATO now actively in the fight against the remnants of the Taliban. We are much better off today because Afghanistan is not the safe haven for terror that it was on 9/11.

It seems as if the world where Cheney lives is one unmolested by facts, truth, or reality—the kind of world where TV networks like ABC get to re-create the events leading up to Sept. 11 out of whole cloth and broadcast them as fact.

Today in Afghanistan the elected government is propped up only with the aid of American weaponry, and outside of Kabul the Taliban are in resurgence. Al-Qaida has re-formed and is thriving within the boundaries of our "friend," the nation of Pakistan, whose leader, Pervez Musharraf, admits that the terrorist group moves back and forth between his country and Afghanistan. And George W. Bush's greatest failure, the albatross who will surely stalk him to the end of his days in office, Osama bin Laden, still lives, waits and plots, alive and mocking.

Once again, look back over five years and see the ways the president and his political advisers have used money, lies and lives to advance an agenda that has failed in nearly every measurable way. Are we safer? Hardly. Are we stronger? Not really. Are we better? No. On five years of Bush's watch, the military has been depleted, nightmare scenarios have occurred in two American cities, an icon of our military strength was scarred psychologically if not permanently and more than 2,600 U.S. troops have died in the sands of the Middle East.

When your child drives your car into a tree, you don't give him the keys to the other car. When he lies about driving the car into a tree, you consider taking away his license. How long will we keep giving this administration the keys? Five years of lies should have been enough.

Tar Baby
November 29, 2006

Finally, somebody gets it.

It's been ugly, it's been long, it's been brutal, and mostly it's been pointless, but somebody finally realized that we're not "in it to win it." At this point, we're like the cop on the beat—right now we're there to make sure the marital spat doesn't turn into murder. Sadly, however, we're a little bit late on that count.

What I'm talking about, of course, is Iraq. And the "somebody" I'm talking about is, surprisingly enough, a Republican U.S. senator. Chuck Hagel of Nebraska might be the most sensible member of his party at this late juncture to realize that not only can you not bring democracy to the Middle East at the point of a gun, but you certainly can't try and maintain one that never took root in the first place.

"The time for more U.S. troops in Iraq has passed," Hagel writes, in a Nov. 26 *Washington Post* op-ed. "We do not have more troops to send and, even if we did, they would not bring a resolution to Iraq. Militaries are built to fight and win wars, not bind together failing nations. We are once again learning a very hard lesson in foreign affairs: America cannot impose a democracy on any nation—regardless of our noble purpose."

Well, how about that? Sanity from Washington! Except for the fact that we went and punched the tar baby (in the classic, Uncle Remus sense) three years ago, and, sadly, there's no unsticking ourselves any time soon. The sheer dunderheadedness of obstinate know-it-alls like Donald Rumsfeld compounded the problem begun by a juvenile president with an Iraq fixation. Even Daddy's fair-haired boy, James Baker, and the Iraq Study Group aren't going to get us out without some penalties to be paid down the line for a good long time.

At this point the wing nuts will shriek, "Well, isn't it a good thing that Saddam Hussein was removed from office?" Maybe so. But also maybe not—this is one of those questions without a good answer; sort of like the one posed a few years ago when the Bushies handed us that tax cut by buying off individual Americans with $300 checks. Back then, when the GOP was taunting us by asking if we'd rather not get $300, the question should have been, "Do you want a punch in the mouth now or later?" In Iraq, George W. Bush has guaranteed that not only have we taken the punch in the mouth now, but that we're going to continue getting rapped about the kisser long after he's out of office.

Partitioning Iraq into Shi'ite, Sunni and Kurdish sections right now might be the absolute worst of all the options—and that's the best option there seems to be at present. The Turks would like having a Kurdish state on their southern border the way we'd like it if Fidel Castro annexed the Miami suburb of Kendall. And the Shi'ites and the Sunnis would get along about as well as, well, think about how that whole West Bank/Gaza Strip thing is working out. Remember Tito and Yugoslavia? Boy, those are looking like the good ol' days now, aren't they?

Years ago I remember a lot of talk about how to solve the

problems in Africa—Hutus and Tutsis, the famine in Somalia and the troubles we encountered in Mogadishu. None of those situations were anything that the United States itself engendered; we simply tried to impose our own solutions on problems that were not of our own making. Even today, the genocide in Darfur still is a heart-wrenching matter that no individual concerned with the welfare of mankind can overlook—but we're already in a hole of our own making, and it's hard to even think about the people in other ones until we extract ourselves first.

Sadly, in addition to the fact that we're neck-deep in Iraq, Sen. Hagel also notes that the Muslim world seems to think, and with good reason, that we are at war with its religion as well. When six Muslim imams get thrown off an airplane in Minneapolis for the heinous crime of praying, it shows that it's not just our leadership that has a long way to go. But Bush has used all the wrong words far too many times (and been egged on by the worst angels of our worst nature, the religious right), and now much of the Middle East holds a grudge against us. And the Middle Eastern nations aren't much prone to grudges that last a few millennia or so, right?

It will be interesting to see how long it takes for Bush to come around to the Hagelian way of thinking when the new Congress convenes in January—if he does at all. Bush has made it clear that he plans on staying his course all the way through to January of 2009. How much worse we'll all be by then isn't something pleasant to look forward to.

General Malfeasance
July 18, 2007

PA News Service—July 13, 2007—The White House announced today that, as part of the duties of the commander in chief, President George W. Bush has allocated the U.S. postmaster general new duties in fighting the Global War on Terror.

"He's a general, right?" President Bush said. "And I'm the commander in chief, which means I outrank him, and he's got to do what I say, because I'm the Decider, and I decided that I needed more troops for this war."

White House spokesman Tony Snow said the new duties of the postmaster general's office include ensuring that all Americans who have dealings with the post office "will be appropriately informed about all the good news this president is creating." "We see it as only right that one of the largest government agencies does its part to ensure that the administration's message is being transmitted without having to go through the filter of the liberal media," Snow said. "This way, any time you go in to get stamps, send a package, or apply for a passport, you'll be able to know that President Bush is working for you."

When queried about former U.S. Surgeon General Richard H. Carmona's testimony before Congress that he was required to mention the president no fewer than three times on every page of every speech he delivered, Snow responded, "The president is the commander in chief, and Carmona's a general. I know you wimps in the press never served in the military, but the way rank is structured, a president still outranks anyone in the officer class." Snow said that since the surgeon general serves "at the pleasure of the president," it was only appropriate for the medical official to remind his audiences as to whose policies he was committed to upholding.

"He's a doctor, isn't he? Which means he's pretty educated and can figure out who he works for," Snow said. "Besides,'Bush' is only four letters long—I don't see how he'd have much problem saying that, and it doesn't take up all that much space. Perhaps your headline writers could remember that while they're writing their defeatist headlines in your newspapers."

The White House has long considered Attorney General Alberto Gonzales to be part of its Global War on Terror. Administration sources say Gonzales has already opened up new fronts on the enemy with his deft and imaginative lack of answers to congressional questions regarding the firing of more than eight U.S. attorneys, and his creative obliviousness and forgetfulness dealing with the administration's domestic wiretapping plan. A Justice Department official who agreed to be interviewed on the condition of anonymity told PA News Service, "Gonzales sees Congress as an obstacle to the president's authority, the same as the news media or the Constitution. The president feels that future historians will see Gonzales as one of the nation's most effective attorney generals due to his incredible ability to accept responsibility for the actions of his department by not really owning up to being in the loop on anything."

Newspaper editorials from all over the country during the last month have taken the administration to task over the president's commutation of the prison sentence handed down to the vice president's former chief of staff I. Lewis "Scooter" Libby. White House spokesman Snow told reporters in an off-camera press briefing, "B-F-D. The only opinions this president cares about are the ones he gets from aides who tell him what he wants to hear. What do a bunch of newspaper people know about running a war?" When it was pointed out that Snow himself used to be a newspaperman, he retorted, "So, you got me. What's your point?"

Late Friday night, the White House also released a statement saying that under the president's authority as commander in chief and unitary executive, no congressional subpoenas apply to any business, entity, officer, papers, actions, or materials so designated by the president. In addition, the president issued posthumous pardons for President Gerald Ford's reputation, for Sen. Joseph McCarthy's good name, and for himself, for trading the 20-year-old Sammy Sosa when Bush managed the Texas Rangers.

"Remember," Snow said, "the president's authority to pardon in the Constitution is unlimited, and not restricted to details such as time, place, or event. If the president saw fit to pardon a ham sandwich, you can believe that sandwich would be free of all guilt—it might even be kosher afterward."

When asked what the president plans for the final 16 months of his term, Snow was forthright: "We think that there is a lot more this president can accomplish unencumbered by the shackles of democracy. Iran is still there to be invaded, gas prices can go up at least another dollar a gallon and we can probably think of one or two more tax cuts that need to be passed. And of course, there is the legacy that this president has where any time you think of the city of New Orleans, you'll think of George W. Bush. I think this presidency will go down as one of the most memorable in American history."

Religion

One of the consequences of the failure of the modern school system to teach anything other than how to answer multiple choice questions by filling in small ovals with soft pencils is that we all have to suffer a real life version of "Groundhog Day."

Those who forget history may not necessarily be doomed to repeat it—we are just forced to watch endless and painful variants of stupidity we should have moved past long ago. When President John Adams submitted the Treaty of Friendship to Tripoli back in 1797 (back when we apparently *did* negotiate with terrorists, except that back then they called them "pirates"), the beginning of its Article 11 stated succinctly that "The government of the United States is not, in any sense, founded in the Christian religion." The Senate approved the treaty, and there was no debate over the clause.

Yet here we are again, in the middle of yet another election season in which religion has yet again been shoved to the forefront. We spent a good part of an election season where one political party fought it out between an ordained Baptist minister, a Mormon former governor of one of the most liberal (and Catholic) states in the country and a (once) pro-choice twice-divorced Catholic man who moved out of his house and took up residence with two gay men once his affair became public. One candidate, Mike Huckabee, the former governor of Arkansas, actually told a Michigan audience that "[We need] to amend the Constitution so it's in God's standards rather than try to change God's standards."

Here we are in 2008, and someone running for the presidency of the last of the superpowers (until China calls in its markers) thinks that our founding document needs a little tune-up in order to conform to his bible. This alone serves as an example why it's probably best to build a few more blast walls in-between church and state in America. That Constitution was good enough for the Founding Fathers, many of whom I'm sure could figuratively kick Mike Huckabee's ass when it came to theological expertise.

On the Democratic side, one candidate was beaten up by another candidate in the media because he should have to reject and denounce sermons he didn't attend from a pastor whose opinions he has already stated he doesn't agree with. This is when he's not having to constantly remind people that he's not Muslim. (As if he could be *both*, which would be an act of religious contortion not seen since the Spanish Inquisition.)

I've now been writing about politics in two separate decades, and in each of them—and beginning in the decade before that—there has been a concerted effort to force religion into the classrooms, first under the guise of "creation science" and then as "intelligent design." You'll note that the effort follows the standard practice on the conservative side for advancing a policy issue: first the frontal assault ["God has been taken out of the schools"], then the lateral attack [adding "creation" to "science" as if the two weren't opposing ideas] and then finally, the obfuscatory muddling of the message with "intelligent design." The only thing to follow is to turn the entire idea on its head with Orwellian newspeak, like gutting civil rights bills by calling them civil rights bills, or proposing lighter standards on polluters while calling it "Clear Skies." Any time now we should be seeing the "Real Science" movement to include biblical teaching in biology classes.

One of the things I firmly believe has set the United States apart from the old oligarchies of Europe and the Third World is that the church has had such little power in the actual running of government. A lot of that changed in the 1980s with the rise of Jerry Falwell and his so-called Moral Majority, and Pat Robertson and the 700 Club. Now that the megachurches have had a taste of power, and the Christian conservatives have seen how far they can go after eight years of George W. Bush in office, we shouldn't be surprised if they continue to try and insert themselves even further into the political sphere. It doesn't require a close reading of Niccolo Machiavelli to know that power is not given away willingly—it must be taken. At some point in the future, if this is to remain the secular nation it was at its founding, the American people may be forced to take back what has already been ceded.

Right now, it continues to be a series of pitched battles between the forces of theocracy and the rationalists. At worst, let's hope it remains so.

*   *   *

More Equal Than Others
August 2, 1995

Were not the ultimate consequences so grave, it would be amusing to see the "religious equality" types get their way for a short while. In other words, can't you see the fundamentalist Christians, who are petitioning Congress to pass their "Religious Equality Amendment" to the Constitution, have to deal with those who want passages from the Koran read over school loudspeakers or football games interrupted by Islam's required five-times-a-day prayer?

The term "religious equality" itself is somewhat Orwellian, coming as it does in a nation founded by people trying to get the hell away from a monarchy where a previous king had split with the dominant church and declared himself divine. And *that* church already was dealing with its own schism after the Pope of Rome told the Patriarch of Constantinople to hit the highway, thus divvying up Europe between the Roman Catholicism and Eastern Orthodox views. And we know how tolerant *they* all are—when's the last time the Pope admitted he was wrong?

The Christian Coalition, the guiding force behind the movement to amend the Constitution, has silently worked behind the scenes to pressure members of Congress and the media to take them seriously on the issue. It has commissioned studies and polls with findings that conclude 78 percent of Americans favor a religious equality amendment.

The main problem with the beliefs put forth by the religious right is not necessarily in what they say, but what they aren't saying. The first "point" in the Coalition's "Contract with the American Family"—"Restoring Religious Equality"—mentions only two religions or symbols thereof: Christianity and Judaism.

The attitude toward the world's other major religions remains unstated, and it's not hard to understand why, even though they're not talking about it.

It could have been voiced unwittingly, however, in a comment made to a Newhouse News Service reporter after the Supreme Court overruled a decision that forbade the University of Virginia from funding a student-run Christian magazine.

Ron Rosenberger, 25, had fought his case all the way up to the nation's highest court and won, and was still glum because the decision was 5-4 and he had hoped for a more "overarching principle" instead of a slim majority and a dissent that noted that for the first time, there had been "direct funding of religious activities by an arm of the state."

Rosenberger hit the nail right on the head when he told the reporter "If universities are going to have (student activity fees), we should have equal access," he said. "(But) to be honest—I go back and forth—we would have preferred that the university fund no one. (Otherwise) everybody gets funding and you get all these crazy wacked-out groups with any kind of fanatical belief imaginable."

Those "crazy, wacked-out groups" may not be exactly what the framers of the Constitution had in mind, but in this enlightened 20th-century era, it has come to be believed that the First Amendment's "Congress shall make no law respecting an establishment of religion, or prohibiting the free exercise thereof" has pretty much meant hands-off and no favors to anyone.

Part of the problem stems from the grounds on which the Christian right is making its argument. They feel that it is a "free speech" issue, where students are not being allowed to exercise their right to practice their religion in school, in atmospheres such as graduation, before football games, at the start of the day and such. This leads to the natural rebuttal that for some, "freedom to…" must also be balanced by "freedom from…" which is a tenet noticeably absent from those promoting school prayer. Of course, had students been leading a Wicca prayer over the loudspeaker in Jackson, Miss. instead of a Christian one, then the school principal who got fired for letting them do it probably would not only not be getting his job back, but would be ridden out of town on the end of a rope attached to the rear of a Ford Bronco with a "God, Guns & Guts" bumpersticker on it.

The "Restoring Religious Equality" section of the "Contract" specifies that the amendment "would not restore compulsory, sectarian prayer or Bible-reading dictated by government officials." "Instead," it says, "we seek a balanced approach that allows voluntary, student and citizen-initiated free speech in non-compulsory settings such as courthouse lawns, high school graduation ceremonies and sports events."

Would you want to be the student in Jackson, who is, say, a Mormon, a Jehovah's Witness (the religion whose court cases originally started schools on the road to secularity), or even a member of the Nation Of Islam, and who objects to such "citizen-initiated free speech"? Considering that the student body of the school there voted 490-96 to allow the over-the-air prayers, it is fairly clear that what is being pushed as "equality" is solely the right for a loud and proselytizing majority to spell out the religious rules for all. This is religious equality, all right—as practiced in Saudi Arabia.

This amendment, perhaps the most odious of the three proposed in the last eight months, may bring about a form of equality, but George Orwell certainly presaged it in his book "Animal Farm": Some religions may wind up being "more equal" than others.

In All Their Ignominy
October 18, 1995

No protected status based on homosexual, lesbian, or bisexual orientation. Neither the State of Colorado, through any of its branches or departments, nor any of its agencies, political subdivisions, municipalities or school districts, shall enact, adopt or enforce any statute, regulation, ordinance or policy whereby homosexual, lesbian or bisexual orientation, conduct, practices or relationships shall constitute or otherwise be the basis of, or entitle any person or class of persons to have any claim of minority status, quota preferences, protected status or claim of discrimination. This Section of the Constitution shall be in all respects self-executing.

There is it is—read it for yourself. That's the text of Colorado's "Amendment 2," the constitutionality of which was argued before the United States Supreme Court last week in the case of *State of Colorado v. Evans.* It is the bellwether of a new era, that which seeks to begin denying whole classes of people equal protection under the law instead of granting them the same rights as everyone else.

In the face of their eroding Stone Age beliefs, a segment of society seems to think that in order to restore things to "the way they ought to be," we must start pushing whole groups of people outside the envelope of protection guaranteed by our own Constitution. With blacks no longer considered three-fifths of a person, both blacks and women "given" the right to vote and nearly everyone allowed to work where and when they please, the so-called morality of a threatened few began to crumble under the weight of modern reason. But no longer—they're fighting back, and Amendment 2 is the clarion call, sounded by a group called Coloradans for Family Values.

The fight to deny rights to gays and lesbians in Colorado is being waged under a variety of illegitimate legal arguments, all of them mostly a front for cultural flat-earthers to proclaim the moral superiority of their beliefs and lifestyles over the rest of the nation, and the CFV has declared Colorado the first battleground.

The first of their arguments says that Colorado should not be "fragmented" over the divisive issue of homosexuality. This is a shameless cover for the fact that they wish to stifle debate by ramming the beliefs of a simple majority down the throats of all—call it moral sodomy if you will.

If anything, free and open political debate is the prime pillar of democracy. Denying the give and take of ideas over *any* political issue, even one as admittedly incendiary as homosexuality, is admitting intellectual impotence. Ignorance is mostly fostered through silence.

Another facet of the CFV's argument is the belief that without the statute, government will be supporting the political objectives of a "special interest group," namely, homosexuals.

The problem with that is, nearly any law could be seen as a benefit to a so-called "special interest group." Those three words have been used negatively since the heady days (for conservatives) of Ronald Reagan and George Bush, who managed to make them, "liberal" and "ACLU" into pejoratives equivalent to "socialist" and "communist" in the post-war lexicon. Just by labeling a group a "special interest" doesn't give the government a legal reason for excluding that group from protection of the laws. It's a sleazy way of saying "Us, good guys. Them, bad guys."

After that argument comes the real doozy: it reveals the core bigotry of the Colorado petitioners for the amendment. They have argued before the Court that the amendment is necessary to promote the "physical and psychological well-being of our children."

Talk about a pandering appeal to fear-mongering! In the initial argument before the Colorado Supreme Court (which struck down the amendment, thus prompting the appeal to the high Court), the CFV and the state argued that homosexuality begets pedophilia and child-molestation. Frankly, if we were to accept that (groundless) argument, the same case could be made against the Catholic Church. Needless to say, the court tossed that out as well.

Finally, the CFV resorts to the hoary old defense of the status quo—that they need to protect the prevailing preferences of the state's population and preserve social norms. This argument is mostly used by those landlords and businesses who feel they shouldn't have to rent or cater to people whose lifestyles and beliefs they find repugnant or immoral.

It won't wash. Despite the fact that the First Amendment to the Constitution grants us a right to be a bigot under the free association clause, it also does not afford us any protection under the law to be such.

For centuries, prejudice has been cloaked in religious and moral terms. As recently as 1967, petitioners argued to the Supreme Court that the separation of the races was ordained by God (*Loving v. Virginia*). Some of the most heinous acts in history have been sanctioned in the name of religion—why would anyone think they would stop now?

It's a sad road we're walking, America. Pray for a day when we fight to give people equal rights under the law instead of taking them away.

That is, if you think it will help.

God's Food Fight
April 27, 2005

Now that the media has concluded its Popeapalooza, we can sit back and mull over what it all means to have a new pope. We here at Animal Control have never been called the most pious on the block (quite the opposite, actually), but we do understand what this pope means in political terms.

Someone of our acquaintance asked, "What's the big deal, especially if you're not Roman Catholic?" At first glance it would seem that the election of a 78-year-old German cardinal to the highest office of his church wouldn't mean much to a protestant in Northern Virginia, a pagan in Ellicott City, or an atheist in Baltimore, but there are larger things at stake and greater issues beneath the surface that can't be ignored.

In essence, we all are about to get caught up in the world's biggest cafeteria food fight. Over the course of the last two months, the evangelical fundamentalist Christians and their acolytes, represented by people like Senate Majority Leader Bill Frist and Focus on the Family leader James Dobson, have set up in one corner, hurling the chicken entrée. To the side is President George W. Bush and his administration, which is quietly egging on the fundamentalists, yet making soothing noises to the other side of the room, which is where the Vatican and the conservative branch of the American Catholic community are deflecting the barrage with lunchroom trays.

What the evangelicals don't realize is that the Vatican has been sneaking into the back door of the kitchen and has loaded up with a good-sized load of old meatballs and is waiting for the right moment to launch them. And in the middle of it all are the rest of us, with our hands over our heads trying to come out of it all with as few stains on our clothing as possible.

Many of America's leading evangelicals have quite the history of anti-Catholic statements under their belt. You see, according to an April 22 *New York Times* report by David D. Kirkpatrick and Sheryl Gay Stolberg, the Christian conservatives have accused new Roman Catholic U.S. Sen. Ken Salazar (D-Colo.) of tolerating anti-Catholicism because he puts up with fellow Democrats who are pro-choice, and thus not following the Vatican on abortion. In other words, the fundies think they can tell the Catholics their business.

This past Sunday's *Justice Sunday* telecast to Christian churches and radio networks featured the Rev. R. Albert Mohler of the Southern Baptist Theological Seminary in Louisville, Ky. Mohler is renowned for making comments like, "The Roman church is a false church and it teaches a false gospel," and, "The pope himself holds a false and unbiblical office." Pretty funny, huh? Frist also appeared on *Justice Sunday*.

You probably wouldn't want to be where Bush is at this point, either. He just came back from sucking up to the Catholic Church by breaking precedent and being the first sitting U.S. president to attend a pope's funeral. Judging from how everything in this White House is run through a political filter first, it can only be seen as an act to try and suck up to conservative American Catholics. Right-wingers made a big deal last year about how Sen. John Kerry, a Roman Catholic and the pro-choice Democratic candidate for president, was going against the edicts of his faith. And don't forget the temporary union of fundamentalist evangelicals and the conservative Catholics over the whole Terri Schiavo mess for a moment seemed like a match made in, well, you know...

Now, with the conservative Pope Benedict XVI firmly installed in Rome, for now—he is 78, remember—the right wing thinks that all is good (except for hard-liners like Mohler, Dobson and company). But they may be surprised.

Benedict has made it clear that religions other than Roman Catholicism are not to be considered true faiths, which puts him squarely at odds with our Religious Right. And Bush shouldn't get too comfortable, as this pope may not be diplomatic about his dislike of the war in Iraq.

Thus might come some small consolation to all of us stuck in the middle of this food fight. With the Vatican on one side and the fundies on the other, it's less likely that they'll again violate the principles of federalism as blatantly as they all did in Florida over Schiavo's feeding tube.

Oh, and think about this: Suppose the Republican nominee in 2008 is a divorced, pro-choice Catholic like Rudolph Giuliani, running against, say, Hillary Clinton? Will the Right be so predisposed to the Vatican's decrees about whether or not pro-choice American politicians should be taking communion? With their fondness of hypocrisy, it's quite likely they won't be.

So remember, sometimes a good old religious schism isn't necessarily a bad thing, politically. Take it as an article of faith.

Swear to Doug
May 18, 2005

We here at Animal Control have a friend named Doug. Doug is a hard-core pagan and proud of it. If at any time someone takes the Supreme Being's name in vain (you know the one), Doug will blurt out, "Why'd you have to go and bring up the old dead guy?"

Yes, we know—Doug's a subtle one. But we love him for it. It's why we like to substitute his name now when we swear: "Oh,

Doug-damn it!"

There are people out there who think that Doug and his kind aren't "real Americans." They're the ones proposing bills to put the Ten Commandments in courthouses and claiming that Christians are being persecuted. This in a country that has plenty of religious TV, "One Nation Under God" on all the currency and pastors who kick Democrats out of their congregations because they won't "repent and vote for George Bush." We have reached a time when Christian evangelicals feel that anyone who questions them is "persecuting" them.

Unfortunately, bits and pieces of their crusade—and really, that's what it is, a crusade, in the classic sense—are making their way into the body politic. The fundamentalists are trying to enshrine their beliefs in the law.

Don't believe us? Google "S.520." The Constitution Restoration Act of 2005 would basically disallow the Supreme Court from reviewing any federal or state case "concerning that entity's, officer's, or agent's acknowledgment of God as the sovereign source of law, liberty, or government." This bill is virtually identical to the "Religious Liberties Restoration Act of 2003," which also would have specifically authorized display of the Ten Commandments in courthouses. And last year they had S.3920, which would have allowed a congressional two-thirds majority to overturn Supreme Court rulings, effectively gutting the Constitution.

Remember, folks, these bills are being proposed by people who swore an oath to uphold, protect and defend the Constitution—and they are pushing bills designed to eliminate the separation of powers and nullify the very checks and balances enshrined in that document. Breathtaking, isn't it?

Years back, when conservatives didn't like something, they

came right out and said so. They hated Social Security when it was proposed: In 1936, Alf Landon, the GOP nominee for president against Franklin Roosevelt, called Social Security "a cruel hoax." They hated it in 1964, when then-Republican presidential candidate Barry Goldwater said, "Perhaps Social Security should be abolished." Some even admit that they hate it now: GOP Congressman Chris Chocola of Indiana has said, "Eventually, I'd like to see the entire system privatized."

Nowadays, they follow the Reagan Rule: If you don't like something, mouth platitudes about how you're for it and what a great institution it is, but that it needs reforming—and then gut it from the inside. They did it with labor law, they did it with civil rights, they're trying to do it to Social Security. And now, for their coup de grâce, they want to do it to the Constitution.

The fundamentalists' newest and latest tactic, dubbed "judicial nullification," would allow Congress to pass laws and exempt them from judicial oversight. This gets right down to the heart of judicial review, the only real power behind the judiciary. If it weren't for judicial review, Congress could pass whatever laws it wanted, constitutional or not, the president could sign them, and that would be that. Slavery, women's suffrage, miscegenation laws—think of how many modern institutions could be overturned and odious practices of the past could be resurrected if the courts were prevented from doing anything. And remember: The people who were against the women's right to vote? Back then, they were called "conservatives." Against civil rights? They were called "conservatives." It didn't matter what party they came from, really. Many Democrats deserted the party and became Republicans right after Lyndon Johnson signed the 1965 Voting Rights Act. And "the old dead guy" was always on their side.

The advance battalion for the principle of judicial nullification is, as you would expect, buried within a provision of the Real ID Act, which itself is buried in another unkillable bill, HR 1268, the Emergency Supplemental Appropriations Act for Defense, the Global War on Terror, and Tsunami Relief, 2005. Inside the Real ID Act is a provision that would cut the courts out of any review of how the Department of Homeland Security deals with illegal immigrants above the district court level, unless very specific conditions are met. So the battle is coming.

First the trickle, then the flood. Check for yourself: You too might start saying, "Doug-damn them!"

Ho Ho No
December 6, 2006

Dear Santa,

It's been a long year, and I've managed to be good enough to stay out of Gitmo. And I know that list I sent you might seem long now, but it really isn't when you think of what I might be asking for otherwise. For instance, I could ask for some kindness and tolerance from my fellow man. What brings this to mind is a right-wing radio host and newspaper columnist by the name of Dennis Prager.

Prager writes a column that is published on the wingnut site Townhall.com, a gathering place for the kind of foaming-at-the-mouth conservatives who have cheered on every bad move made by the country's commander-in-chief, no matter how many citizens in New Orleans had to suffer for it. On Nov. 28, he published a column slamming one of the newly elected members of Congress, Keith Ellison, an African-American Muslim from Minnesota, who plans on being sworn into office with his hand on the Koran.

Prager writes, "He should not be allowed to do so—not because of any American hostility to the Koran, but because the act undermines American civilization."

Hold on a minute—it gets better. Prager writes, "First, it is an act of hubris that perfectly exemplifies multiculturalist activism—my culture trumps America's culture. What Ellison and his Muslim and leftist supporters are saying is that it is of no consequence what America holds as its holiest book; all that matters is what any individual holds to be his holiest book."

This is all very nice. Right-wing wack job hears about man of different religion getting elected to Congress. Wack job hears of man wanting to be sworn in on his religion's main text. Wack job says this undermines the nation, and then goes on to put words in Ellison's mouth.

Sadly, the Constitution, the founding document of that civilization Prager says is in such utter danger, says in Article VI that "no religious Test shall ever be required as a Qualification to any Office or public Trust under the United States." Which means that those hard-line cultural conservatives so up in arms about multiculturalism spreading like a rash all over their country (are you listening, Bobby Ehrlich?) might just have to find something else to rail about.

If you're wondering how to find these like-minded individuals, you could simply do like Washington, D.C. radio host Jerry Klein did. He opened his show last week by arguing that Muslims in America should be made readily identifiable by being tattooed with crescent marks or being required to wear armbands.

His second caller, according to a Reuters story, congratulated Klein and said, "Not only do you tattoo them in the middle of their forehead but you ship them out of this country…they are here to kill us." Another caller said that tattoos, armbands and other identification (such as markings on their driver's licenses) weren't enough to do the trick. The caller said, "You have to set up encampments like during World War II with the Japanese and Germans."

Klein's hour-long show on the Sunday after Thanksgiving brought out the ugliest in the ugly American hordes that have been fed by the anti-immigrant rantings of the Rush Limbaughs and the Tom Tancredos. But at the end of the show, Klein turned the tables. It was all a hoax.

"I can't believe any of you are sick enough to have agreed for one second with anything I said," Klein said. "For me to suggest to tattoo marks on people's bodies, have them wear armbands, put a crescent moon on their driver's license, on their passport or birth certificate, is disgusting. It's beyond disgusting. Because basically what you just did was show me how the German people allowed what happened to the Jews to happen....'We need to separate them, we need to tattoo their arms, we need to make them wear the yellow Star of David, we need to put them in concentration camps, we basically just need to kill them all because they are dangerous.'"

It's disheartening to know that there are Americans, raised within the rich tradition of a nation born of immigrants, who believe, in this day and age, that there's only one "American religion" or "American bible." It's disgusting to think that there are people—like outgoing Virginia Sen. George "Macaca" Allen, for instance—who think Americans should only look like themselves. And it's saddening to think that every day there are still people who think like this, egging on the haters and the so-called "culture warriors."

Pat Buchanan, one of the prime movers behind this thinking, is yet again considering a run for president, and already the right wing is gearing up to smear Sen. Barack Obama, who is considering a run for president in 2008. On the MSNBC talk show *Hardball* last week, Republican consultant Ed Rogers began using Obama's middle name, Hussein, as a not-so-subtle jab at Obama's heritage and to link it to Bush bête noir Saddam Hussein.

So Santa, if you think about it, my list of goodies isn't so bad compared to having to give enlightenment to these kinds of people.

Love,

the Political Animal.

Labor

When I started out in full-time professional paying journalism, at all-news WTOP radio in Washington, Jamie MacIntyre, now the Pentagon correspondent for CNN, was our union shop steward. He handed me and the other guy who got hired that day the union handbook for the station. On the first page was a simple declarative statement that I have carried with me for the rest of my professional life:

WE DO NOT WORK FOR FREE.

Since then I have come to realize that the fight between labor and management (and I've been on both sides of that equation) is quite simply the front lines of one of America's longest-lasting and ugliest battlefields. In the modern day, the average American seems to have been convinced that all labor leaders are a bunch of fat, pinky-ring wearing non-working Tony Soprano-style crooks, and unions are all out to drive honest businessmen out of business.

What has happened because of that is that wages have steadily eroded, jobs have been shipped out of the country and CEO paychecks and golden parachutes have gotten obscenely more lucrative every year to the point of making The Gilded Age look like something out of Dickens. Paris Hilton may waggle her ass in TV commercials for fast-food joints, but she didn't start out rich from that—she's a heir to the Hilton fortune. That she gets TV commercials and cable reality shows after a sex tape and a stint in jail shows you how ridiculous it's gotten. Hello, they're *waving it in your face*, people! The rich are different from you and me, and they intend on *staying* that way. Public Citizen and the public interest lobbying group United for a Fair Economy issued a report back in 2006 showing that the lobbying effort to repeal the estate tax was financed primarily by 18 superwealthy families attempting to fix the merry-go-round so only they get the ride and the rest of us get to push. But nobody cares about them because, hey, everybody wants to be rich someday, me included. It's All About The Benjamins.

But heaven forbid a bunch of people band together and try to get paid fairly for it—oh, no. That's *socialist*, gol-durn it.

I'm a big believer in the capitalist system, but I also know that given half a chance, the big guy will put his boot on the little guy's neck and try to take his money. It's what America was founded on, if you recall. No, I'm not talking about King George, I'm talking about all that free labor the South was built on for the first 89-plus years of our nation. It's easier to have a plantation with a mansion if you happen to *own* the labor.

So I'm a labor guy, from start to finish. Whether it's baseball, workers at Wal-Mart or Hollywood writers (and especially Hollywood writers), I come down on the side of the employee. Maybe when I've inherited Paris Hilton-type money then I'll reconsider. But I really doubt it.

*   *   *

It's A Business, Sport
February 2, 1994

If you want to get into an easy argument, just bring up sports, politics or religion. Of course nowadays, when sports is a business, it's almost impossible to keep politics out of it, especially when the sport is baseball and the boobs who run the game think they're the cardinals and ersatz commissioner Bud Selig of the Milwaukee Brewers is the pope. Oops—it didn't take long for religion to crop up, did it?

With the publication of an ad in the Capitol Hill newspaper *Roll Call* last week, the self-delusion of the major-league baseball owners appears to be complete. The third and fourth sentences of the informational ad cut right to the heart of the illusion the owners would foist upon a cynical public (especially when you consider the primary readership of *Roll Call* is Congress):

"...This unhappy situation is not about labor versus management. It is about the game and its fans, about preserving our national pastime and promoting its growth..."

There you have it—lying, pandering and dissembling all in one and a half sentences. It *is* about labor versus management, the game has been taking it on the chin leaving the fans on the mat and the best way to preserve the pastime would be to take it out of the hands of the greed-head hacks running it.

Simply put, it's as if your boss wants you to limit the amount of profit you can make from your labors on behalf of the company when it does well, but suffer more when he or she runs it down the toilet. Call it the San Diego Padres School of Management and Economics.

Later in the ad, the owners state that "skyrocketing costs in baseball have doubled over the past five years and threaten the long-term viability of MLB franchises." No one is arguing that baseball players make an obscene amount of money. It's the tribute to the American system: if you can make it or if you are worth it, grab it. Every Republican and most Democrats with functioning brains can agree on that. It is the basis on which the Kennedy and Rockefeller families made their fortunes.

The problem here is, the owners refuse to open the books. "We're losing money," they cry on one hand, while already debating future expansion on the other. What business talks future franchises while pleading poverty?

A study by the Congressional Research Service, the information resource of the Library of Congress, shows specifically how the owners are blowing smoke. "The Baseball Strike and Federal Policy: An Economic Analysis," written by Dennis Zimmerman and William Cox of CRS says the owners' salary cap plan would have decreased the amount of money going to players by $198 million in 1994, cutting the players' share of revenue from 55 percent to 44 percent. What's more, it said just $38 million of the reduction in the money going to players would have been split among the teams in revenue sharing if the cap had been in full effect last year. "Much of the remaining $160 million presumably would accrue to the large-revenue teams,"

The cap, the report said, "has the effect of reducing baseball owners' potential losses from a bargaining impasse and subsequent unilateral action." Boy, who wouldn't want to run a business with fail-safe guarantees like that?

Now despite the defiance of Orioles' owner Peter Angelos (cue cheers) and Canada's Toronto Blue Jays (respectful nods, just this once), Selig and the other teams plan to use replacement players to fill out the '95 season if the strike isn't over by Opening Day.

Currently there are three bills pending in Congress that would let the nation's lawmakers horn in on the act: measures by Sen. Daniel Patrick Moynihan (D-NY) with bipartisan co-sponsorship from Sen. John Warner (R-VA), and on the House side from Rep. Pat Williams (D-MT) that would completely strip baseball's anti-trust exemption, and also one from Rep. John Conyers (D-MI) that would simply allow players to take their grievances to court.

Selig and the owners take the high renewal rate of season ticket plans as a sign from fans that their anti-labor moves are being met with approval. An Associated Press story cites owners as claiming a 71 percent renewal rate as of Jan. 13, with ten clubs higher than 80 percent and four at 90 or above.

The reality is, fans know this little game of pepper will only go on so long. Spring training opens in two weeks, and fans know if there's any serious chance that the major leaguers won't be in uniform come Opening Day, either the White House or Congress will butt in. *That's* why they're renewing. Already President Clinton is showing more vertebrae with the owners than he has with the GOP, which is something of an encouraging sign.

The coming weeks should prove exciting. One way or another, Bud Selig and the rest of the gang will be caught between angry fans and an angry Congress if duffers in cleats show up to the ballparks this spring. If puffs of white smoke are seen to be coming from the chimney of the next owner's meeting, it could mean one of two things: either a new Pope has been chosen…or the owners have accepted terms of surrender.

Labor Pains
November 8, 1995

If you drive by the Omni hotel in downtown Baltimore this week, take a look out the window at the people out on the sidewalk. Rain or shine, they won't look happy.

The Omni, the only hotel in Baltimore with unionized employees, is being struck. "So what?" you may ask. But before you write off those people as members of an outdated organization (a union) who you may believe are overpaid and under-worked, think about a few things.

We here in Baltimore have been virtually prostituting ourselves for a football team for well over ten years. We have offered parking money, we have offered concessions, we have offered to build a giant stadium with natural grass and a built-in audience for professional football.

And we kept getting stiffed, until the events of this week proved that, if you whore yourself long enough, they will come

Football, like anything else in today's economy, is a business—a big business, with overall revenues in the billions of dollars. And it's a seller's market.

The state of Maryland and the city of Baltimore are in competition with every other state and major city out there, trying to lure businesses and jobs. And the companies know this.

America has been desperate for jobs in the 90s—droolingly, slavishly desperate, with every company looking to move trying to eke out so many concessions, tax breaks and incentives out of the prospective state or city that we may as well dress our mayors and governors in cheap nylon mini-skirts and gaudy lipstick and send them off to Chambers of Commerce to ask "Wanna date?"

The bottom line is that companies know they can get anything they want, and to please their shareholders, they do. And "costs"—meaning workers—be damned.

If you don't own stock, if you don't own property, if you don't make the big bucks, you're screwed. It's not a matter of race anymore as it is of class. According to Census Bureau figures, in 1960, the senior executive of Fortune 500 companies made 12 times more than the non-supervisory worker or line employee. In 1975, it was 35 times more. Last year, the big shots made as much as 135 times more than the grunt who did the hourly work.

Is it worth it? You tell us. Last month, according to stories in the Associated Press and *Mother Jones*, IBM announced layoffs of 1,100 employees in order to cut costs. Their stock rose on the announcement. In 1994, they cut 36,000 jobs. Their chairman, Louis Gerstner, made $2,800,000 before the cuts. His new salary: $4,600,000.

No one is safe anymore, because if companies aren't laying off employees to cut costs, they're laying off employees because of mega-mergers. But then again, we don't need to tell you that here in Baltimore.

Just last week, Crestar Financial Corp., after eating Loyola Capital Corp. (parent of Loyola Federal Savings & Loan), announced it will cut 40 percent of the workforce once the merger is complete. Back in August, Chemical Bank and Chase Manhattan Bank announced a merger, which would also cause the elimination of 12,000 jobs, while the combined banks go on to become the biggest bank in the nation. This came not long after Chemical merged with Manufacturers Hanover Trust, leading to 6,000 layoffs, according to reports in the Associated Press.

During the months of June, July and August of this year, there were a combined 96,920 layoffs nationwide, reports a Chicago-based international outplacement firm, with one-third of those due to mergers.

What's the matter? Why is this happening? The Dow Jones last week went to a record high, breaking the 4800 mark. Unemployment is at the 5.5 percent mark—something the experts call close to "full employment."

It's beginning to appear that there are two classes of Americans going into the millenium: those who are stockholders, and those who are not. Unions have been destroyed in the name of "competitiveness," and workers are no longer assets but costs. Employee loyalty is to be prized by management when it is cheap, but otherwise valueless. Labor department statistics show that this is the 12th consecutive quarter that collective bargaining settlements called for smaller increases than the ones they replaced.

Can we honestly say anymore that companies are working for anyone other than the people who receive the annual report? With all our talk of the decaying moral structure of our families and our children, can we afford to forget the blame when it reaches the door of the executive suite?

Apparently not. We must, after all, remain "competitive" in the global marketplace. The question is, who in America can buy anything if they can't afford to?

If you drive by the Omni hotel in downtown Baltimore this week, take a look out the window at the people out on the sidewalk. Rain or shine, they won't look happy.

Look at their faces. Someday, like the lottery used to promise, it could be you.

Ain't That The Truth?
December 6, 1995

Let's see if we've got this straight:

A bunch of millionaires not accountable to the public (NFL owners) want to be able to move their football franchises wherever they can and wherever a (stupid) community wants to pay them obscene amounts of tribute in the name of "civic pride."

The NFL (starring Paul "Baltimore Sucks" Tagliabue), then goes to a bunch of millionaires accountable to the public (Congress) asking them to give that millionaire owners' organization (the NFL) a limited anti-trust exemption, so those millionaire owners won't lose a passel of money fighting the cities who got screwed out of a team in court when said millionaire owners sell out to the next city dumb enough to give away the store. And supposedly that will stop those "renegade" owners from leaving their stadiums full of loyal fans in the dust.

So, in essence, they are asking that the economic process be subverted, and the league be treated as an entity instead of the bunch of greedy venal millionaires that they are. Sort of like baseball, actually.

Well, almost exactly like baseball, except the baseball players have a union that functions and the owners have the century-old protection of a government that refuses to see that that sport has ceased being a pastime and has become, like everything else in our bottom-line oriented culture, a business.

Sen. Mike DeWine of (where else?) Ohio, in sponsoring the limited anti-trust exemption, says he wants to hold the NFL to its own stated standards.

"The NFL should enforce its own rules," DeWine said, according to a report in the Knight-Ridder newspapers. "If they allow the Browns to move, the rules are useless. It means they have no rules. It means that no community in the country is safe from having its team getting up and moving,"

"Bingo!" shouts the little old lady from Baltimore. Didn't we say this 11 years ago? Didn't we kvetch long enough about how our last football team owner skipped town in the middle of the night?

What is truly ironic, but not surprising, is the amount of across-the-aisle goodwill generated in a state's delegation when something of this world-shaking magnitude happens to a city. Mike DeWine and Louis Stokes (both former mayors of Cleveland, now members of Congress in the Senate and the House, respectively) probably are miles apart when it comes to the issues of cuts in the growth of Medicare, inner-city job training programs and how long we should take to balance the federal budget. But, by gum, let their football team split town because they can't renovate a stadium that's been in service since Jesse Owens laced up his track shoes, and they're all wearing Dawg Pound masks.

It's kind of comical, really. Probably nothing does more to negatively influence people's opinions of politicians more than seeing long-held principles of non-interference in the marketplace and laissez-faire capitalism dissolve when the visceral desire for professional sports and the passions that accompany them enter the picture. Voters love football. Politicians love voters. Cogito ergo pander.

What it really comes down to is that the free-agency that began on the field has extended to the owner's box. As the players got more money for doing what put people in the seats, the owners needed more money to keep the players while still making (ridiculously large sums of) money. In order to do so, they need to be able to get more money out of the people sitting in those seats, up to and including licensing to them the right to sit in the seat they'll have to pay a ticket for anyway.

Should that community not be able to pony up the cash, the owner wants the right to be able to go elsewhere to get it, "fans" be damned. And now the organization wants the government to step in by saying "Stop Me—Before I Move Again."

If there is such a thing as personal accountability anymore, we need to be able to call a spade a spade, no matter whose garden it's being used to dig up. Wellington Mara, the owner of the New York Giants, said as much to the New York Daily News upon notice that Art Modell planned to move his team to Baltimore.

"I don't like the idea of free-agent franchises," Mara said. "But I do feel like we have free-agent franchises. It's really hard to believe. It's one of the penalties that comes with affluence, I guess."

Ain't that the truth. And we're stealing a team, too. And if the members of Congress think that an anti-trust exemption will stop owners from moving their teams, they're dumber than we think they are (which is saying a lot in the '90s). Anyone who wants a team bad enough will wave the money it takes to get one.

Printed on our money it says, "In God We Trust." What it does not say, but should, is, "All Others Pay Cash."

Wal-Mart, *The Sun,* and You
July 2. 2003

Why do baseball teams always cry poverty? Because they can. They rarely pay for the new stadiums they play in, they get millions in TV revenue, and they enjoy an anti-trust exemption afforded no other sport. But they're always saying they're losing money. When you ask them to open the books and prove it, they decline. Who says they're poor, then? They do. "Trust us," they say.

Last week, Nike lost an appeal to the Supreme Court, where it wanted the court to slap down a consumer activist who says Nike was engaged in false advertising when it denied claims that the sportswear company uses abused and underpaid workers in Southeast Asia to make its products. Nike turned on its massive public-relations machine to deny the charges—letters to editors, press releases and a 30-page pamphlet about their labor practices—and Marc Kasky, the activist, sued, calling Nike's rebuttal false advertising.

Why did Nike take the case all the way to the U.S. Supreme Court? Because, in this day and age, companies say whatever the hell they want, and damned if anyone will stop them.

Take Wal-Mart, for instance. Last December, the mega-retailer was told by a federal jury to pay more than 400 of its Oregon employees for the unpaid overtime it made them work between 1994 and 1999. CBS reported that two years prior to that decision Wal-Mart was forced to pay a $50 million settlement covering 69,000 employees in Colorado and another $500,000 settlement for another case in New Mexico—both for making employees work overtime without pay.

So what did Wal-Mart say after the decision in Oregon? Company spokesman Bill Wertz said, "Wal-Mart has a strong policy of paying its associates for all the time they work." Uh-huh. And baseball is losing money.

You may have heard recently about the labor troubles over at that newspaper on Calvert Street. The employees there recently accepted a new contract, after coming down to the last few hours before a strike deadline.

Now we here at Animal Control were not privy to any of the labor negotiations, and haven't spoken to any of the principals on either side, but we did take more than a passing interest in the circumstances surrounding the contretemps. Newspapers in the United States may have to deal with declining readership and the rising cost of newsprint, but believe you me, they aren't hurting for money.

But when negotiators for Chicago-based Tribune Co., *The Sun*'s parent company, came to Baltimore, they had already prepared ahead of time—they went to their other properties and told the employees that, in essence, Trib would pay them double salaries to come and work in the place of Sun employees if the locals went on strike. And then Trib went into the negotiations with the local Newspaper Guild and offered wage cuts, wage freezes, less job security and less vacation. This was considered "bargaining in good faith."

Baltimore is legendarily a union town. And Maryland is considered to be a progressive, labor-friendly state. Even rock-ribbed Republican and former Congresswoman Helen Bentley knew enough to go to union picnics and make nice, due to her years covering dockworkers, some of the hardiest union people alive.

So, for the Tribune Co. to come to Baltimore, insult its employees by claiming that they're "underperforming" and make it clear that it is prepared to pay its other employees double salaries in order to break the local union, it tells you something about what the company considers to be "good faith."

On a side note, we find it funny that in negotiations, the Tribune people were supposedly calling *The Washington Post The Sun*'s biggest competitor (while offering up only the worst and most regressive parts of the *Post*'s labor contract with its employees). Back in the early 1990s, this writer, then a radio reporter, posed a question to then-Sun publisher John Carroll at a professional association meet-and-greet: "Who do you consider to be The Sun's biggest competitor?" His reply: "The Yellow Pages."

It tells you something when the Guild, after voting to accept Trib's final contract offer, released a statement saying they "accept this contract under bitter protest" and they "condemn the Tribune Company for its demeaning and destructive conduct, and for negotiating in bad faith."

It is a hopeful sign that the Supreme Court has still not elevated commercial speech to the protected status of individual free speech, as demonstrated in their decision not to render an appeal of the Nike case in California. But it's very clear that almost all the weapons are on the side of the companies. When the government lets media conglomerates metastasize like cancer, allowing them to ship workers anywhere to break unions, while simultaneously making bald-faced PR statements professing innocence and honor, the little guy and his coworkers are on the shakiest of ground.

The next company to do this may be yours. Why? Because it can.

More Labor Pains
January 21, 2004

Just under a century ago, if you were an American wage laborer, it sucked to be you. Over the next 50 years, the work landscape changed: Child labor laws were passed, the 40-hour work week became standard, a minimum wage was established and employees got such previously unheard of things as pension plans, health care and paid vacation time. Because of this, the United States' standard of living surpassed the rest of the planet's. The concept of "leisure time," before these labor innovations, was almost nonexistent for the working class.

What was the driving force behind this revolution? The U.S. labor movement.

Nowadays, unions spend every hour waging a battle akin to that of Helms Deep. The grocery strike in California is past its 100th day, and two of the stores involved, Albertsons and Vons, have lost a projected $1 billion. One of the points of contention: employee health care.

In July of 2003, the Bush administration repealed a Clinton-era rule that mandated employers track, document and report repetitive stress injuries. The Bush Labor Department said at the time that the data collected would be useless in identifying the causes and preventing the injuries. Yet one more step backward for the worker.

For every retreat the labor movement is forced to make, the top echelon of management seems to take four steps forward. In this space in 1995, I pointed out that in 1960 the average senior executive of a Fortune 500 company made 12 times more than the average non-supervisory worker or line employee. In 1975, it was 35 times more. And in 1994, the big shots made as much as

135 times more than the grunts.

What has changed? Pretty damn little. An April 2001 *New York Times* article pointed out that by the end of the 1990s the average head of a big company took home more than $10 million before taxes. When sales slowed in 2000 and '01, those same chief executives did...better. When the recession caused investors to lose 12 percent of their portfolios in '00, CEOs got an average 22 percent raise in salary and bonuses—not even counting stock options, the free candy for the rich in the new millennium. That year, according to the federal Bureau of Labor Statistics, the typical hourly worker got a 3 percent raise, with 4 percent raises for salaried employees.

More? You want more? Sure! The year following Sept. 11, 2001 was one of the worst financially for airlines. For their troubles, the airlines received two federal bailouts totaling about $18 billion dollars, but all five of the top airlines that reported losses in '01—United, Delta, Northwest, Continental and US Airways—upped the salaries and benefits of their CEOs, according to *The Washington Post*. As the *Post* put it, "While executives were earning more, they were slashing jobs, salaries and pensions.... US Airways, for instance, shut down its pilots pension plan and replaced it with one that provided benefits at about half the original level. United has laid off 9,000 workers."

Pension plans have been raided, employees are increasingly seen as "costs" and unions are being assaulted by both corporate management and an administration that loads its Department of Labor with people hostile to the very tenets the agency was founded to protect and nurture. You, the little guy and gal, are getting screwed.

And still, the conservatives repeat the mantra that unions don't benefit anyone—another lie that has become standardized in public discourse dominated by the right.

A study recently published by the nonprofit, nonpartisan Economic Policy Institute shows that unionizing raises the wages of workers by nearly 20 percent, and total compensation—pay and benefits—by about 28 percent. Strong unions even help nonunion workers. If you're a high-school graduate who works in an industry that's 25 percent unionized, even if you're not in a union yourself, you're getting paid on average 5 percent more than similar workers in less unionized industries.

One of the saddest trends of the '90s was unions giving back, giving up and giving in. Which is why, more than any other organized group in the United States, 2004 has to be seen as a critical battleground. If you want a pension, if you want decent health care, if you want a future greater than simply standing and reciting 27,649 times a day, "Hi, welcome to Wal-Mart," you can see that the movement that made life better for the American worker in the last century is the last, best chance at making a change for the better in this one.

The American dream was the idea that life for each successive generation could be easier, freer and better than the previous one. In three short years, this administration has bankrupted that dream. As Vice President Dick Cheney told former Treasury Secretary Paul O'Neill, "Reagan proved that deficits don't matter." Whose side are *you* on?

Remember Inglewood
April 14, 2004

This time the smaller army won, but it may not be like this again. Last week, the Los Angeles suburb of Inglewood turned back the behemoth that is Wal-Mart, which wanted to open a

Wal-Mart Supercenter on 60 acres of land next to the Hollywood Park racetrack.

Like everything Wal-Mart does, it did it on a grand scale, and on its own terms: The megastore project was an attempt to circumvent the Inglewood City Council, which blocked the world's largest retailer's effort to ram through a store that would have run roughshod over the city's environmental, traffic, labor and public safety concerns.

Opponents noted that Wal-Mart paid the army of canvassers it used to gather enough signatures to bring the issue to a public vote more than the company pays its average clerk, and then spent more than a million dollars blitzing the community with ads in order to try and sway votes.

It's likely that you've set foot in a Wal-Mart before. Sadly, you might have even bought something. But as you watch U.S. jobs dry up and head overseas, and see corrupt CEOs and conscience-bankrupt boards of directors reward themselves with raises and stock options whether or not their companies ever see a good year, think of how Wal-Mart really reflects this nation's business marketplace.

As noted before in this column, Wal-Mart is being hit left and right with charges of forcing employees to work overtime without pay. CBS News reported in 2002 that more than 39 class-action lawsuits had been filed at the time in 30 states against the company in back-pay related cases. In 2000, the company reportedly settled one off-the-clock lawsuit for $50 million in Colorado, and another one in New Mexico for $500,000.

Last November, Wal-Mart was hit with a racketeering lawsuit in New Jersey for conspiring with cleaning contractors to cheat immigrant janitors out of wages. The suit claims Wal-Mart didn't pay workers' Social Security payments, didn't withhold federal payroll taxes and, as *The New York Times* reported, engaged in a "pattern of racketeering activity" to keep government officials from enforcing wage and immigration laws.

Last January, the *NYT* reported that for 15 years Wal-Mart has had a policy of locking in its employees overnight, and the paper cited instances where workers had broken bones and sustained other severe injuries yet were threatened with dismissal if they vacated the premises via alarmed fire-escape doors.

Last week, the *Los Angeles Times* won a Pulitzer Prize in national reporting for a three-part series looking into Wal-Mart. The series pointed out that while company founder Sam Walton started a "Bring It Home to the USA" program in 1985 that offered domestic suppliers as much as 5 percent premiums for U.S.-made products, Wal-Mart now forces Third World countries to compete against each other in a race to the bottom in order to deliver on items like an $8.63 polo shirt. Playing factories in China against operations in Bangladesh and Vietnam, Wal-Mart nickel-and-dimes its way across the globe, threatening to close factories and move if employees and employers can't shave more and more off the costs of making the items it then sells by the millions.

And speaking of shaving, when *The New York Times* reported on a growing practice of shaving time off workers' timecards, guess which company popped up not far into the story? There it was—more than a dozen former Wal-Mart employees stating in interviews and court depositions that stores had altered time records to shortchange employees.

The sad part is how much Wal-Mart reflects modern political America. The Arkansas-based corporation went from not even cracking the top 100 in political donations in 2000, to ranking 71st in 2002, to second in the 2004 election cycle, according to the nonprofit, nonpartisan research group Center for Responsible Politics. It is a company that, in order to serve stockholders, does everything up to the line of legality to squeeze workers (who are seen more as costs than assets) of every penny, no matter whether they live in Bangor or Bangladesh. When thwarted in City Hall, it pays to go around the system and pushes its will at the ballot box. And when thwarted there, it complains, as it did on NPR this past week, that the voters were not really exhibiting the will of "the people." When you lose 3-2 at the polling place, what is left to spin?

In the wake of the vote, Jay Nordlinger, the managing editor of the conservative magazine *National Review* took to the pages of the *Los Angeles Times* to blast the citizens of Inglewood for their rebuff of Wal-Mart. Nordlinger superciliously stated, "If the people of Inglewood would rather have 60 acres of nothing instead of a Wal-Mart Supercenter, that's their business. But I can't help feeling that they were badly misled."

The registers will still rack up sales for Wal-Mart, bad publicity or not. Maybe the people of Inglewood did their small part in holding off the tide, but the fact remains, just like we are Americans who want services but don't want to pay taxes for them, we also want our polo shirts for $8.63.

No Money, No Funny
November 14, 2007

It serves as only part of the bitter irony of the American entertainment history that the man who began the modern-day assault on the union movement served as the president of a union for six years and to this day is the only president who was ever a union member.

Ronald Reagan is quite likely the paternal grandfather to the corporations trying to break the Writers Guild of America in its members' quest to be remunerated for the work they do that gets ported to new media. Of course, Reagan was the president who broke the air traffic controllers' strike in August 1981, after his transportation secretary had trained replacements secretly ready to take over—this after both the controllers' union and the Teamsters endorsed Reagan over Jimmy Carter in 1980. Considering that Reagan, while head of the Screen Actors Guild, was also a squealer to the FBI during the House Un-American Activities Committee, it only adds that much more grim irony in an era when Hollywood is constantly being tarred, by blow-hards like Bill O'Reilly, as a hotbed of liberal sympathizers and pro-terrorist effetes.

Normally, strikes are over the simple things that have been fought over for almost a century: time, wages and benefits. But in the entertainment industry (think of the baseball strikes), the issues are not always as clear to the consumer as they are in the case of the truck driver, the factory worker, or the prison guard. And it is always in the interest of the corporate fathers to make sure that the strikers are looked upon as poorly as possible—something relatively easy to do in a world where most of the media is owned by barely a handful of companies.

Responding to snide coverage of the strike in *The New York Times*—a recent news article on the strike pointed out that "instead of hard hats and work boots, those on the barricades wore arty glasses and fancy scarves"—Joss Whedon, the creative mastermind behind Buffy the Vampire Slayer, Angel and Firefly, slammed that characterization in a blog post.

"[T]his is exactly the problem," Whedon wrote. "The easiest tactic is for people to paint writers as namby-pamby, arty-scarfy posers, because it's what most people think even when we're not striking. Writing is largely not considered work. Art in general is not considered work. Work is a thing you physically labor at, or at the very least, hate. Art is fun. (And Hollywood writers are overpaid, scarf-wearing dainties.) It's an easy argument to make. And a hard one to dispute."

But in the new millennia, when the Bush presidency has driven the national debt to new skyrocketing heights, when China owns a mortgage to our future, and when it takes $1.10 to buy one Canadian dollar, there may not be much the United States creates anymore except intellectual product. The backbone of that intellectual product is the entertainment industry, and people all around the world are buying it up by the pallet. That is, when they're not pirating it they way they do in China.

And the way of the future isn't television anymore, or even cable for that matter. It's the Internet. And the companies that have done business the same way for decades now want to change the rules.

Think of it this way—if you've ever watched a snippet of Comedy Central's *The Daily Show* online, you know that before you watch any of it, you have to watch an ad. So the studio is making money off that—but not the writers, who don't see a dime. When a show airs on regular television, the writers get paid. When it airs in reruns, the writers get paid a residual, which is less, but they still get paid. But right now, when it airs on the net, or on your phone, or heaven forbid in the future, they beam it right into your skull, the writers get *bupkis*. And the studios like it that way. In essence, that's what we're talking about.

Like the baseball players said, no one ever went to the game to see an owner. Nobody ever watches *Desperate Housewives* or *Heroes* or *Lost* to see some suit take a piece of the real action, and that action is created by the writers. The studios created the garbage that is "reality TV" in order to get around writers, even though, when you listen to the participants later on, it's clear that "writers" juiced the storylines at every stage of the game. From *Dancing With The Stars* to *Survivor*, the fix has been in.

Last week on the picket lines, the writers for the late-night talk shows in Manhattan chanted, "No money, no funny" as they walked carrying their signs. If you can't muster up any sympathy for the Writers Guild, then perhaps you deserve to watch *The Biggest Loser*. There's your irony for you.

City Politics

Little did I know when I moved to Baltimore on a cold, grim April fifteenth back in 1990 that I would become a proud and permanent resident of this city. In the 1990s, my *City Paper* colleague Van Smith nicknamed Baltimore, "The City Of Swirling Trash." My neighborhood back then, a bastion of historic brick rowhouses lit by old-fashioned gas lanterns, sat around a square made famous by the home of its late literary resident H.L Mencken. But we were the oasis. Just one block to the north and two blocks to the south lay slums. One of my oldest friends came to town and while walking to the Mt. Clare Junction shopping center through the edges of Pigtown, he facetiously joked "Hey—look! You got white people living as poor as black people!"

My first years here were the era of Kurt Schmoke and his laissez-faire attitude toward drug decriminalization. Baltimore has been "Junkietown" for years now—finding heroin "works" on the floor tucked in behind the men's toilets at local restaurants and miniature crack vials in the gutters of the street was as regular an occurrence as the sound of the drug couriers on minibikes ferrying packages from the north side to the south side.

Schmoke's re-election campaign in the mid '90s against city council president Mary Pat Clarke was a masterpiece of using race in an election without mentioning the word at all. Larry Gibson, Schmoke's campaign manager and political Svengali, had apparently crunched the numbers and realized that if Schmoke held onto his African American base, for the most part, he didn't need any of the city's white vote at all. So Schmoke's bumper stickers featured the pan-African colors of red, green and black and blared in capital letters, "MAYOR SCHMOKE MAKES US PROUD." So crime and drugs and quality of life never really entered into the equation at all, and Clarke never stood a chance. And nothing changed.

Oh—and an aside. This chapter is about Baltimore politics, true, but if you'll notice, the 1995 election between Schmoke and Clarke also shows us how a race between a black man and a white woman should *not* be conducted. Take from this what you will when you think about the Democratic presidential primary of 2008.

When I worked at the drug policy office of the White House under Barry McCaffrey, I learned that the average heroin addict had to steal about nine hundred dollars a day worth of stuff to support a three hundred dollar a day drug habit. What this meant was a lot of property crime, and in places like my neighborhood of Sowebo, we knew about it firsthand. Every party you went to, the homeowners would stand around over their wine or homebrewed beer and trade stories of the latest break in, robbery or thwarted larceny attempt. As residents, we learned how to tell one caliber of weapon from another, simply by the sound, since we heard gunfire so regularly, and so close by, that you knew when you might want to sink to the floor when some gangbanger decided to pop off his new .45 into the air on New Year's Eve.

Later in the decade, when then-councilman Martin O'Malley challenged the two frontrunners, city council members Lawrence Bell and Carl Stokes, in his first election campaign, nobody really thought he had a chance. But poll leader Bell spent too much (Charging suits purchased out of town to his campaign? What was he thinking?) and made too many mistakes. When in their debate Bell talked about getting "new ideas," Stokes, in a finishing punch worthy of Lloyd Bentsen crushing Dan Quayle's allusion to Jack Kennedy, retorted, "I don't need to go to New York to get new ideas. Just like I don't need to go to New York to get a new suit" and Bell was *done*.

By that time O'Malley's emphasis on public safety had taken hold and he managed to slipstream between the two and capture the fifth floor office in City Hall, and we started noticing, in our little west side bunker, that things had changed. Outside of the standard New Year's Eve gunfire into the air, we started hearing less of the street-side rat-a-tat. Property crime started dropping. Home values started going up.

Almost ten years now have passed since that time—O'Malley has moved on to the governor's mansion, and Sheila Dixon vaulted into the mayor's office in an election featuring some of the lowest turnout of voters in a generation. Crime has leveled off, even if the murder rate (then as now comprised mostly among the ever-present gangbangers) has started to inch back up again. We're in the middle of the giant subprime mortgage crisis, but Baltimore still remains a better deal when it comes to home buying than the insane real-estate prices commanded in the DC metropolitan area.

The final column in this chapter was written right when the Clinton administration was taking over Washington at the start of 1993, and an influx of young liberals and Democrats were surging toward the nation's capital—and sometimes even eying our little

"Smalltimore" as a possible place to set up. Time has passed, and some, like *Post* book critic Jonathan Yardley, have decamped down the highway to DC. Over the last five years, Washingtonians have steadily moved here, finally discovering the lower home prices and cheaper cost of living (and the crime and the trash). Right now I look out my window and I can see the "Taxation Without Representation" license plate on the back of my new neighbors' car. But a lot of what I wrote in the piece is still accurate, even if DC now has its own baseball team and a brand new stadium to go with it (where I'll wager the prices are *still* higher than those in Baltimore's Camden Yards).

Baltimore still has a lot of the quaint, the humble, the poor, the charming and the offbeat that it had when I moved here nineteen years ago.

And it's still a fun place to live.

*   *   *

It's Beginning To Smell A Lot Like Christmas
December 21, 1994

Christmastime may be a season for forgiveness. But we here at Animal Control probably think a good number of people are finding it hard to feel that way toward politicians. And especially toward newly minted felon and former city comptroller Jackie McLean.

Although year in and year out the trust people feel in our political leaders drops faster than a rock from the top of the World Trade Center, there still seems to be some way that McLean and her attorneys feel she'll be forgiven by a public that elected her and then was betrayed by her. And then this lingering resentment will be carried around in the bloodstream of the body politic like the cholesterol after too many pork rinds until the next election, when talk radio will heat up once more and people running for office who actually want to do something will wonder where all the vitriol came from.

What is probably the most disgusting part of the whole sorry affair is M. Cristina Gutierrez's performance once the verdict was announced, with the multi-media, multi-channel revision of reality that she put on Friday for the television cameras. Like the line from Shakespeare, "Methinks the lady doth protest too much," Gutierrez has been insisting that her client has been punished enough, that she has paid back what she stole and her life and her business are in a shambles.

Now wait just a minute—almost a year ago wasn't McLean playing the race card for all it's worth, claiming that these charges were all politically motivated and aimed at her because supposedly people couldn't stand to see a strong, powerful black woman in office? Didn't she run for the office of comptroller based on what she claimed was her competence and her savvy business skills? And didn't she turn tail and run for the hospital only when the checks started turning up as evidence against her?

There's a fine tradition officeholders follow when sentencing time comes around. Usually it's some form of abject contrition, accompanied by a religious revival. That lasts as long as the object of scorn's name remains in the public eye. Then comes the period of contemplation of options before returning to the public arena.

There's no shortage of Marylanders who have gone through the judicial and media merry-go-round before making attempts at returning to a position of political influence. Nathaniel Oaks made a run for the legislature again. Tommie Broadwater, a state senator from Prince Georges County, takes a stab at reelection every two years only to be fondly rejected by the constituency that still remembers his fraud conviction. And Marvin Mandel is still a lobbyist in Annapolis.

Except the difference is that Jacqueline McLean will not serve any time in jail.

This is a time when guns are seen as great holiday gifts, when elected officials are being turned out all across America for being "too liberal" and the only cure for crime is considered to be mapping out the space for the next thousand prison beds. And yet when a city comptroller, the person who holds the purse strings for more than 700,000 people gets snagged for heisting city cash and steering same said city toward buying the building that held her failed travel agency, where's the swift hand of justice?

Three years prison, suspended, and 750 hours of community service is what rock stars and actors get for trashing hotel rooms and consensual sex with 15 year olds. It's a slap on the wrist. There's more than a message that is sent when elected officials are not jailed for abuse of office—there's a knowledge among the electorate that, yes, politicians *are* different from you and me, and what's more, they can get away with it.

Former Speaker of the House Tip O'Neill wrote in his book "All Politics Is Local" that a politician's word is his bond. Although that may sound so assured and cheerful in the light politics is held in these days, it means something. It means that leaders are held to a high standard, and all they have to keep them there is that they promise to do right by the people that put them there.

Jackie McLean was haughty in victory, aloof in office and non-conciliatory when first presented with accusations of wrongdoing. Now she has been humbled, and through the largesse of a retired Carroll County judge presiding over her sentencing, she will not serve any jail time, which is what any ordinary person who filched 25 grand from a bank would get.

McLean will now go back to Sheppard Pratt and vanish into her 750 hours of "community service." The odds are, we'll see her again. We always do. There are second acts in American lives, despite what the husband of another Sheppard Pratt alumnae, F. Scott Fitzgerald, wrote years ago.

And when we see her, we'll say, "That's Jackie McLean. She used to be comptroller. I hear she's doing better now." And maybe she won't run for office again. And we can forget about her.

Because when it comes to abuse of office, perhaps the only way we can forgive is to forget.

Running On An Island
June 14, 1995

The late-afternoon sun was beating down on the eastbound drivers like bad campaign rhetoric, and the traffic on Eastern

Avenue was moving about as fast as affluent couples deciding to settle in the city, which means of course, not at all.

After Darth Vader thanked me for using Bell Atlantic (I didn't return the favor—they're closing down the convenient office on St. Paul St. and laying off the workers), the Death Star voice at the other end told me it was 81 degrees outside. That and a cloud of Friday evening exhaust fumes made it feel like it was 82…inside someone's muffler.

The reason I was stuck in last week's traffic gotterdamerung in Highlandtown was to see a politico doing what has to be one of the most inane and ridiculous campaign inventions imaginable: The Wave. Candidate stands on street corner, surrounded by loyal followers with placards, and waves at traffic. Traffic obligingly responds by waving back. Hopefully traffic pays at least an equal amount of attention to the roadway, else said candidate becomes hood ornament.

At the corner of Eastern and Haven, just when the roadway ducks under the railroad tracks before emerging into the swirl of Greek and Latino restaurants, two young black men stand, trying to hail a cab and failing miserably. After the fifth empty one passes, its driver a swarthy study in disinterest, the stockier of the two gives him the finger.

Across the street, unaware of this, surrounded by eager acolytes bearing orange signs, stands Mary Pat Clarke. Her heels are together, her slightly faded red blazer is buttoned at the waist, and The Woman Who Would Be Mayor is giving The Wave her Highlandtown best.

What's more, it's working. Despite the fact that this part of town can hardly be called Schmoke country (lest we forget, Schmoke's last adversary, William Swisher, has his offices less than a mile down the road), people of all colors stream through the Eastern and Haven intersection, and in equal amounts they honk back, and that is what is marking the candidacy of Mary Pat Clarke. If her handlers were to make the mistake of paraphrasing former presidential candidate Michael Dukakis, they might put it: "It's Not About Race, It's About Competence."

Clarke is as well received in East Baltimore legion halls as she is in West Baltimore pulpits. In 1991, during her re-election as city council president, she pulled in more votes than any other politician in the city, a fact her staff trumpets in their releases and on their World Wide Web site when they call her "the most popular elected official in Baltimore." She is accessible and can be found popping up in neighborhood association meetings and merchants' association gatherings like a red-blazered mushroom.

But her biggest strength is also her biggest weakness. Her biggest strength is that she can point out all the things that have happened—or haven't happened—in Baltimore while Kurt Schmoke has been mayor. Her biggest weakness is that she's been there, as city council president, almost as equally culpable, at the same time. City council meetings have often looked like circus acts, and Clarke's trademark red blazers only point out which one of the performers is the ringmaster.

Her campaign manager has had to defend herself against charges of naivete after their offices were broken into and their laptop computer stolen (Who leaves a laptop out and unlocked in a downtown Baltimore office?) Their communications director came from the Sauerbrey camp in a city that delivered the saving grace for Parris Glendening. And they filed campaign reports so late, it led people to question Clarke's administrative skills. After all, she *is* running for mayor.

But some neighborhood activists, community leaders and political trendwatchers refuse to count her out. Clarke has definitely gained some strength in communities in what was previously Schmoke country, as residents feel the mayor has been either inaccessible or inattentive. Also, Clarke can simply say, "Baltimore has been run the same way for years—the mayor controls the show." William Donald Schaefer has proved that the mayor's office can be a chamber of power. Clarke can say that, under Schmoke, it has been a distant ivory tower, aloof to the needs of the everyday citizen.

The problem for Clarke is, political attacks are dangerous. Nearly all of Clarke's campaign themes are destined to be negative, and as anyone who has ever seen a Marx Brothers movie can tell you, at the end of the pie fight, hardly anyone escapes unscathed. Each time she launches an attack on Schmoke, she opens herself up to charges of complicity in a city that has gotten more dangerous, less educated and less affluent each year.

So that is why this woman in a faded red blazer standing on a three-foot wide piece of cement in the center of evening rush hour traffic is linked both to a good chance at success and the level possibility of failure. Mary Pat Clarke is standing on an island and waving like her career depends on it. Like anyone who finds themselves trapped on an island, there's nowhere else to go.

It's No Kid's Game
August 23, 1995

"Politics ain't beanbag," said Mr. Dooley, the fictional Irishman and saloonkeeper creation of the writer Finley Peter Dunne. "'Tis a man's game; and women, children and prohibitionists do well to keep out iv it."

Well, despite the correct assertion that politics is not a children's game, it appears that one woman in town is playing it by some of the hardball rules, and is doing well by it. The question is, will the people be doing well by her?

The individual is Joan Pratt, running against former state senator Julian "Jack" Lapides for city controller. This race is being run against the backdrop of the last person to acquit herself with dubious distinction in the job, convicted felon Jacqueline McLean. Mrs. McLean, ever to keep herself foremost in our hearts, is now angling to get her pension reinstated after embarrassing both herself and the city with her actions before her conviction. Let's just say thanks, but no thanks.

For those who like to sit on the sidelines and watch the political game as it is played, it's kind of masterful to see what the Pratt campaign is doing to push their candidate. For the record, Pratt is a certified public accountant—a fact prominently placed on all her signs and literature right under her name—and has worked as the controller for the Legal Aid Bureau for 10 years. Legal Aid is kind of a sacred cow of sorts: no one can assail what they do, as it's kind of like dissing Mother Teresa.

What the use of politics does in a race such as this one is it makes the people forget that it's not about Mother Teresa, so to speak, it's about what Mother Teresa's job is supposed to be.

Pratt, in her stump speech, goes on about her qualifications as an accountant as if it is the most valuable asset for the job of comptroller. The fact is, it's not. If anything, Pratt is *redefining the job* to make it fit her, rather than explaining what of herself is fit for the job. She's playing to her strengths.

The position already exists that matches the qualifications extolled by Ms. Pratt—that of City Auditor. Except that it's a position that reports to the comptroller! Why redefine the position downward, to make it that of an auditor?

When Pratt spoke to the members of BUILD at their

candidates' forum, the candidates were each given a set amount of time to state their positions and record, and explain if and how they would work toward BUILD's agenda.

Pratt's competition in the race, Lapides, basically went through the agenda, and while supporting its tenets, noted that in a race such as that for comptroller, there was little bearing on any of the items when it came to the actual duties of the job for which they were running.

From all reports given, Pratt—not once, but twice—failed to address even a single item. At the start, she simply stated, "I fully support BUILD's agenda." When it came time for a follow-up question, which naturally asked for more specifics, she tersely reiterated, "As I said, I fully support BUILD's agenda." And continued with the listing of her resume.

BUILD associate organizer Carol Reckling, while noncommittal on either of the candidates, did note that the generic answer given was off-putting to some in the crowd.

"Many didn't take it well," Reckling says, "…Our instructions were to listen for specifics [or see if you] are getting a campaign speech."

"It was a mixed reaction," she said later.

The other exhibition of power politics displayed by the Pratt campaign is kind of a mass spin control. As *City Paper's* Van Smith reports, it was if every member of the Pratt organization in the hall was coached to rise in unison and wildly applaud a speech that was somewhat monotone at best. Given this kind of aural support, it can leave other participants with the feeling that the bandwagon is rolling and they'd best get aboard.

But the real issues here are behind what's playing on the political stage and cut to the heart of how people feel both about race and competence in this city. It is true—Joan Pratt may be a perfectly good CPA, and could make a fine comptroller. *But she has no experience in true public office.*

This is the city's money—all of our money—involved here. Once before a woman ran on the platform of "I'm a strong, independent and successful black woman. How dare you challenge what I've achieved." In that race was also a white male, who went down to defeat.

What bearing does race or gender have on this? *None whatsoever!* But the subtext remains, and is being played out yet again.

Who can act best as a watchdog over the city's finances? Who can act as the check on authority as the third member of the Board of Estimates? Match the records and the *real* qualifications against the position.

Politics, serious as it is, is a game. Governance is a science. We've let the game take precedence before, and look where it got us.

Truth, Lies and Videotape
August 30, 1995

"Tell the truth," they yell. "Tell the truth!"

"The truth" is an interesting concept, depending upon whose version you happen to be accepting. The whole advantage to the cry of "Tell the truth" is that it merely *implies* the one being accused is lying, without the rhetorical, emotional and legal baggage that goes along with it. It's so much *nicer* to say "Tell the truth" than to hit someone with the brute harshness of "You're lying."

It did Bob Dole no good back in 1988, when asked if he had anything to say to his primary opponent George Bush, to reply, "Tell him to stop lying about my record." Bush, the Miss Manners of American politics, went on to be president, and Bob Dole only enhanced his long-standing reputation for being mean.

The added advantage of asking an opponent to "tell the truth" is that it leaves the attacker with the option of ignoring the response. If the person so being accused is baited into a response, the attacker need only repeat the initial call—reinforcing the stance that the person is *still* lying. It's a no-lose play for the attacker and a no-win proposition for the defender.

The whole "truth" ploy all rests on the assumptions of the onlooker. The first person to lob the grenade avoids the burden of proof that "the truth" requires, while getting the sympathy or kudos of being the "honest" one in the debate.

What brings us to this is the televised debate on WMAR a week and a half ago, wherein Kurt Schmoke asks Mary Pat Clarke to specify exactly where she will get the funds for all the new police officers she is promising to put on the streets.

"From the waste you've made," she answered, with what appeared to this onlooker to be an almost smug smile.

For all intents and purposes, Clarke scored a very clear point in the exchange—she played to the galleries, she got in a concise response and she made the evening news and the papers. Bat hit ball, and over the fence it went. Home run for Clarke.

But it only *looked* like a home run—if you roll back the tape, you'll see why.

With nearly all taxpayers in the modern era, there is the assumption that government is wasting money. No matter how much any administrator cuts back because of tough times, political pressure or reorganization, there is always the hardcore belief on the part of John Q. Public that his money is being wasted.

People running for election know this and key on it. Parris Glendening, Mickey Steinberg, Ellen Sauerbrey—all of them ran on the issue that there was excessive waste in government and the savings could be transferred back to the taxpayer. Hardly any of them needed to cite specifics, because, hell, we all know it's there, don't we?

For Clarke to hit Schmoke with "...with the waste you've made" plays right to our assumptions. "Tell the truth," she's telling Schmoke. "Tell the truth!" But the lie is the *assumption*. There is no specific attribution behind it.

Where is the waste? Where are the specifics? Rolling back the tape of the debate only shows Clarke constantly playing for the bleachers without any consideration for specifics on her own part. It's not like Clarke doesn't have access to the figures—they cross her desk all the time. She is, after all, president of the city council.

In one instance where a questioner arrived with his own facts (a Baltimore City police officer claiming 11 instances of Clarke voting against police budgets containing funds for more officers), Clarke failed to answer the question. She responded with the equivalent of "I'm not aware of those figures...." and then charged forth, ignoring the request for clarification on a significant part of her record.

We've known Mary Pat Clarke for a long time. We know the part about being a teacher, we know the 20 years of public service, we know she lives here. Hell, we all do—we're just not running for mayor.

What we don't know is the specifics—things she plans to do or say. How much more money will the schools get? How much more money for police in communities? How much more for the libraries? Where will the money come from—and not from some pie-in-the-sky claim of "waste." One person's waste is another person's livelihood. If you don't think so, ask Parris Glendening about the DALP program.

Every candidate running knows to attack a predecessor on "waste." But unless specifics are given, it's an attack based on assumptions. Kurt Schmoke is a wonk, and we've known it for a long time. His campaign has come out with a slick tome of "accomplishments" that he may or may not be able to take credit for. Already the chorus is starting: "It's in the book!" Mary Pat Clarke needs to do the same. She can run only so far playing to the crowd, but she should remember that numbers mean a lot too. Ask her to provide some.

And to tell the truth.

Image Ain't Everything
September 6, 1995

Campaigning is a cynical pursuit.

It is all at once as challenging as baseball, with one man facing nine, and as exasperating as golf, with the only opponent being oneself and nature.

Each candidate hires the consultants to help them figure out what is the public perception of who they are, and then hires staff to go out and exploit that image. Then they get pollsters to tell them what part of it you think is working.

It is filled with terms such as being "on message," which is what happens when a candidate, campaign manager or spokesperson constantly repeats key positive attributes of their campaign and the negative ones about the opponent—usually within the same sentence. There are "hot button" topics, like crime, that hit everyone on their doorstep, and "wedge" issues like race, which can separate a candidate from his or her core group of supporters.

There are some black people in Baltimore who, no matter how poorly they may have felt Kurt Schmoke has run Baltimore over the past eight years, simply will not vote for Mary Pat Clarke because she is white. They look at race as an all-encompassing prism through which all else is viewed, and in the larger scheme of things, they feel that white people have run the city long enough. End of discussion.

There are some white people in Baltimore who are the reverse, who feel that Kurt Schmoke, for all his glowing resume and powerful friends, has not and could never approach what William Donald Schaefer did for the city. They measure Schmoke's tenure against then memory of a glowing and rosy pre-integration time when streets were safe and downtown Baltimore was predominantly white. These people will never speak their bias, because the change in the times has made it impermissible to say this without social scorn and the threat of being ostracized—unless you're Mark Fuhrman talking to a screenwriter.

Both of these two groups will never change. It is a testament to the ugliness of our racial past that we have poisoned the well, and the water we drink from it perpetuates a cancer on the political leadership of our future.

It is then up to the candidates and their handlers to manage our expectations of them, and to exploit our beliefs for their gain. Crime is up, one of them says, brandishing numbers. Crime is down, the other says, also brandishing numbers. Both sets of numbers come from the same book put out by the FBI, but each has broken out specifics sets of figures to buttress their point. Lies, damned lies and statistics. And when a public, slow to process information, sees that the crass manipulation of information by both sides is designed to prejudice its views, that public gets cynical.

In this campaign we have seen attacks over issues as seemingly innocuous as the color of campaign signs. "Seemingly" innocuous, because enough white voters felt that by use of colors (one of the strongest, and yet subtlest methods of persuasion), the Schmoke campaign was making racial overtures and appeals solely to the black community, after running for two terms on a platform of inclusivity. After nearly months of denials, the Schmoke campaign has turned on the attackers (but tacitly admitting the use of the strategy) by in effect saying, "So what? If the Robert Curran and Wilbur Cunningham campaigns can use the Irish green, why can't we use African red, green and black?" Race began the attacks, and unashamed ethic appeals ended it.

By this time, the negative spiral of campaigning has progressed too far to reverse. Professional campaigners know that negative campaigning, for all the complaints about it by the public, works and works well. Hammering an opponent four days before the election can turn the tides around for a candidate; it has worked time and time again. The one who refrains from doing it can only watch from the sidelines in defeat and prepare for the next battle a few years later, stronger in resolve not to be caught so weak ever again. Michael Dukakis is now a professor who instructs political neophytes not to let an attack go unchallenged.

But image ain't everything, folks. The one thing, the *only* thing that can subvert the machinations of a trained campaign strategist and highly paid advertising and marketing specialists is a voter with an open but skeptical mind, a good memory and one who likes to read. That's it.

After that, it just becomes a list of which appeal becomes more craven, which charge has no merit, who has run the hardest on their record or distorted the reality that the voter knows to be true.

Who's going to win? Who do *you* think? If you simply want to know who's going to win, better start dialing Dionne Warwick and her Psychic Friends, whose guesses could only be as accurate as flipping a coin.

We all have to live with our decisions for the next four years, so don't accept what others tell you to think. We'll tell you what we think—it takes up newsprint and pays the bills. But the final decision is made by you when you enter the booth and pull the lever. *Nothing else matters.*

GOPers Bearing Gifts
November 1, 1995

That squeaking noise you hear each November following a Baltimore City primary election is that of the Baltimore City Republican Party, and this year they're vowing to squeak louder than ever.

We say squeaking, of course, because the Baltimore GOP makes itself known like mice in the kitchen: literature droppings appear on your doorstep, faint noises in the media about not being irrelevant and the usual chewings-on about how there needs to be a real two-party system in the city.

It is too true that since Theodore McKeldin last passed this vale, the Republican Party in the city hasn't really drawn breath either, and that perhaps some of the residents may cling too closely to party lines. But there may be a reason for this, and much of it stands to reason with the attacks made upon the urban environs by the national Republican Party since Ronald Reagan turned the money tap off.

But if you examine the latest manifesto put forth by the city GOP, you see maybe there's something else to it as well. They're calling it the "Agenda for a Better Baltimore", and if you didn't know any better, you'd think this was the product of someone as liberal as, well, maybe Connie Morella.

There are a number of items on the "Agenda" that are sound recommendations that strike sensible chords, but so many of them are intertwined with other ideas that can only serve to try and politically build a stronger base for the GOP. As always, term limits for elected officials is at the forefront of "Agenda," despite being buried in the sixth point in the first section, titled "Return Influence and Control to Neighborhoods."

As we here point out time and again, if citizens feel the officeholder isn't cutting it, they can always elect someone else. Calling for term limits is always the first argument made by those whose sets of ideas aren't cutting it in the regional marketplace, so then they have to remove the opponent by other means. The Republicans at the national level called for term limits for years— until they took control of the Congress, and then suddenly it's not as important an issue anymore, is it?

The first section, dedicated to decentralizing city power by allegedly returning control to the neighborhoods seems to almost mimic the "states' rights" arguments made at the national level, where instead of a strong central bureaucracy, they say city power should be divvied up among regions, or in this case, neighborhoods.

We aren't aware of a lack of neighborhood administration in the city—if anything, Baltimore has proved itself to truly be a "City Of Neighborhoods," with regional associations and political clubs so prevalent and vocal you'd have to be a hermit to get away from them. Divesting the city of power only to hand it to an amorphous body of non-elected citizenry is only an appeal to factionalism.

The one reasonable point in the first section is a call for single-member council districts, which is a more direct and effective method of legislating. Unfortunately, getting to that point would mean redistricting, which is tantamount to legal warfare, especially considering how racially polarized the city has become after the last election. But true, just because the means may be ugly, that shouldn't be a reason to avoid a fairer end.

The next section, "Create Economic Development and New Jobs for the 21st Century," once again calls for decentralization and depoliticization of economic development functions (such as BEDCO and the convention board), calls for a load of task forces and studies to see where the city is wasting money and calls for a "volunteer mentor and incentive program" to get people off welfare and into "productive work in the private sector at decent pay."

Once again, the Republicans' buddies at the national level are sabotaging the motives of those here in the city. "Volunteer," of course, means "free," and remember, you get what you pay for. What we aren't getting is "productive work in the private sector at decent pay," considering the anti-union climate of business and the rush for profits at the expense of things like health care and pension plans. We've heard that "Thousand Points of Light" hooey before, thank you.

Nearly all of section three, "Restore Civil Order," is dedicated to cracking down on crime with more cops, specialized cop squads, etc., along with a few tweaks of the court system, most of which would be reasonable to anyone—after all, who's in favor of crime?

Sections four and five start out the call for privatization, ranging from the HUD programs to what they call "trial experimentation with alternative education delivery systems" which sounds suspiciously like the school voucher program advocated by failed gubernatorial candidate Ellen Sauerbrey, who, unsurprisingly, was listed as a participant in the agenda's committee.

In short, this is a moderate mission statement being put forth—the Baltimore GOP has to try and play to the obviously skeptical masses. But look deep inside the seemingly palatable ideas, and you see their whole load of anti-urban policies raring to come out. This is a Republican Trojan Horse, and judging from the ratio of Democrats to Republicans in this town, Baltimore knows to beware of GOPers bearing gifts.

Living for the City
October 18, 2006

I moved from Greenbelt to a second-floor rear apartment in Sowebo on a blustery spring Sunday, April 15, 1990. My upstairs neighbors were fun-loving, libertarian-leaning Republicans with a penchant for home brewing and cats; one was a museum curator and the other a newspaper editor.

As my brother and a buddy struggled to move in the giant railroading-era wooden desk I had purchased in a Fells Point antique store, the neighbor who was the museum curator filled me in on the neighborhood. "Don't leave anything in your car. Watch who's around you on the street at all times. If you have to bring in groceries, do it one load at a time, and lock your car in-between each trip. If you see someone coming up the street at you and you don't like how they look, feel free to cross the street. Pay attention to what's happening around you—you're living in the city now."

Over the five years I lived in that apartment, I doled out that same advice to any number of people who moved into the little six-apartment building on Hollins Street. Most were college students, though there were a few young couples, even a teacher or two. And they learned what it was like on the streets of Southwest

Baltimore in the early and mid '90s. I used to be able to identify the caliber of a weapon by the sound of the gunfire echo from Baltimore Street. Later on, when my fiancée moved in, she learned how to as well.

We jokingly used to guess what kind of crime had occurred when passing a scene, simply by counting the number of police cars. One car: property crime. Two cars: domestic disturbance. Three cars: violent crime. Five cars: homicide.

Neighborhood parties nearly always featured a gathering in the kitchen over beer or wine where we'd regale each other with stories of the latest break-in or altercation with some crackhead or wino.

These were during the Kurt Schmoke years, back when Mayor Schmoke was one of the nation's leading proponents of decriminalizing drug use. I recall having a discussion with him at a campaign event in 1991, when he again ran against the man he beat in 1987, Clarence "Du" Burns. Schmoke and I stood outside Penn Station, and he corrected me when I accused him of wanting to "legalize" drugs. He argued for treating drug abuse as a health problem and not a criminal one.

From my vantage point now, years later, I can see part of his point, but not all of it. The streets of Baltimore were a petri dish of crime under his laissez-faire decriminalization policies. His police commissioner, Ed Woods, came on a reporters' round table program broadcast by WJZ-TV, and when I peppered him with questions about the drug-related crime on the streets, Woods looked like a deer caught in the headlights.

In 1999, Martin O'Malley won the job of mayor of Baltimore. From January 2000 to New Year's Eve on the cusp of 2001, the only gunfire I heard was from the usual celebratory revelers firing off weapons in the air at the start of the new year, and I don't think it was a coincidence. Property crimes dropped precipitously. The number of expensive late-model Nissan Maximas and Jeep Cherokees with darkened windows and New York license plates cruising past Stuart Hill Elementary School dwindled almost to nothing. On summer days, we heard less of the drug couriers on little stolen dirt bikes ferrying their deliveries from the north side to the south side.

This isn't to say that crime disappeared—it didn't. But the quality of life in the neighborhood improved enough that the house my wife and I bought for a song during the Schmoke years went for a sizable profit four years after O'Malley was elected mayor.

It's seven years later, and I can't tell you that O'Malley has been a perfect mayor. I read the stories in this newspaper about the arrests being made by the city's police department, and it makes me angry, as it does a lot of other African-Americans in Baltimore. Ed Norris might have been an excellent police commissioner had he not chosen to make the same mistakes many big city police commissioners do, what with slush funds and the high life. But the changes he brought when O'Malley hired him away from New York made Baltimore a more livable city.

Now Gov. Robert Ehrlich is trying to hang Baltimore around O'Malley's neck like an albatross. The way Ehrlich plays it, Baltimore is the repository of all the state's ills, filled with lousy schools, crooked cops and high taxes. Ehrlich thinks that he can carve out a hole in the center of the state at the end of the Patapsco River and claim that everything else that has gone well is because of him.

Me, I'm sick of people like Ehrlich bashing the crap out of Baltimore. He became governor, and since then has claimed credit for a whole host of things that he fought against. O'Malley turned a city around. That counts for a lot more in my book.

Welcome to Washington. Now Stay There.
Unpublished, January 1993

So you've arrived in Powertown. And even if you haven't landed that prime appointment yet, you know it's on the way. You've gone down to the Government Printing Office and forked over the 13 bucks and change for the Plum Book, and highlighted, circled and dog-eared the thing until it's thicker than a phone book left out in the rain.

You started house- or apartment-hunting while you were still buried under mounds of paper in the old Gazette building in Little Rock. The amount of old *Washington Post* real estate sections littering the back porch and recycle bins of the friends' house where you have been staying is starting to cause local volunteer fire departments to mark the spot as a potential four-alarmer. You've spent every spare hour outside of the transition or inaugural offices (and there ain't too many of them) cruising the back streets of Cleveland Park, Dupont Circle and Eastern Market (Georgetown is out—after all, you're a staffer, not Kay Graham) for chi-chi places to live.

What it comes to is, you've arrived in Washington. And we residents of your stepsister-cum-twin to the north, Baltimore, have a message for you:

Stay there.

We mean it. Stay there. Discover the joys of the Smithsonian and the Kennedy Center, fill your face with all the gastronomic joys of the area, revel in cheap dry cleaning, talk on cellular phones 'til you get as hoarse as the president-elect the day before the election and gridlock your little heart out in the traffic. Maybe even duck a bullet every now and then; heck, it *is* the murder capital. Live dangerously once in a while.

Just stay away from Baltimore.

Oh, sure—come visit during baseball season. We've already realized that you'll make the drive to the new ballpark at Camden Yards, buy the overpriced crab soup, sit in the club-level mezzanine that has all the ballpark ambience of your dentist's waiting room or the first-class lounge at National Airport, watch about six and a half innings of play and then head out for your car if there's a difference of more than four runs in the score. We expect it from you. Come to think of it, we almost hope for it (but not too much; many here in Crabtown already think there's a conspiracy that gives all the best seats to DC area ticket buyers) because it's the best way to buy tickets after the game's begun without getting scalped too badly. Good-natured Washingtonians don't always want to make a profit on that spare ticket. Besides, you live in *Washington*. It's *understandable* if you have to spend that Sunday power-wonking your way through some policy analysis of state-supported business activity in Tadjikistan.

But when you're done, go home. Honest. But you don't need us to tell you that, do you? Why would you stay in *Baltimore*?

Even though now the whole Baltimore-Washington corridor (and believe you me, you ain't gonna find a Bawlamorean worth his Old Bay who will say it the other way around) has been annexed into one complete metropolitan area, anyone who has lived in either place will show you, by the look on his or her face, what they think of that "other" city to the south/north.

About Baltimore: "No class." About Washington: "Too snooty." About Baltimore: "Too cheesy." About Washington: "Too status-conscious." About Baltimore: "Too much crime." About Washington: "Too much crime." About Baltimore: "Too far." About Washington: "Too *near*."

So we wouldn't want you to destroy those closely held beliefs about Baltimore's second-class status, would we?

For instance, what would your "friends" (Hoover was right— if you want a real friend in Washington, better buy that dog) think if they found out a two-bedroom apartment in some decent sections of downtown Baltimore cost one-third to one-half less per month than in the DC area? Of course, they'd think you were slumming! You wouldn't want that, want them feeling you just aren't tony enough for them, now, would you?

And about that commute: it's almost sacred water-cooler conversation, a veritable badge of honor to kvetch about how long it took you to get to work. Like New Yorkers who complain about the Big Apple in one breath and in the next tell you there's no where else on earth worth living, Washingtonians are bound by the fraternity of bad traffic. For those in Shady Grove, the trip in on I-270 is regurgitated like the expensive but bad salmon at last night's dinner. Virginians shriek about HOV in terms reserved for purse snatchers and people who work for the Department of Motor Vehicles. For those who live in the city, it's the regular rant about potholes the size of Humvees, bike messengers with a collective death wish and cabdrivers that cross lanes like it's the evening rush hour in Istanbul.

So if you could hop on a MARC train and be on the Hill in an hour-plus-ten, that would leave you out of the kaffeeklatch, wouldn't it? You'd be standing there while the rest of the gang conducts their morning bonding routine about how the bottleneck at I-495 and New Hampshire Avenue at the P.G.-Montgomery county line left them sitting like last week's stale bread for fifty-three minutes. You wouldn't be *one of them*.

Forget it! Baltimore? No way!

When people who live in Baltimore tell you about the great crab cakes, about bars where you can still buy a beer—imported, no less—for under two dollars, where you can get apartments with 16-foot ceilings, tell them you'd rather live where the action is.

When someone mentions how both Senators Barbara Mikulski and Paul Sarbanes commute from Baltimore, or how Channel 9 news anchor Frank Bond or *Washington Post* book critic Jonathan Yardley or author Taylor Branch live in the sob-sister city 35 miles to the north, tell them there's always room for a few eccentrics up there. Heck, isn't that where John Waters lives? The guy made movies about a drag queen who ate dog poop!

In short, tell 'em to hit the highway!

Besides, think what would happen if everybody <u>did</u> move to Baltimore.

Competition would mean there goes the bargain rents for restored, hundred-year-old apartment buildings with the foyers that you can play volleyball in.

There would be more hassles getting your kids into those grand old private schools like Gilman and Boys' Latin than there is now.

More Washington-style expensive luxury import cars would line the streets, prompting more car theft and higher insurance rates.

Train stations would be filled with impatient, camel-colored, trenchcoat-wearing Schedule C clones with their ears stapled to cell phones, not even bothering to say "Hi" or "Good Morning" like the soulless droids that stand next to one another during the morning commute on the Metro from Wheaton to Farragut North.

A shorter ride to the ball park would mean more tickets being snapped up in a shorter amount of time, leaving more real fans to watch the games on TV, where singing and dancing news anchors in Orioles' promos on Baltimore stations might have to get serious for a change.

You'd still root only for the Redskins, causing no small amount of grief among those people who still remember exactly what they were doing on that snowy March night back in 1984.

Two dollar Heinekens? *No mas.*

So, really. Stay there. You love Washington. Washington loves you.

Because if you discovered what it's *really* like up here, it would hurt us a lot more than it would hurt you.

About the Author

Brian Wendell Morton is an award-winning radio reporter and newspaper columnist. He began his career as a student journalist at the University of Maryland where he and a partner won the national spot-news award for print journalism from the Society of Professional Journalists for covering the drug trial following the death of collegiate basketball star Len Bias.

He continued as a reporter at all-news radio station WTOP in Washington where, while covering everything from local politics to the inauguration of George H. W. Bush, he won awards from the Chesapeake Associated Press and the Dateline Chapter of the Washington Society of Professional Journalists. At WBAL Radio in Baltimore he distinguished himself with another AP award for his coverage of a freak tornado landing in a Baltimore suburb.

In 1994 he originated the "Political Animal" column for Baltimore's *City Paper*, which he wrote until 1996 and then resumed in 2002. In 2006 he also he hosted the "Weekly News Roundup" for Baltimore's public radio station WYPR.

Acknowledgments

This would never have happened if it weren't for the three editors I have had at the Baltimore *City Paper*: Sono Motoyama, Andy Markowitz (GO TERPS!), and Lee Gardner. I'm proud to say that if it weren't for a dead alternator in upstate Western New York and a computer server glitch while I was on a crazy Christmastime bus trip to Manhattan, I would be batting .1000 on deadlines, instead of the annoying .997 over seven years (okay, so I pushed it a little). Thanks also go to CP publisher Don Farley for not paying attention to all those seditious rants that have run right after the letters page since 1994.

On the radio journalism side, thanks to the late Paul Michael "Mike" Rushlow, WTOP radio desk editor extraordinaire, who taught me that keeping your cool is one of the smartest things you can do under pressure. Thanks to Karen Gray-Houston, who put up with my immature ass when I wanted to be a big-time radio reporter. And thanks to the late, great Jamie Bragg, who always knew when it was time to have your resumé on the copier.

On the political side, my thanks go to former congressman

and former NAACP president Kweisi Mfume for a front-row seat at the table during some really cool moments in history. Also, thanks to retired Gen. Barry R. McCaffrey, who provided me with many "general rules" I still quote to others today ("Stay in your own lane," "Often wrong, but never in doubt"), and for being a man who has dedicated his life to serving a great country.

For Carla Mutu and Pamela McDowell who watched it happen.

Lastly, humble thanks to Kevin King and Gregg Wilhelm at Loyola College's Apprentice House, for giving me the opportunity to make all of this typing last a little longer than a week.

The future of publishing...today!

Apprentice House is the country's only campus-based, student-staffed book publishing company. Directed by professors and industry professionals, it is a nonprofit activity of the Communication Department at Loyola College in Maryland.

Using state-of-the-art technology and an experiential learning model of education, Apprentice House publishes books in untraditional ways. This dual responsibility as publishers and educators creates an unprecedented collaborative environment among faculty and students, while teaching tomorrow's editors, designers, and marketers.

Outside of class, progress on book projects is carried forth by the AH Book Publishing Club, a co-curricular campus organization supported by Loyola College's Office of Student Activities.

Student Project Team for *Political Animal:*

Kevin King, '09
Thomas R. Conigatti, Jr., '08
Andrew Zaleski, '11

Eclectic and provocative, Apprentice House titles intend to entertain as well as spark dialogue on a variety of topics.

Financial contributions to sustain the press's work are welcomed. Contributions are tax deductible to the fullest extent allowed by IRS.

To learn more about Apprentice House books or to obtain submission guidelines, please visit www.ApprenticeHouse.com.

Apprentice House
Communication Department
Loyola College in Maryland
4501 N. Charles Street
Baltimore, MD 21210
Ph: 410-617-5265
Fax: 410-617-5040
info@apprenticehouse.com

www.ingramcontent.com/pod-product-compliance
Lightning Source LLC
Chambersburg PA
CBHW051726260326
41914CB00031B/1758/J